52 European Wildlife Weekends

A YEAR OF SHORT BREAKS FOR NATURE LOVERS

James Lowen

Bradt Travel Guides Ltd, UK
The Globe Pequot Press Inc, USA

Bradt

Author

Wildlife expert **James Lowen** (⌖ jameslowen.com 🐦 @JLowenWildlife) has been immersed in all aspects of natural history since he was able to walk. This eventually persuaded him to ditch a high-flying career in public service in favour of becoming a fully fledged (and award-winning) wildlife writer, editor, guide, and photographer. James's most recent book for Bradt Travel Guides, *A Summer of British Wildlife: 100 Great Days Out Watching Wildlife*, scooped Travel Guide Book of the Year at the 2016 Travel Media Awards.

A member of the British Guild of Travel Writers, James's travels and writing commissions take him all over the world. His previous books cover the British Isles (*Badgers*, *Hedgehogs* and Bradt's *52 Wildlife Weekends: A Year of British Wildlife-Watching Breaks*), South America (Bradt's *Pantanal Wildlife: A Visitor's Guide to Brazil's Great Wetland*) and Antarctica (*Antarctic Wildlife: A Visitor's Guide to the Wildlife of the Beagle Channel, Drake Passage and Antarctic Peninsula*). A book about wildlife travel in Europe was long overdue!

Acknowledgements

A large number of people have suggested experiences to cover, provided me with information, endured travelling with me, facilitated or sponsored my recces, or commented on draft chapters of this book. With apologies to anyone I have inadvertently omitted, I thank Dave Andrews, Tormod Amundsen (Biotope), Malcolm Ausden, Steve Babbs, Roger Barnes (Bird Holidays), Phil Benstead, Richard Bonser, David Bradnum, Graeme Buchanan, Stephen Burch, Stuart Butchart, Andy Butler, Dave Capper, Sara Cernich, Robin Chittenden (Limosa Holidays/Harlequin Pictures), Graham Clarke, Rob Clay, Mark Cocker, Stephanie Coghlan (Snail's Pace Tours), Sean Cole, Carl Corbridge, Kiki Deere, Vladimir Dinets, Lee Dingain, John Dixon, Jen Donelan, Jon Dunn, Guy Dutson, Sandra Eleksius (Estonian Tourist Board), Martin Fowlie, John Geeson, Bob Gibbons (Natural History Travel), Harry Grabenhofer, Gaidis Grandāns (Dabas Tures), Jon Hall (mammalwatching. com), James Hanlon, Ben Hoare, Matthew Hobbs, Mike Hoit, Gill Hollanby, Mark Hows, Terence Ilott, Josh Jones, Claudia and Martin Kelsey (Birding Extremadura/ Casa El Recuerdo), Guy Kirwan, Sophie Lake, Paul Lambourne, Keith Langdon, Mark Lawlor, Andy Lawson, Hannah Lawson, Jono Lethbridge, Ben Lewis, David Lindo, Durwyn Liley, Adrian Long, David Lowen, Marika Mann (Estonian Nature Tours), John McLoughlin, Dougal McNeill, Richard Moores, Steve Morgan, Andy

Feedback request and updates website

Why not write and tell us about your experiences using this guide? Post reviews to ⌂ bradtguides.com or Amazon. You can send in updates on out-of-date information or suggestions for your own recommended wildlife-watching days to ☏ 01753 893444 or ✉ info@bradtguides.com. Any contributors will be thanked by James Lowen in future editions. We may also post 'one-off updates' at ⌂ bradtupdates.com/52eww.

Musgrove, Peter Oefinger, Vanesa Palacios (Extremadura Turismo), Ed Parnell, Yoav Perlman, Philip Precey (Wildlife Travel), Stuart Reeves, Ian Robinson, Chris Sharpe, Alick Simmons, Olly Smart (SmartImages), Will Soar, Jeroen Speybroeck, Domen Stanič, Paul St Pierre, Andy Symes, Marianne Taylor, Mark Telfer, Megan Tierney, Uudo Timm, David Tipling, Joe Tobias, Chris Townend (Wise Birding), Colin Turvey (Crete Birding), Mike Unwin, Howard Vaughan, Paul Veenvliet, Ilze Vilšķērste (Dabas Tures), David Walker, Tarvo Walker (Estonian Nature Tours), Nick Watmough, Rob Williams and Matt Wilson.

A raft of photographers contributed images for potential incusion in this guide. Whether or not their images made the final cut, I am grateful to them all for taking the time to demonstrate their prowess with the camera – even if their pictures made me embarrassed to call myself a photographer. Those whose images are used are credited alongside their photos.

From Bradt Travel Guides, I thank Sue Cooper, Rachel Fielding, Carys Homer, Anna Moores and Adrian Phillips. For design, I thank Pepi Bluck at Perfect Picture. Finally, my biggest gratitude goes to Sharon and Maya Lowen. Without my brilliant wife and wonderful daughter, research trips would never have happened, would have been far worse informed and/or would have been far less pleasurable.

Hefty, scruffy, yet slightly endearing: the wild boar features in several weekends. ▲

FRANK SOMMARIVA/IMAGEBROKER/FLPA

Introduction

Brown bear padding. Two-tailed pasha nectaring. Great bustard displaying. Sperm whale fluking. Alpine ibex rutting. European bison chewing. Common cranes yodelling. Striped dolphins bow-riding. Red-breasted geese massing. Iberian lynx slinking. Raccoon dog trotting. Siberian jay bossing. King eiders swirling. Mirror orchid dazzling. Imperial cave salamander clinging. Dragon arum protruding. Corsican crocus proliferating. Long-tailed mayflies rushing. Wolverine marauding. Lilypad whiteface basking. Alpine marmot alarm-calling. Apollo enchanting. Musk ox hulking. Zino's petrel caterwauling. European souslik begging. Ocean sunfish bewildering. Wildcat prowling. Honey buzzards kettling.

What's in, what's out

The geographical reach of this book is the whole of Europe west of Russia, Belarus, Ukraine, Moldova, and Turkey. It includes the Atlantic and Mediterranean islands under the rule of European countries (Azores, Madeira, Canaries, Balearics etc) because these are well-established holiday destinations. Where I have not included a country, it in no way implies an absence of great wildlife-watching – but rather that either another experience elsewhere has pipped its offering to the post (eg: Croatia), or I lacked sufficient personal feel for the country to be comfortable writing about it (eg: Bosnia and Herzegovina).

That said, I have intentionally excluded some countries. The UK does not feature because I have explored it extensively in two previous books (*52 Wildlife Weekends* and *A Summer of British Wildlife*). Despite desperately wanting to cover snorkelling in Gozo, I excluded it because of Malta's inaction on halting the illegal killing of migrant birds. The same applies to Cyprus.

Hopefully attitudes will change in time for their inclusion in any sequel to this guide (*52 More European Wildlife Weekends*, anyone?).

Certain brilliant experiences have had to be omitted because they cannot be shoehorned into the timeframe – weekends – imposed by this book. Examples are spring bird migration in Lesbos (to where there are currently only weekly flights, making even a long weekend impossible) and the circumnavigation of Svalbard, in Arctic Norway. I have not suggested weekends that involve visiting beaches to see turtles or Mediterranean monk seals, as these species are vulnerable to human disturbance. I have also been deliberately shy of giving location details for some reptiles and orchids – as there remain misguided individuals who, respectively, collect or dig up these amazing life forms. Nothing would distress me more than people abusing the information in this guide. This book is about wildlife-*watching*.

Nose-horned viper coiling. Olm unsettling. Sea daffodil flourishing. Long-eared owls roosting. Orcas chasing. Starlings murmurating. Wallcreeper butterflying.

This book is a celebration of Europe's abundant wildlife riches in the age of low-cost, high-frequency international travel. It is an ode to their survival despite manifold human threats. It packages the very best nature-watching experiences into 52 convenient, short-break-sized chunks. It inspires you to travel, then informs you how, where and when you should go, and what you should see. Each trip is carefully timed to optimise the experience. So whenever you have a weekend free to immerse yourself in all things European and natural, this guide has a suggestion for you.

Encompassing 21 European countries, recommendations stretch from the Arctic to the Mediterranean, from the Atlantic to the Aegean. Weekends cover the breadth of European wildlife – from massive mammals to ostentatious orchids, from migrating birds to cave-dwelling amphibians. There are lizards and butterflies and dragonflies and moths and owl-flies. Whatever your wildlife interest and wherever you wish to travel, there is something for you.

I have selected weekends for a variety of reasons. All provide unforgettable wildlife-watching experiences. But that's a given. Their number includes trips that would work as (all or part of) a family holiday or on a city break. There are hiking excursions and waterborne cruises, breaks that are best guided by an expert and those where you explore off your own bat. The landscapes visited – cherished, eulogised – are varied: there are woodlands and wetlands, mountains and oceans.

Critically, all suggestions are feasible within a long weekend – two full days (only) 'in the field' with international travel either side of that. Accordingly, all destinations are within easy reach (2–3 hours' drive, generally) of transport termini – normally airports (and how low-cost airlines have revolutionised pan-European travel!), but also major train stations where this is feasible. There is a bias towards locations easily accessible from airports in countries where the expected readership lives (British Isles, Low Countries, Scandinavia).

Hirsute and heavily built, brown bears feature in several weekends. ▲

52 European wildlife weekends

The coloured circles identify the location of each weekend. Each circle contains the weekend number (ie: 1 = January, weekend 1). The colour of the circle varies, following the colour scheme used in this guide.

ICELAND 24

11
9
49
32
29

NORWAY 31

SWEDEN

FINLAND 27

10 19
ESTONIA
LATVIA 8
LITHUANIA
RUSSIA

DENMARK 39

IRELAND 21
46

UNITED KINGDOM

NETHERLANDS

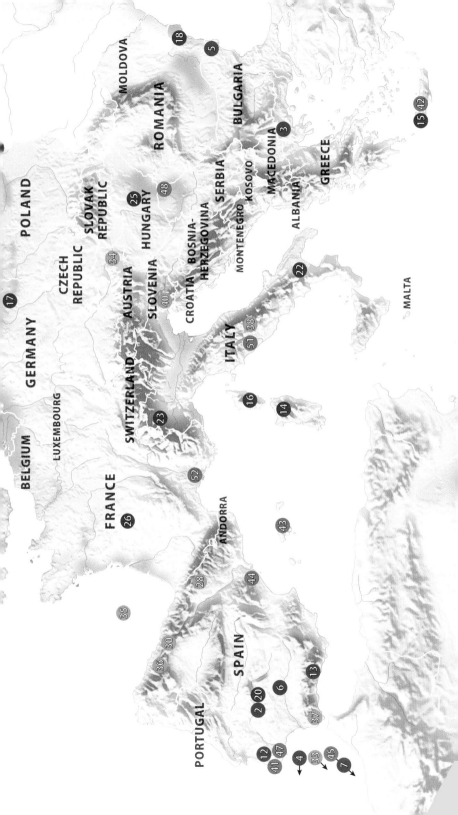

Which binoculars are best for me?

You're probably well aware that binoculars are a fabulous tool for getting close to nature. But choosing the right pair can be daunting — particularly if you are thinking of upgrading. This guide aims to help.

Buying binoculars: the basics

Three guiding principles may help. First, what's right for me may not be for you. Binoculars are a personal thing, so never buy without testing. Second, prepare for trade-offs between weight, performance, practicality and price. Third, buy the best you can afford. You get what you pay for. My Swarovski 'bins', bought in 2004, remain as brilliant as on day one.

Binoculars are described in off-putting jargon. Their names include two numbers, the magnification factor and objective lens diameter (in mm). An 8x56 binocular magnifies objects by eight times through a 56mm-wide lens. Larger numbers usually mean heavier, more cumbersome binoculars. I advise sticking to the ranges 7–10 (magnification) and 30–56 (lens). The ratio between the numbers influences how much light the binocular lets in — and thus how bright the image. The larger the ratio, generally, the better low-light performance. I favour a ratio of 1:4 (eg: 8x32) or 1:5 (eg: 8x42), but up to 1:7 (eg: 8x56) may enhance use in shady forests or at twilight.

Numbers aside, binoculars are either 'roof-prisms' (H-shaped, slimline) or 'porro-prisms' (M-shaped, chunky). For tight budgets, porro-prisms arguably offer better value. Although pricier, roof-prisms tend to be better quality, easier to handle and more compact. They get my vote.

Testing binoculars: what to look for

Pick them up: is the weight evenly distributed? Can you hold them steady? Spectacle-wearers need eyecups that roll or slide so that the binocular offers 14–17mm of 'eye relief'. Now look through the optics. You want a wide field of view — but no need to go overboard. Ensure the image is sharp, ideally right to the edge of vision. How close can you focus? If you anticipate watching insects, choose a pair that focuses on your feet. Check that colours look natural — with no blue or yellow cast. Finally, examine a backlit object: if it is fringed yellow or purple, choose another pair.

What makes binoculars really good?

Consider each candidate binocular's finer characteristics, which sort wheat from chaff across years of service. 'Fully multi-coated' lenses and prisms are recommended; they maximise light transmission, contrast and clarity. Look for an image so sharp it sears your eyes. Extra-low dispersion (ED) or high-density (HD) lenses correct colour fringing. Depth-of-field is important: you want to minimise time spent refocusing. Durability is key: seek high-strength but ideally lightweight housing. Weatherproofing keeps out dust and water. Finally, if things go wrong, you want the manufacturer to stand by its product, offering a lifetime warranty. There's a reason why my Swarovskis go on… and on…

How to use this book

In this book I suggest a year's worth of brilliant wildlife-watching breaks across Europe – one for you to enjoy each weekend of the year. Eight months have four weekends; four (March, May, July and August) are indulged with a fifth. To help frame your visit, I suggest up to five wildlife 'targets' for each trip, focusing on the special, the rare and the spectacular. There is usually plenty of pace to each weekend. Should you prefer a more leisurely itinerary, simply pick 'n' mix.

Each weekend has my subjective take on its **accessibility** and **child-friendliness**. For the former, I have thought about the ease of the weekend for a wheelchair-using friend. For the latter, I have used my young daughter as a barometer: how much would each weekend excite her (or did!) – and thus how realistically could this be a family-based trip? A score of 1 means the experience is not particularly accessible or child-friendly. A 5 means it is highly accessible or child-friendly.

The main text

Each entry walks you through the weekend, bringing to life the sites, scenery and species involved. Sometimes these are textured with my own personal experiences or with perspectives from experts. Other entries are contextualised with musings – on the nature of rarity, the merits of conservation, the ethics of a particular visit and so on.

Practicalities

Each entry contains a box on practical considerations. This gives you the nuts and bolts needed for planning the trip.

GETTING THERE gives details of international travel, focusing on the nearest airport but specifying land-based transport options where these make sense (bearing in mind the shortness of the trip). In most cases, I assume you will hire a car from the airport, so distances and times (unless otherwise specified) relate to driving.

Follow us

Use the hashtag #wildlifeweekends to share your adventures using this guide with us and to make your own suggestions – we'd love to hear from you.

- 📘 www.facebook.com/BradtTravelGuides
- 🐦 @BradtGuides and @JLowenWildlife (#wildlifeweekends)
- 📷 @bradtguides (#wildlifeweekends)
- 📌 pinterest.com/bradtguides

Flying green

Low-cost air travel has revolutionised how we explore Europe. It makes possible nature-orientated trips that would have been unthinkable (or, at least, much harder) a couple of decades ago. This book wouldn't exist in the absence of easyJet, WizzAir, Ryanair and their brethren.

But, as an environmentalist, I feel guilty about encouraging wanton air travel, given that this exacerbates global warming. My pain is all the more intense because of my previous professional life. This involved negotiating on behalf of the UK Government in United Nations discussions on climate change, helping design the European Union carbon trading scheme, and advising airlines on how to adapt to a carbon-constrained world.

I seek to mediate the tension by identifying viable alternatives to air travel, where these exist, and by encouraging you to fly green. The latter involves choosing the most fuel-efficient airline for your route (check ✏ tinyurl.com/atmosfair-index) and offset greenhouse gas emissions resulting from your journey (use online tools such as ✏ tinyurl.com/atmosfair-calculator). Purchasing carbon offsets from organisations such as Carbon Fund (✏ carbonfund.org), ClimateCare (✏ climatecare.org) or World Land Trust (✏ worldlandtrust.org) won't stop global warming – but doing so goes some way to compensating for your carbon footprint. Let's minimise the environmental cost of cheap air travel.

WHERE TO GO summarises access details for sites mentioned in the text. This includes both relevant websites where you can get more information and GPS points that you can type into internet- or app-based mapping services (eg: Google maps or the app maps.me).

SUGGESTED BASES offers ideas about where you should spend the night. This is usually a town or village (often with a website where you can learn more) but sometimes includes specific accommodation.

MAKE IT A WEEK suggests ways in which you could expand the weekend into a full week of nature-based exploration. A proper holiday!

FLEXIBILITY acknowledges that not everyone can make the trip on what I reckon is the optimum weekend. This section summarises your room for manoeuvre, with respect to the seasonality of the weekend's most special creatures. Can you travel a week later and still see the target wildlife? Or a month earlier?

TITBITS encompasses any other information that I think useful. This might comprise, for example, details of nature guides to escort you or books where you can learn more. Suggestions for additional *generic* information can be found in *Further information* (page 228).

Great weekends for...

JAMES LOWEN

LAND MAMMALS
January 1, February 1–2, March 2, March 5, May 2, June 1, July 1–5, August 3, August 5, September 1–2, September 4, October 2

BIG NUMBERS OF BIRDS
January 2–3, March 3, July 3, September 1, September 3, October 4, November 4, December 2–3

WACKY CREATURES
February 3, March 4, April 1, June 1, June 3, July 4, September 4, November 3

FLORAL EXTRAVAGANZA
March 5, April 1–2, May 4, June 1, June 4, July 2, September 1, September 4, October 2

LIFE IN COLD BLOOD
February 1, February 3, March 4, April 1–3, May 1, May 3, June 3–4, July 2, August 2, September 4, October 2–3, November 3

BUTTERFLIES AND MOTHS
February 3, May 3–4, June 1, June 3–4, July 2, July 4, August 1, August 5, September 1, October 1

DRAGONFLIES
May 1, June 3–4, August 3, October 1–3

FAMILY ADVENTURES
February 3, March 4, April 2, May 5, June 2, July 3, August 1–5, September 1, September 3, October 1, October 3–4, November 1–3, December 3

MOUNTAIN WALKS
April 3, June 1, July 2, July 4–5, August 5, September 2, October 2

FABULOUS FORESTS
January 1, March 1–2, August 1, September 2

GREAT WETLANDS
January 3, February 1, May 1, June 3–4, August 3, December 2, December 4

ISLAND VISITS
January 4, February 3, April 1, April 2, May 4, June 2, July 3, August 2, October 2, November 1–2

AVOIDING AIR TRAVEL
May 4, June 4, November 2, December 2, December 4

CITY BREAKS
April 4, May 5, August 3, December 3

WATERBORNE WILDLIFE-WATCHING
January 4, April 1, May 1, June 2, July 3, August 1–2, August 4, October 1, November 1–2, December 1

CONSERVATION SUCCESS STORIES
January 4, February 2, June 1, July 5, August 2, September 1–2

HEAVENLY GRASSLANDS
January 2, March 4, April 2, May 3, May 4, June 3, July 4, October 2, December 2

One of Europe's prettiest birds of prey, the lesser kestrel. ▲

Contents

January

February

◀ Ural owls are stars of the Latvian winter (weekend 8).
ROBIN CHITTENDEN www.robinchittenden.co.uk

March

April

Spanish ibex, one of several species of hill-climbing 'goat' featuring in weekend suggestions. ▶
ALEX BERRYMAN

xiii

May

June

▶ The glowing coals of a transparent burnet moth, a star of weekend 21.   JPS/S

July

OLIVER SMART www.smartimages.co.uk

August

Walk high then look up to see a lammergeier, the famed bone-breaking vulture (weekend 28). ▲

September

October

◀ Different populations of Ibiza wall lizard exhibit different coloration (weekend 43).

55

November

December

STEFAN SCHARF/S

Preposterous, yet real: a greater flamingo (weekends 41, 47 and 52). Nature is more bizarre than we can even imagine. ▶

Arguably Europe's most stunning duck, the drake Steller's Eider (weekend 11). JAMES LOWEN

January
February
March

European bison – common crane – Dalmatian pelican
greater spotted eagle – Azores bullfinch – sperm whale – golden jackal
Iberian lynx – European free-tailed bat – monarch
blind squat lobster – pygmy owl Siberian jay – Eurasian lynx
Eurasian elk – Steller's eider – great bustard – mirror orchid

Into the trees

WHERE Białowieża Forest, Podlaskie, Poland
TARGETS European bison, Eurasian beaver, black woodpecker, three-toed woodpecker, northern long-tailed tit
ACCESSIBILITY ③ (car-based, but snow)
CHILD-FRIENDLINESS ② (but snowballs!)

'Come closer and see/See into the trees.' Goth-rock pioneers The Cure provided the primary soundtrack to my teenage years. My favourite song, 'A Forest', recounts the protagonist's quest for an ephemeral lover amid the dark wood of his mind: introspective romance at its most harrowed. Thirty years later, and Robert Smith's lyrics career through my head as I reflect on Europe's most troubled forest, the old-growth marvel that is Białowieża.

This *puszcza* – which roughly translates as 'huge primeval forest' – straddles the border of northeast Poland and west Belarus, and has played a pivotal role in conservationists' successful efforts to rescue the European bison from extinction. Białowieża is the largest remnant of a diverse forest that, ten millennia hence, sprawled across much of lowland Europe. As such, it is a vital, world-famous refuge for a remarkably broad spread of European wildlife – and one that, wretchedly, is perpetually trying to stave off destruction.

▲ Snow forces herds of European bison out of dense forest into the open. DANM12/S

Old-growth forests are those that have remained undisturbed for longer than any of their individual trees have grown. Their mosaic of habitats, from steepling giants to a lush herb layer, from dead wood to light-filled glades, offer a great diversity of niches for wildlife to exploit. Białowieża first received protection in the 15th century, when King Władysław II Jagiełło declared the forest as royal hunting grounds.

Such halcyon years are long gone. The period during and between the two world wars saw rampant poaching, timber extraction and infrastructural development. The latest crisis is the decision by the ruling Law and Justice Party (PiS) – flying in the face of a European Court of Justice ruling – to fell a million trees a year, ostensibly to protect the forest from an invasion of beetles. Such logging threatens to destroy Białowieża once and for all.

So experiencing this remarkable area – and seeing its exhilarating wildlife – is a priority.

And so to your visit. Freshly fallen snow starts the year anew. The dense

> **66 In the 1920s, European bison was extinct in the wild 99**

white blanket smothers the ground and fringes dingy branches with light. The paucity of vegetation serving as concealment or nourishment forces Białowieża's most famous mammalian resident into the open. They are normally reclusive forest denizens, but winter's harshness concentrates small herds of European bison (aka wisent) into particular meadows, where they chew the cud of specially provisioned silage.

That any of us can still see this bovine at all is remarkable. In the 1920s, European bison – a different species to its prairie-dwelling American cousin, lest you be

WILDLIFE WORLD/S

wondering – was extinct in the wild. Diligent captive-breeding programmes resulted in the mammal's reintroduction to Białowieża (first, then to other suitable sites across Europe) in 1952. The forest's contingent of free-ranging animals now stands at around 400, almost one-quarter of the total world population. Back from the brink, indeed.

There are several good areas to search for bison (see *Practicalities*), typically on the edge of villages such as Olchówka, Teremiski and Narewka. When you locate a herd, admire their hump-backed, curly-horned might from a respectful distance. Fifty metres is more than close enough: you neither want to stress the bison nor risk injury by inciting their wrath.

GETTING THERE Nearest airports are in Warsaw. Chopin (aka Okęcie; ⊘ warsaw-airport.com) is the main one, but budget airlines fly into Modlin Mazovia (⊘ en.modlinairport.pl), conveniently located 20km northwest of the capital. From here drive 3½ hours (240km) east to Białowieża village.

WHERE TO GO Białowieża Forest (⊘ bialowieza-forest.com) lies east of Hajnówka towards (and beyond) the Belarus border. A national park (⊘ tinyurl.com/bialowieza-np) includes a strict conservation area to which access requires a permit and guide (book through the tourist information office at Park Pałacowy 11, Białowieża; ✳ 52.702946, 23.846790). Good meadows and/or feeding stations for European bison lie near **Olchówka** (✳ 52.852205, 23.821869), **Teremiski** (✳ 52.731118, 23.770452) and **Narewka** (✳ 52.832668, 23.765492). For night drives, spotlighting for mammals, you must stick to public roads. A good route is from Białowieża, via Teremiski and Budy (✳ 52.732396, 23.730027), north to Narewka. Surrounding Białowieża town are several good areas for forest birds. Head northeast along **Browska** (✳ 52.703264, 23.879422), follow the tracks leading east from ✳ 52.694354, 23.881737, or walk the **Zebra Zubra trail** from

▲ Spotting evidence of Eurasian beavers is easy; seeing the real thing may demand patience.

Spend the rest of the weekend driving public roads at night to spotlight for other mammals, checking the ground for their footprints, and wandering forested paths looking for woodpeckers and other sylvan birds. The legacy of hunting pressure means that Białowieża's mammals are mainly active during darkness.

Roe and red deer are the most common herbivores, with the wild boar population currently beleaguered by disease. Evidence of Eurasian beavers is widespread in and near wetlands. Spend an hour by a dam, lodge or gnawed trees, and the typically elusive architect may reward your patience with its presence. Among carnivores, you are most likely to see red fox and probably pine marten. But careful perusal of indentations in the snow may attest to the proximity of grey wolf – several packs roam the forest – and even Eurasian lynx. Like the protagonist in Robert Smith's love song, you should relinquish hope of seeing your quarry itself, instead contenting yourself with piecing together the clues it leaves.

Then explore on foot for special forest birds. Białowieża harbours all bar one European woodpeckers, so set high expectations. Black woodpecker – with its ivory eyes and flaming crest – is a must. More subtle but enticingly scarcer are three-toed and white-backed woodpeckers. The latter specialises in exploiting old-growth woodland, while the former lacks the fourth toe common to almost all other woodpeckers worldwide.

Three good areas to search fringe Białowieża village; a fourth lies near Kosy Most. Small forest birds will doubtless also attract your attention. Flocks of bullfinch and siskin splash colour. Crested tits purr at feeders. The star, however, is northern long-tailed tit. This beautiful bird displays a head as pure white as the driven snow that coats the amazing yet ever-vulnerable *puszcza* of Białowieża.

the car park at ✳ 52.703813, 23.829914. Another excellent walk is the **Carska Tropina trail** near Kosy Most, 2.5km southeast of Narewka (park at ✳ 52.798911, 23.812701).

SUGGESTED BASES Ample lodgings in Białowieża, including the **National Park guesthouse** (⌀ tinyurl.com/bialowieza-guesthouse) and **Stoczek 1929** (⌀ stoczek1929.pl/en/).

MAKE IT A WEEK Go mammal-watching in **Bieszczady Mountains** (where Europe's Big5 has a carnivore hide ⌀ europesbig5.com), **Puszcza Borecka** or **Kampinos National Park**. At **Osowiec Fortress**, 125km northwest of Białowieża, ask a guide to show you the bat hibernacula (species include barbastelle, Natterer's and Daubenton's). Search for Eurasian elk along the first 40km of road between Osowiec and Warsaw.

FLEXIBILITY All targets are resident but best seen December to April when foliage is minimal.

TITBITS Recommended local guides include **Wild Poland** (⌀ wildpoland.com) and **Pygmy Owl Nature Tours** (⌀ bialowiezaforest.eu). Wild Poland sells an excellent site guide. The Crossbill Guide *North-east Poland* is also good.

SERGEY URYADNIKOV/S

Hundreds
and thousands

WHERE Extremadura, Cáceres province, central-west Spain
TARGETS Common crane, great bustard, Iberian imperial eagle, red deer, otter
ACCESSIBILITY ⑤ (almost entirely car-based exploration)
CHILD-FRIENDLINESS ②

You hear them before you see them. And even if you have never heard them before, you just *know* what they are. There is simply no mistaking the call of common cranes, nor even the faintest possibility of remaining unbewitched by the chorus of thousands that resounds across Extremadura's rice fields.

Carrying effortlessly for kilometres through the sobriety of this winter day, the voice of this stately bird – long of both neck and leg – is peculiarly tricky to describe. Some say that cranes 'bugle'. For me, the sound is more that of a reedy wind instrument – a rippling oboe perhaps. Unfettered by hubbub, the voice is wild and remote, emphatic yet imbued with fragility.

Each winter, cranes shape Extremadura's land and soundscapes. More than 130,000 winter here between November and early February – by far Europe's mightiest congregation and one that has doubled in the past decade – and you

▲ Visit a roost site for the ultimate common crane spectacle and soundscape.

could see one-fifth of them this weekend. Yet it is not merely the number of *grullas* that mesmerise, but the myriad ways to experience them.

A pair yodelling to each other, their heads thrown back. A family moseying in maize stubble, within strides of a smallholding outside Madrigalejo. A score tiptoeing through earthy rice fields near Vegas Altas, a monoculture instigated by General Franco. The subdued, wary whistling of youngsters, seeking counsel from their parents. A single bird beating overhead, silently and purposefully winging between feeding grounds. A gathering of hundreds mooching between sturdy holm oaks near Moheda Alta, each Afro-crowned tree dispensing acorns for leggy birds. Or a flock of a thousand flapping into roost, all oboe and limbs and grace.

> **The crane's voice is wild and remote, emphatic yet imbued with fragility**

However you enjoy them, cranes are measured yet emotive. Hefty yet insecure. Rumbustious yet orchestral. 'I can't imagine ever tiring of cranes,' says Martin Kelsey, who runs Birding Extremadura. 'I feel bereft when they depart.' Bespectacled and bookish, Kelsey has the air of a genial professor. He knows as much about the region's wildlife as anyone – and treats me to the highlights. As we watch hen harrier and merlin hunting in tandem on flocks of small birds (sparrows, waxbills and avadavats), Kelsey jests that 'in Extremadura, we have big birds, we have little birds, and we have big birds eating little birds'.

Despite the predators' attentions, the rice fields frequented by many cranes are dripping with small feathered bodies. Chiffchaffs and bluethroats flit along the ditches, hoopoes pose ostentatiously, and penduline tits peep plaintively from reedmace. There are even great bustards here – a bird of the plains, not the paddies – plus stone-curlews in dry fields around the village of Campo Lugar.

Start your second day in Monfragüe National Park, northwest of Trujillo. January often dawns misty, making for somewhat unsettling views of griffon vultures hunched on the Peña Falcón escarpment, one of two impressive protrusions at the Salto de Gitano. These huge birds suspend their crooked, coat-hanger wings, harnessing the wind as a feather dryer. Acoustics excel: mating vultures roar like red deer and flap wings as noisily as beating a carpet. You can even hear their toenails scratch the rocks.

DENNIS JACOBSEN/D

Iberian imperial eagles are a highlight of Monfragüe National Park. ▶

If you think griffons are big, you ain't seen nothin' yet. In swoops a cinereous vulture. It spacehoppers across a rock ledge, tummying griffons out of the way before goose-stepping on outstretched legs to its co-opted vantage point. Now check the river below the cliff; this is a great site for otter.

If you can drag yourself away (and rock buntings, firecrests, black redstarts, Iberian magpies and blue rock thrushes seek to prevent you), head northeast. Around the River Tiétar dam, look for red deer, which are impressively tame in the absence of hunting pressure. Continue to Monfragüe's back door, Portilla del Tiétar, a regular nesting site for Iberian imperial eagle. Muscular and self contained, this is probably Europe's rarest raptor. January sees pairs nest-building and displaying. As will become a refrain this weekend, your ears may detect them before your eyes.

For the weekend's final quarter, explore the plains – the Iberian pseudo-steppes in which you dabbled the previous day. Modern agricultural practices have so traumatised the landscape that one-time special denizens such as little bustard are struggling to survive. Some cling on, just, and your chances of seeing a small flock somewhere west of La Aldea del Obispo are reasonable. The big, tawny fields here also provide decent real estate for pin-tailed and black-bellied sandgrouse. Listen for their calls – respectively, a nasal whine and a purring churr.

Sound is the predominant feature of Extremadura's winter plains: calandra and crested larks sing in abundance, and corn buntings jangle their keys everywhere. Great bustards are easier to encounter than their smaller relatives: you might even see a hundred or more bustling through fields around the hide lying southwest of Santa Marta de Magasca. Almost alone among this weekend's birds, these turkey-like giants are silent. You may rest your ears at last.

GETTING THERE Nearest airports (2–3 hours' drive) are Seville (⌂ sevilla-airport.com) and Madrid (⌂ aeropuertomadrid-barajas.com).

WHERE TO GO A good crane area centres on side roads around **Madrigalejo** (✻ 39.140974, -5.627250), 35km southeast of Trujillo, along the EX355. The area around **Vegas Altas** (✻ 39.129178, -5.565813) is also productive. The crane information centre at **Dehesa de Moheda Alta** (✻ 39.151080, -5.489987 ✉ moheda.alta@gmail.com ⌂ tinyurl.com/moheda-alta) is worth a visit. For **Monfragüe National Park** (⌂ parquedemonfrague.com) follow the EX208 northwest from Trujillo. Salto de Gitano is at ✻ 39.828526, -6.057419, Portilla del Tiétar at ✻ 39.856847, -5.959511. The best area of the **Cáceres plains** flanks the CC99, between km35 of the A58 Trujillo–Cáceres motorway and Santa Marta de Magasca (✻ 39.510851, -6.099478). The hide is on a side road north of the CC99 at ✻ 39.469716, -6.188516. Another good area of plains lies west of La Aldea del Obispo (✻ 39.563065, -5.913380).

DAVID KJAER/NPL

SUGGESTED BASES Neatly located for sites covered, **Trujillo** (⟨⟩ trujillo.es) has ample accommodation. In Pago de San Clemente, 11km east, is the excellent **Casa Rural El Recuerdo** (⟨⟩ casaruralelrecuerdo.com), run by Claudia and Martin Kelsey.

MAKE IT A WEEK Double the amount of time you spend in each habitat: rice fields, dehesa and pseudo-steppe. Look for little bittern, black-winged kite, purple heron, purple gallinule and bluethroat at **Arrocampo Reservoir** (✷ 39.848713, -5.676984), and black-winged kite around **Saucedilla** in particular. Scan through thousands of wildfowl at **Alcollarín Reservoir** (✷ 39.249320, -5.743178).

FLEXIBILITY Cranes: November to early February (biggest numbers December to January); others: resident.

TITBITS Moheda Alta holds a crane festival each November (⟨⟩ festivaldelasgrullas. gobex.es). **Oriole Birding** (⟨⟩ oriolebirding.com; see ad, page 235) run popular winter tours to Extremadura.

Great bustards are gregarious outside the breeding season. ▲

GLADYS KLIP

Big mouth strikes again

WHERE Lake Kerkini, Macedonia, Greece
TARGETS Dalmatian pelican, greater spotted eagle, lesser white-fronted goose, sombre tit, rock nuthatch
ACCESSIBILITY ④
CHILD-FRIENDLINESS ④

I am trapped in a staring competition. My rival flourishes a tousled, bleached 'hairstyle' that originates somewhere between 1960s pop-art icon Andy Warhol and 1980s popster Howard Jones. Shadowed with yellow war paint, the beadiest of ivory eyes fix me with an unrelenting gaze. I – well, we – have fish. My adversary knows it. Wants it. And gets it. The Dalmatian pelican tosses up the scaly morsel with the most humungous bill I have ever been within inches of, encases it within a vast crimson pouch… and swallows. Then looks back at me. And resumes staring.

More Dalmatian pelicans – a thousand – winter at Lake Kerkini than anywhere in Europe. Nowhere else in the world can you get closer to this massive bird than at Greece's largest national park. And in no month does this globally threatened waterbird look more splendid than January. It is the indisputable star of this fabulous mid-winter escape.

▲ At Lake Kerkini, Dalmatian pelicans have become accustomed to handouts of fish.

You can watch the pelicans (actually two species: Dalmatian and white) easily from the shoreline. They show little fear in winter, and come agreeably close. Good locations include Mandraki, Vyroneia and Lithotopos dam, where they encircle fishermen. But the finest way to experience pelicans is to take a boat into the middle of the lake, carefully approaching the throng and trading tasty morsels for photographic opportunities. And there are many images to capture. Low down, close up, head on. Pelican swimming. Pelican flying. Pelican gobbling. Pelican mirror-imaging. Pelicans squabbling. And pelican staring.

> **66** Pelican swimming. Pelican flying. Pelican gobbling. Pelican mirror-imaging. Pelicans squabbling. And pelican staring. **99**

Lake Kerkini is often a millpond, sheltered by the Belles, mountains that soar two kilometres towards their snow-crowned peaks. Kerkini is among Europe's most important sites for wintering waterbirds. Numbers of flamingos, grebes, ducks, geese, cormorants and – of course – pelicans may defy credulation. Remarkably, Kerkini didn't even exist until 1982, when it was created by damming the River Strymónas to mitigate flooding and irrigate cultivated land. Sometimes – if only sometimes – inadvertent consequences are happy ones.

I'm not normally a fan of cormorants – wretched scarecrows with raggedy wings – but Kerkini's brace puts me straight. There are ample pygmy cormorants (rather dapper, I feel obliged to admit), but lots and lots and lots of great cormorants. Vast seething masses of black, fish-eating feather swarm through the lake in dense feeding flocks, beating wings against water to panic the fish. Crowds of cormorants stand astride stunted trees forming the 'flooded forest'. Quite stupendous, I am forced to confess.

Estimates of ducks at Kerkini have reached 50,000. These are serious numbers. I can't think of a single inland waterbody in the UK that even gets a sniff of that total. There are internationally important concentrations of mallard, teal and pochard – the latter particularly significant now that this burgundy-headed diving duck is stuttering towards extinction. The whole northwestern sector of the lake excels for ducks but smew and the scarce ferruginous duck (the male chestnut with a staring white eye) tend to favour the dam near Lithotopos.

Meanwhile, a thousand white-fronted geese graze in fields around the lake. Excitingly, given the species's global rarity, more than 100 lesser white-fronted geese now seemingly join them for the entire winter. Good areas to find geese are from Mandraki south to the lake shore, and on the 'delta' at Strymonas, viewed from the northern stretches of the embankment that hems the eastern edge of the lake.

KIT DAY

To raptors, such waterfowl concentrations are a vast buffet. Kerkini thus excels for birds of prey, notably greater spotted eagle, which is probably as easy to see here as anywhere. Most are youngsters, their dark chocolate plumage dusted ('spotted'!) with sugar crystals. True teenagers, some like to hang out near the harbour at Mandraki and atop the flooded forest, viewed from Megalochori. Golden eagles often descend from the mountains to hunt the plains, and other hook-billed brethren frequently seen include goshawk, eastern imperial eagle, hen harrier, and peregrine.

With a couple of a boat trips and an entire lake to circumnavigate, there is more than enough to fill a weekend. But its surroundings also whisper your name. On Kerkini's southwestern flank, several dirt tracks lead to hills that prop up Mt Krousia. Woodland and scrub along these can be great for small landbirds such as sombre tit – a speciality of southeastern Europe – and woodlark.

Another site for the former is an old quarry northeast of Vyroneia. It's also a great place to encounter another star of this region – rock nuthatch. This bizarre bird breeds in crevices in cliff faces and the like, securing its nest hole from predators by sealing it with mud. Hang around this quarry until dusk and you may be surprised by an eagle owl. The bisyllabic booming call of this night bird carries for a few kilometres, yet – oddly – seems to grow fainter the closer you get. Should you track one down, it will probably fix you with a steely glare. Another staring competition with which to end this fine weekend break.

▲ The beginning and end of each day are perfect times to explore Lake Kerkini by boat.

GETTING THERE Nearest airport is Thessaloniki (⚬ thessalonikiairport.com). From here it is just over 1 hour (95km) along roads 2, 25 and 12 to Lithotopos at the southeastern extremity of Lake Kerkini.

WHERE TO GO For an overview of **Lake Kerkini National Park**, see ⚬ kerkini.gr. The following summary of sites works clockwise from the southeast corner of the lake. **Lithotopos** (✽ 41.138906, 23.222716) has the dam and fishermen, and is popular with pelicans and ducks. Follow the western shore of the lake along Epar.Od. Rodopolis. After 4km, a good track heads southwest into scrubby hills inhabited by sombre tit. Back on Epar.Od. Rodopolis, the road passes through **Korifoudi** marshes before reaching **Kerkini** village (✽ 41.215579, 23.086536). Here roads ply east to an embankment that parallels the lake north to the pumping station (✽ 41.247304, 23.102393). This area drips ducks. On the northern shore, explore the area south of **Mandraki** village, and view the lake from ✽ 41.256025, 23.140590. Around **Vyroneia**, east–west tracks worth exploring include those starting at ✽ 41.259287, 23.251094 and ✽ 41.256492, 23.250356. **Vyroneia quarry** is 2.3km north of the village. Park just west of the church at ✽ 41.283536, 23.256982 and walk 200m west. Back at Vyroneia, continue south across the river to reach Megalochori, from where you join the western embankment at **Triangle Megalochori**, (✽ 41.250202, 23.211919). Heading south you get views over **Strymónas Delta** and the **flooded forest** (✽ 41.230119, 23.187341). Then follow the embankment south all the way to Lithotopos.

SUGGESTED BASES A bald list of hotels is at ⚬ kerkini.gr/eng/accommodation. Most people stay in Chryssohorafa, Kerkini or Lithotopos. Two hoteliers are wildlife experts who operate the boat services listed below: Vasilis Arabatzis runs **Hotel Oikoperiigitis** in Kerkini (⚬ oikoperiigitis.gr) and Nikos Gallios owns **Limneo Hotel** in Chryssohorafa (⚬ limneokerkini.gr/en).

MAKE IT A WEEK Nearby **Sidirokastro** has rock nuthatch and blue rock thrush. Explore coastal wetlands at **Kalochori** for wildfowl and waders. Visit the **Evros Delta** for large numbers of wintering ducks and geese.

FLEXIBILITY Pelican, tit and nuthatch: year-round but December to February is best for tame pelicans; eagle and goose: November to February.

TITBITS UK operators offering Kerkini tours include **Greenwings** (⚬ greenwings.co.uk; see ad, page 233) and **Bird Holidays** (⚬ birdholidays. co.uk; ad, page 237). Good-value **boat trips** – fixed departures and pre-arranged charters – depart Kerkini (⚬ oikoperiigitis.gr/en/activities/boat-tour) and Chryssohorafa (⚬ tinyurl.com/limneo-boat).

The well-named rock nuthatch shuns the trees favoured by almost all other nuthatches. ▷
GEORGIOS ALEXANDRIS/D

Mid-Atlantic Europe

WHERE São Miguel, Azores, Portugal
TARGETS Azores bullfinch, Atlantic canary,
vagrant American birds, sperm whale, short-beaked common dolphin
ACCESSIBILITY ③
CHILD-FRIENDLINESS ①

> 66 Azores bullfinch was so nearly a textbook example of Anthropocene extinction 99

N ew Year, (almost) New World. Out here in the mid-Atlantic, the Azores rather stretch this guide's definition of Europe. The Portuguese archipelago lies a thousand miles from the national capital, Lisbon. Indeed, the islands are barely further from New York than Hawaii is from San Francisco. But there's an outstanding – indeed, unique – reason for coming here. For the *priôlo* occurs nowhere else.

Moreover, not only does Azores bullfinch – a tubby, caramel-coloured, sparrow-sized bird – occur solely on the Azores, but it actually resides on just one of the nine islands. As if respecting the constraints of the weekend wildlife-watcher, the priôlo inhabits São Miguel, also conveniently home to an international airport. Pickier still, it now lives only in that island's dampest, windiest, easternmost laurel forests. And – the *coup de grâce* (or, given where we are, *golpe de misericórdia*) – as few as 700 bullfinches may remain. Which is why people are prepared to fly such a long way out into the Atlantic Ocean to see this particular bundle of feathers – and why I encourage you to follow suit.

But there's another reason too – and this one poignant. Azores bullfinch was so nearly a textbook example of Anthropocene extinction. In the 19th century, the bird was so locally abundant that it got in the way. São Miguel's human colonisers demolished the *laurissilva* (or laurel forest) so they could plant fruit-bearing trees and other crops. The bullfinch's habitat shrank – as did its food resources. Its taste for fruit – its need to eat – led it into those self-same orchards… and thus into conflict with cultivators, who hunted it as a pest. As if this double whammy were not enough, non-native, invasive plants (kahili ginger, sweet pittosporum, etc) have

▲ Endemic and iconic, Azores bullfinch has long attracted visitors to the Atlantic archipelago.
DOMINIC MITCHELL www.birdingetc.com

wreaked havoc on what little laurel forest remains – pushing the *priôlo* to the edge. By the early 1990s, as few as 120 bullfinches remained.

As such, for my generation and others, Azores bullfinch became an icon of how we can mess up the planet – and here in Europe too, not in some far-flung rainforest. This explains both the long-harboured aspiration to see the *priôlo* 'before it's too late' and the more-recent hankering to observe it now that its future seems – if not secure exactly – then certainly less parlous. As a result of intensive conservation efforts, there seems to be a recent population recovery. To reflect this, the official conservation status has improved from Critically Endangered to Vulnerable. Accordingly, seeing Azores bullfinch equates to celebrating both its existence and the value of conservation efforts.

In which case… how and where to find the bullfinch? Let's be upfront. Plain sailing this is not. These are small, undemonstrative birds and – despite forest clearance – there's still a lot of trees in which they can hide. But with two days at your disposal, you should be fine. So set off from your digs in the blackness to arrive in the Serra da Tronqueira at dawn.

Seven kilometres east of Povoação, turn north off the main cross-island road (EN1-1A) on to a dirt track (EN1-2A) towards Nordeste. Most tracts of forest should produce Atlantic canary – originator of the coalmine songster – plus the local endemic races of chaffinch and goldcrest (the finch looking quite different to birds in northern Europe). Blackcaps, robins and blackbirds will also all abound – but their presence may give little hint as to the whereabouts of your principal quarry.

GORKA OCIO Verballenas.com

The Azores excel at cetaceans such as this short-beaked common dolphin. ▲

For bullfinches, the trick is to drive slowly, watching for birds feeding by the roadside, and to pause regularly in good-looking laurel forest to listen for their plaintive call. With a combination of persistence and luck, you should succeed. When you do, admire these small birds. Though not shockingly coloured like European bullfinch, the *priôlo* has its own charm. Its immense bill shouts out for fruit seeds to crack. Its sooty cap, tail and triangle on its wings stand out on the milky-tea plumage. Here is Europe's rarest songbird, all for you.

When you have succeeded, celebrate with a half-day boat trip offshore. Although low season for cetaceans, you should encounter short-beaked common dolphin, common bottlenose dolphin and sperm whale. You are even in with a chance of fin whale.

Then it's a case of hunting down some of the transatlantic vagrant birds for which the Azores has become famous. Each year, strong westerly-based winds jet North American birds across the Atlantic, well off their normal north–south migration route. Many make landfall on the Azores – and the larger birds (ducks and waders, for example) often stick around through the winter. This creates a little piece of the Americas in Europe.

Classic locations for vagrants include freshwater lakes (Lagoas das Furnas, Azul and Verde) plus the jagged black rocky coast of Mosterios. It is a somewhat surreal experience to watch an American waterbird such as a pied-billed grebe, ring-necked duck or green-winged teal against the backdrop of steaming sulphur springs and dripping, misty laurel forest. New Year, New World indeed.

JAMES LOWEN

▲ The Azores is the best place in Europe to encounter vagrant American birds such as this greater yellowlegs.

GETTING THERE Nearest airport is Ponta Delgada, the archipelago capital, on São Miguel ($\oslash$ aeroportopontadelgada.pt). There are direct flights from two London airports on Saturdays (only), but you will need to return via Lisbon if you travel for under a week. **WHERE TO GO** The forest of **Serra da Tronqueira** lies in southeast São Miguel, centred around ✸ 37.780359, -25.192766. From Ponta Delgada, follow the EN1-1A through Povoação, then turn left (north) on to the EN1-2A after 7km (✸ 37.766031, -25.203327). Continue along this dirt track then, after 1.7km, branch right (northeast) towards Nordeste at ✸ 37.773259, -25.197892. Measuring from the EN1-1A junction, good areas include those after 500m and 2.7km. Another regular site is Serra da Tronqueira mirador (✸ 37.796252, -25.184662). A third option is to continue further east along the EN1-1A to ✸ 37.776346, -25.145966 then drive the M1038 to **Pico Bartolomeu mirador** (✸ 37.778097, -25.168695). Alternatively, try the track up to **Pico da Vara mirador**, the island's highest point at 1,103m. Leave the EN1-1A in Algarvia (✸ 37.842256, -25.231410), driving south to the trailhead at ✸ 37.816128, -25.231747. If you haven't seen bullfinches by this point, walk south then east to Pico da Vara (✸ 37.814347, -25.200101; permission needed: $\oslash$ tinyurl.com/picodevara). Sites to search for American vagrants are widely separated. Excellent information for most is at $\oslash$ tinyurl.com/azores-sites. **Lago das Furnas** flanks the EN1-1A, immediately southwest of Furnas (✸ 37.757903, -25.332683). East of Sete Cidades, **Lagoa Azul** is at ✸ 37.857111, -25.786339 and Lagoa Verde at ✸ 37.852850, -25.787917. Also in northwest São Miguel is **Mosteiros** ($\oslash$ 37.898519, -25.821750).

SUGGESTED BASES Ponta Delgada offers plenty of accommodation, most of which can be accessed through $\oslash$ visitazores.com/en/accommodations. You could also stay at **Furnas** or **Ribeira Grande**.

MAKE IT A WEEK Do further **boat trips** offshore. Although January is far from the summer cetacean peak ($\oslash$ azoreswhales.blogspot.co.uk/p/statistics.html), you may strike it lucky with humpback whale, Risso's dolphin or striped dolphin. Island-hop to **Terceira**, where **Praia da Vitória** excels for American vagrants in winter. As you have to fly back via Lisbon, spend a day or two birding the city's **Tagus Estuary**: two wildlife weekends in one!

FLEXIBILITY Bullfinch and canary: year-round, though easiest in fine weather; vagrants: September to March; cetaceans: year-round (but peak April to August).

TITBITS A recommended travel agent specialising in the Azores is **Archipelago Choice** ($\oslash$ azoreschoice.com). The Priolo Interpretation Centre (✸ 37.80150, -25.16318; $\oslash$ centropriolo.spea.pt) is worth a visit to understand conservation in the Azores. Several operators run **cetacean-watching boat trips** off the island (eg: Futurismo ($\oslash$ futurismo.pt/en/program/whale-watching-half-day).

Wild goose chase

WHERE Black Sea coast, Dobrich, northeast Bulgaria
TARGETS Red-breasted goose, white-fronted goose, Yelkouan shearwater, pygmy cormorant, golden jackal
ACCESSIBILITY ④
CHILD-FRIENDLINESS ②

Having risen in the pre-dawn pitch, you take up position by Shabla Lake, adjacent to the Black Sea of Bulgarian Dobruja. You wait. Peering westwards, the argent waterbody glistens from the murk. You wait. Behind you, the sun strains to levitate. You wait. Suddenly it is daybreak. You are alive – and tens of thousands of geese are awake. Yapping and yelping, chattering and squeaking, the winged forms smoke into the air. Swathe after swathe take off vertically, twist acrobatically and stretch upwards and towards you, roaring directly overhead before powering inland to graze amidst vast wheat fields. The sound, the motion, the intensity sear into your soul.

Some 100,000 geese spend two winter months building sufficient fat reserves to power their spring migration northwards to Arctic breeding grounds. The large majority are white-fronted geese – grey in plumage, with adults bearing a snowy blaze around their candy-pink bill. Seeing this compact waterbird in such numbers would be reason alone for the trip. Yet it does not take top billing.

▲ Huge mixed flocks of red-breasted and white-fronted geese are one of Europe's finest avian spectacles.
BAS VAN DEN BOOGAARD/MINDEN PICTURES/FLPA

Red-breasted goose is indisputably Europe's most handsome goose. At range – particularly in the half-light of dawn – it may appear black and white. But such an impression is misleading. This exquisite bird is on fire, exhibiting an intense rufous breast, foreneck and cheeks.

But the 'red-breast' is not merely beautiful – though that too would be reason enough for this weekend. It is also one of Europe's two rarest geese. Estimates of its total world population vary, but a ballpark would be 50,000. That's not a lot. Roughly as few people inhabit the Leicestershire (UK) town of Melton Mowbray.

And even that titchy population – of which more than half winters in Dobruja, a contested region divided between Bulgaria and Romania – remains under pressure. Russian and Kazakh hunters shoot red-breasted geese as they migrate to and from the Arctic. Bulgarian hunters strafe them

> **Yapping and yelping, chattering and squeaking, the winged forms smoke into the air.**

– ostensibly inadvertently, mistaking them for white-fronted geese – on their wintering grounds. The goose's favoured winter-wheat fields are being concreted over or supplanted by wind farms, policies with which the European Court of Justice has taken umbrage. The waterbird may even be poisoned by pesticides applied ever more liberally following the contortion of Bulgarian agriculture by the European Union's environmentally deleterious Common Agricultural Policy.

Little wonder then that this beautiful goose is considered threatened with global extinction. See it now, before it's too late. Once the birds roosting on Shabla or nearby Durankulak lakes have flown to feeding grounds, follow them. This is a case

of driving roads through frosty agricultural fields surrounding the lakes until you chance upon a flock. Watch carefully from the vehicle. If you get out, the geese will probably mistake you for a poacher, fret into the air, and wing to pastures distant. This would be unfortunate for both the geese and your weekend.

As you cruise, scan and watch, you will encounter other exciting birds. Both lakes are important refuges for congregations of wildfowl (and are visited by geese for a midday drink). These include the delightful smew – the punk-crested drakes of which are 'designer ducks', with black mascara and go-faster stripes on otherwise icy-white plumage. Among a thousand pochard – a diving duck that has declined so dramatically to now be in danger of global extinction – look for red-crested pochard. Males of this bizarrely bouffant-headed duck look even more comical with their tonal discord between tangerine head and strawberry bill.

GETTING THERE Nearest airport is Varna (⊘ varna-airport.bg), from where it is 1½ hours' drive (109km) along the E87 to Durankulak. There are flights to Varna from several European cities, including a low-cost airline from London Luton.
WHERE TO GO Durankulak Lake (✳ 43.678839, 28.555047) borders the Black Sea, just east of the village of the same name. **Lake Shabla** (✳ 43.573520, 28.567014) is approximately 10km south. Geese roost on both waterbodies, and occasionally on the smaller lake of **Shablenska Tuzla** (✳ 43.557799, 28.591998), 1.5km southeast, or on the sea (particularly when lakes are frozen). All three lakes are accessed via minor roads east of the E87. South of Balgarevo, **Cape Kaliakra** (✳ 43.360686, 28.466095) is 40 minutes' drive (50km) south of Durankulak. Side roads help you explore the steppe en route to the Cape – but note that military police routinely drive the area.
SUGGESTED BASES Inexpensive accommodation is available in the villages of Durankulak (✳ 43.689149, 28.529874), which includes **Branta Birding Lodge** (⊘birdinglodge.com),

▲ Golden jackals are spreading west through Europe but Bulgaria remains one of the best countries to see them.

Scan the lakes carefully and you may encounter other waterbirds. Pygmy cormorant – a bonsai version of the more familiar and widespread great cormorant – is a scarce species in Europe, but seems to be increasing in numbers. The odd Dalmatian pelican may linger through winter – although these are more easily seen north and south of here. The extensive, golden reedbeds secrete avian interest too. You should have no problem in seeing bearded tit, but stumbling upon a great bittern – camouflaged, concealed and swaying in tandem with the vegetation – demands either fortune or sharp eyes.

You should also encounter a multitude of raptors. There's a trio of buzzards to discern: in descending order of abundance, common, rough-legged and long-legged. Marsh harriers outnumber hen harriers, but both are pleasingly frequent. White-tailed eagles block out the sun as they barn-door overhead. And peregrines and merlins compete for the title of Most Dashing Falcon.

When you fancy something different, two ideas nominate themselves. The first is to drive through the steppe towards Cape Kaliakra, looking for calandra and crested larks *en route*. Once you reach the caramel cliffs at the headland, scan the sea for Yelkouan shearwater, yet another globally threatened bird. And scan the deep gorge just north of the Cape, where wildcat has been seen. Second, drive this same area at night, sweeping a powerful spotlight over the stony terrain in search of exciting carnivorous mammals such as golden jackal (more common in Bulgaria than anywhere else in Europe) and beech marten, plus – conceivably – marbled or steppe polecat. In this land bordering the Black Sea, even inky darkness offers attractions.

and **Shabla** (✳ 43.530952, 28.526401). Plenty of hotels in Balchik, between Durankulak and Varna.
MAKE IT A WEEK There is excellent birding around **Pelican Birding Lodge**, west of Silistra (⚭ pelican-birding-lodge; see ad, page 232), the base of Pandion Wild Tours (see *Titbits* below). To see white-headed duck (another globally threatened bird), visit **Bourgas** wetlands or Romania's **Lake Techirgiol** (30km north of the border). Try the forest around **Lake Varna** or **Brestnica** for sombre tit. Try Lake Srebarna for Dalmatian pelican.
FLEXIBILITY Geese: can be present December to late February, but mid-January to mid-February is optimum. Numbers depend on weather (too warm or cold and they head elsewhere); you want cold but not frozen lakes. Check ⚭ neophrontours.bg/category/news/ for updates. Note also that shooting season lasts until 31 January. Other species: year-round.
TITBITS Local wildlife-tour operators offering guiding services with a focus on red-breasted goose include **Pandion Wild Tours** (⚭ birdwatchingholidays.com; see ad, page 232), **Branta Tours** (⚭ branta-tours.com) and **Neophron** (⚭ neophrontours.bg).

❝ Erect and oddly sphinx-like, the Iberian lynx has long limbs and insanely tufted ears ❞

CARLOS N. G. BOCOS

The lynx effect

WHERE Sierra de Andújar, Jaén, Spain
TARGETS Iberian lynx, mouflon, Schreiber's bat, European free-tailed bat, stripeless tree frog
ACCESSIBILITY ⑤
CHILD-FRIENDLINESS ③ (kids may get bored with long waits)

E arly morning in Spain's Sierra de Andújar. The air smells of blended wild rosemary and lavender – even if I cannot see either plant. What should be rocky hill slopes and a valley are shrouded in the densest of mist. An Iberian green woodpecker laughs at us from somewhere below, and hawfinches call, unseen. Our chances of seeing the world's rarest feline – indeed of seeing *anything* – seem slight. My vision failing to pierce the murk, I slump.

▲ Thanks to conservation action, Iberian lynx is thriving again in parts of Spain and Portugal.

'There's one!' says my companion. I jolt alert. He's right. Scarcely 50 metres away from our perch on white concrete blocks, marginally but euphorically on our side of the fog bank, sits a female Iberian lynx, bold as brass. Erect and oddly sphinx-like, she has long limbs and insanely tufted ears. Mottled and marbled, she could easily pass unnoticed amid the greys, browns and greens of Andújar's botany.

We admire the cat for several precious minutes until she attracts the attention of the local Iberian magpies. Inappropriately clad in a baby's outfit of pink, blue and white, the garrulous gang surrounds the lynx, jeering in alarm from a safe distance. Eventually she tires of the racket and slinks through the bushes… towards us. Padding softly, stumpy tail cocked behind her, cheek frills pointing groundwards. She glances towards us, conspicuously disinterested, passes behind a boulder… and vanishes. We can finally exhale.

For decades, Iberian lynx was a mythical creature – one on the point of extinction, and never seen. Ten of the 12 known populations died out between 1988 and 2004. The two that remained have suffered as a consequence of widespread myxomatosis in the European rabbits upon which the lynx depends. At the lowest point, there were just 1,000 cats left. Inoculating bunnies and translocating captive-bred lynx appears to have turned the conservation corner.

The cat is no longer Critically Endangered – although the world total remains in the low hundreds. Nowadays, the prospects of seeing Iberian lynx within two to three days are very high. Chris Townend of Wise Birding (see ad, page 230) – a seasoned lynx-watcher – had tipped us off about the best spots: 'Focus on the two main viewpoints at La Lancha. I have had most luck in the final valley.' We followed his advice.

For a break from hours of scoping hillsides or scanning bushes for errant 'rocks', bump downhill to the Embalse de Jándula. Approaching the dam, an obvious viewpoint affords views of raptors (including Iberian imperial eagle), vultures (griffon and cinereous) and woodlark. Before crossing the dam, walk southwest and look across the gorge for Spanish ibex posing atop craggy outcrops. If the day is sunny, you should see Geniez's wall lizard here. Then traverse the dam as seething flocks of crag martin encircle you and a rock bunting thrusts back its head and pours forth.

Once over the other side, enter the tunnel for a mammalian marvel. Using a torch sensitively, peer upwards into roof cracks. Several species of bat roost here by day. You may discern Schreiber's, greater mouse-eared and Daubenton's. Visiting bat roosts is the preserve of surveyors in much of Europe, so enjoy the freedom to do so here – but respect the animals' desire for darkness and quiet.

Andújar offers other furry interest. You may bump into mouflon – a stocky, leggy, curly-horned sheep – anywhere, but rarely do they afford close views.

In contrast, abundant red and fallow deer tolerate close attention. Wild boar is shy – the impact of hunting – but trailing around at night will likely bring you into contact with a sounder. Even at this early juncture in the year, Andújar flora is impressive. In addition to rosemary and lavender, there is ample lupin, abundant jonquil daffodil and numerous tiny angel's tears (a *Narcissus*).

The second-best area to try for Iberian lynx is the Sendero del Encinarejo, a little further south. Most visitors come here after trying the honeypot sites to the north. To maximise chances, spend time between the lay-by on the hilltop and the dam during the last few hours of daylight. This is a good site for Iberian imperial and golden eagles, while globally threatened Spanish terrapins often adorn rocks in the Río Jándula below.

Stay beyond dusk for a more varied wildlife experience. As the air thickens, scores of mouse-eared bats wing along the dam wall, while European free-tailed bats coast high overhead. Once light has been vanquished, eagle owls call deeply from cliffs near the dam, mole crickets scissor from subterranean holes – and a veritable amphibian chorus opens up. Carefully follow up each different call to be enchanted by amphibians such as natterjack toad (abundant!), Iberian water frog and stripeless tree frog (usually on the ground in defiance of its name).

Such is the change in the fortunes of Iberian lynx (and lynx-watchers!) that few visitors leave the Sierra de Andújar without seeing its figurehead feline. Should you be among them, however, the supporting acts make for a brilliant wildlife weekend in their own right.

▲ Schreiber's bat is among several species roosting in the tunnel at Embalse de Jándula. Use your torch sensitively.

GETTING THERE 3 hours' drive north of Málaga airport (⊘ tinyurl.com/airport-malaga), which takes abundant charter and scheduled flights from numerous European cities. Sevilla airport is closer, but has fewer flights.

WHERE TO GO Leave the A4 motorway at km 321 (Andújar), follow the A6177 northeast to the JH5002 junction. For **La Lancha** (the main lynx-watching area, which up to a dozen individuals may frequent) follow the JH5002 north, then turn west on the badly potholed, slow JF5004. The best viewpoints are between the white concrete blocks (❋ 38.212883, -3.959642 and the gate (❋ 38.215803,-3.962887). Some have seen tame garden dormice here. **Jándula dam** is 2km downhill (❋ 38.224201, -3.972599). Approaching from **Los Escoriales** the area around the stone troughs is good for mouflon (❋ 38.189943,-3.929651). The other lynx area is **Sendero del Encinarejo**. From the A6177/JH5002 junction continue west along the A6177, turning north immediately after a single-track road bridge. From the lay-by with white concrete blocks, scan the valley. Continue to Encinarejo dam, scanning from the hillside above the car park. Amphibians occur in standing water south of the dam.

SUGGESTED BASES Most stay at **Complejo Turístico Los Pinos**, near the A6177/ JH5002 junction (❋ 38.128399, -3.965730; ⊘ lospinos.es); stripeless tree frogs inhabit the garden. You can eat here and across the road at **El Rancho**. *Casas rurales* include the lovely **Villa Mathilde** (❋ 38.142812, -3.948591; ⊘ villamatilde.org).

MAKE IT A WEEK Go exclusive by paying to access one of the private *fincas* where Iberian lynx reside (⊘ iberianlynxland.com). Look for reptiles: **Mirador El Peregrino** viewpoint is good (❋ 38.131240, -3.977132); so too the area behind the viewpoint above Jándula dam. Look for the globally threatened white-headed duck and other waterbirds at **Río Guadalhorce Nature Reserve** near Málaga airport (⊘ tinyurl.com/rio-guada).

FLEXIBILITY Lynx: year-round although December to March is best. Other species: year-round although January to April is best for amphibians.

TITBITS Weekends can get crowded (and noisy) with lynx-watchers. A useful site guide is at ⊘ tinyurl.com/dingain-lynx.

JAMES LOWEN

Head out after dark to investigate Andújar's amphibians such as this stripeless tree frog. ▲

LEANDER KHIL www.leanderkhil.com

Blind love and headless chickens

WHERE Lanzarote, Canary Islands, Spain
TARGETS Houbara bustard, cream-coloured courser, monarch, blind squat lobster, East Canary gecko
ACCESSIBILITY ④
CHILD-FRIENDLINESS ⑤

Under the insipid sun of Lanzarote's winter dawn, an enormous cotton-wool ball is catapulting across a stony, prickily vegetated, gently sloping plain. Peering through binoculars, you determine that the snowy pom-pom is ruffled with black and borne by two sturdy legs. Those limbs are fairly sprinting for two cricket-pitch lengths, before zigzagging off at a sheer angle. The apparition prompts thought of a cartoon headless chicken, apparently unable to see and dementedly refusing to concede that its life is expiring. But it is actually the marvellous-yet-mad display of the male houbara bustard.

Bustards are hefty, ground-dwelling birds of open areas. Our region's three species are all in trouble, with the African houbara being considered threatened with global extinction. The gritty desert of the easternmost major island in the Canaries – just 125km from Africa – is the world's easiest place to witness this dramatic creature strut its stuff.

This is not 'desert' as in Saharan sands, but arid, rocky plains undulating unto the horizon, thorny bushes dotting the vista. Three fine sites for bustards are El Rubicón (on which the tourist resort of Playa Blanca is sadly encroaching), the goat farm at Guatiza (in the northeast) and El Jable.

▲ Half pom-pom, half chicken: a male houbara bustard displays to a female.

The latter hosts the largest and highest-quality plains, which stretch north from the charming town of Teguise towards Muñique, Sóo and Famara. Spend from first light until mid-morning here, exploring the multitude of dirt tracks. Houbaras occur widely; you may see small groups. For optimum views, stay in your car: birds typically wander within 50m, oblivious to their human admirers, before dissolving into the thorny scrub.

Remain alert to catch sight of other avian stars, all somewhat camouflaged. Cream-coloured coursers – delectable, charismatic creatures – sprint across the bare ground, legs whirring beneath their caramel tones. Represented by a regionally endemic subspecies, the goggle-eyed stone-curlew is common and confiding. Trumpeter finch, with its bugling calls and rosy bill, cannot help but charm. Lesser short-toed larks provide in-flight acoustic entertainment. Berthelot's pipits stride boldly; this abundant bird occurs only in the Canaries and on Madeira.

And all this on 'Lanzagrotty'. The more widely you investigate Lanzarote, the dafter its disparaging nickname becomes. Away from the (admittedly ugly) tourist strip, this island oozes handsomeness – from steepling sea cliffs to low, whitewashed villages, from Timanfaya's tar-coloured volcanic plains to Haría's shockingly verdant valleys with their spurge, cacti and palm.

Although wildlife away from the plains prefers not to thrust itself upon you, there is plenty to admire. Haría's vegetated hairpins are great for birds such as Atlantic canary, African blue tit and spectacled warbler. This area is particularly good for butterflies too; look for monarch, geranium bronze and long-tailed blue. The sheerness of Mirador del Río offers a decent shot at Barbary falcon, but you could come across it anywhere.

ALICK SIMMONS

66 Cream-coloured coursers sprint across the bare ground, legs whirring beneath their caramel tones 99

Cream-coloured coursers are perfectly camouflaged for life in Lanzarote's arid soils. ▲

ALEXILENA/S

Reptiles are intriguing. The terrain looks perfect for snakes, yet none exists here. East Canary skink provides the herpetological nirvana, yet is seemingly never seen (if, indeed, it persists here at all). Focus instead on tracking down Haría (aka Atlantic) lizard, with its blue- or green-spotted flanks. This can pop up anywhere, from a rocky town wall to more natural terrain. When darkness has settled, shine your beam along stone walls to locate East Canary gecko, a sucker-toed speciality that occurs solely on Lanzarote and neighbouring Fuerteventura. You should have a chance in almost any village, and even in more built-up areas. Alternatively, turn over stones by day to find one lurking calmly.

GETTING THERE Tens of scheduled/charter flights daily from many European cities to the capital of Arrecife (⏁ tinyurl.com/airport-lanzarote). Lanzarote is small (60km by 25km); getting around is quick.

WHERE TO GO El Jable plain (roughly centered on ✳ 29.062490, -13.609292) lies northwest of Teguise. Access is along easily drivable tracks east of the LZ401 Tiagua–Muñique–Sôo road or west of the LZ402. Urbanisation means that **El Rubicón** plains (✳ 28.886464, -13.856721) are not what they were, but it is a convenient location to try if staying in Playa Blanca. Take tracks west from the LZ2. A great site for bustards is the goat farm 2.2km south of **Guatiza** (✳ 29.04222, -13.48708); take the turning signed 'Tinamala'. Also in northern Lanzarote, the approach to Haría has rich vegetation (✳ 29.131485, -13.513728), **Jameos del Agua** (✳ 29.156565, -13.430901; ⏁ cactlanzarote.com/cact/jameos-del-agua) lies northeast of Punta Mujeres, and **Mirador del Río** (✳ 29.213124, -13.482838) sits atop towering cliffs.

▲ The glittering underwater 'stars' are tiny, unique squat lobsters with the scientific name *Munidopsis polymorpha*.

The displaying houbara bustard may appear blind, its head and eyes trapped deep within fluffed-out breast feathers, but Lanzarote's most remarkable creature is genuinely sightless. This tiny squat lobster – known formally by its scientific name *Munidopsis polymorpha* – is among the most bizarre animals you will encounter during your year of wildlife-weekending across Europe.

Bleached of colour and cave dwelling, this crustacean lives only on Lanzarote. Accordingly, you might think that tracking it down would be tricky, perhaps requiring snorkelling into dark cavities. But you would be wrong. Thousands of *Munidopsis* can be easily seen at Los Jameos del Agua, a tourist attraction crafted by the island's architectural genius, César Manrique.

> **The blackness of igneous rocks is starred with innumerable glowing crustaceans – an underwater night sky**

Fusing geology with art, there is nowhere like Los Jameos. Descending via a stone staircase through a lava tube, you reach a cave called Jameo Chico. Here, within a mineral-cool, irresistibly clear pool, the blackness of igneous rocks is starred with innumerable glowing crustaceans – an underwater night sky. Atop every square metre of rock there can be up to 150 *jameitos*, as the mini-lobsters have become known. By day, most skulk in crevices, but scores may still be cherished at close range. Should they feel threatened, they shoot through the water with remarkable alacrity. Blind yet speedy, bizarrely like the displaying houbara bustard with which you started this surprisingly rich wildlife weekend.

SUGGESTED BASES Plenty of tourist accommodation in coastal resorts such as Playa Blanca, Puerto del Carmen and Arrecife, but try and stay in a traditional village in the interior. I particularly like **Teguise** (beware: not Costa Teguise!) and **Tinajo**.

MAKE IT A WEEK Take a (brilliant!) submarine safari from **Puerto Calero** to see trigger fish and rays (⊘ submarinesafaris.com). **Seawatch** from Charco del Palo, Punta Ginés or Punta Pechiguera for possible Bryde's whale, spinner dolphins and seabirds such as Bulwer's petrel and Cory's shearwater. Look for vagrant shorebirds at **Laguna de Janubio** or migrant landbirds (and Barbary partridge) at **Tachiche golf course**. Take a day-trip to **Fuerteventura** for Canary Islands chat, or take the ferry to **Tenerife**, watching cetaceans and seabirds *en route*.

FLEXIBILITY Year-round.

TITBITS Bird Holidays (⊘ birdholidays.co.uk; see ad, page 237) run a wide-ranging Canaries tour.

JAMES LOWEN

Originally a New World species, the monarch butterfly has resided in the Canaries since the mid-19th century. ▶

> **66** To see owls,
> pray for windless,
> dry conditions,
> ideally on dark,
> moon-free nights **99**

GERRIT VYN/NPL

Snow?
Go!

WHERE Vidzeme, Latvia
TARGETS Ural owl, pygmy owl, white-backed woodpecker, three-toed woodpecker, raccoon dog
ACCESSIBILITY ③
CHILD-FRIENDLINESS ②

'Latvia in late winter is some of the best birding I have experienced anywhere in Europe.' Coming from a wildlife-tour leader – in this case, Andy Walker of Birding Ecotours – that is high praise indeed.

Latvia is sandwiched between the other two Baltic states (Estonia to the north and Lithuania to the south). The country is rich in wildlife yet oddly remains little visited by naturalists. Those that do come tend to target spring bird migration (typically at the brilliant Cape Kolka) or summer's butterflies and orchids. This weekend takes an alternative tack, focusing on the avian specialities of Latvia's snowy forests.

Although a schlepp from Riga to Druviena in northeast Latvia, it's worth it. The tranquil village is definitively rural, with tree-lined roads and fields partitioning the houses. Focus your time on the dense forests westnorthwest of the village, driving where you can and otherwise walking. Prepare to divide your time between day and night.

During the hours of darkness, your quarry comprises various owls with a side-order of quality mammals. Late winter and early spring are the best times to hear owls calling, as they vocally proclaim ownership of a dominion. Pray for windless, dry conditions, ideally on dark, moon-free nights. Familiarise yourself with the

▲ Europe's smallest owl, the pygmy owl hunts by day as well as night.

voice of Ural, pygmy and Tengmalm's owls and refresh your memory with the array of sounds offered by tawny owl. When you hear an owl, walk slowly and quietly towards it. Late winter is a lean time for owls, and their energy resources are depleted. So resist the temptation to bring it closer by playing a recording.

Each of the owls offers something different. Ural resembles tawny, but is open-faced and long-tailed. It often hunts from exposed trees in clear-fell areas. Pygmy owl is enchantingly tiny, with white eyebrows that make it appear to be constantly frowning. This titch is active by day as well as night, when its rapid, woodpecker-like flight may catch the eye. The star that shines brightest in the Latvian night is Tengmalm's owl. With large pale eyes and an arched brow, it looks surprised to be alive. Rare and reclusive, it is best seen with the help of a local expert such as Gaidis Grandāns, near whose former home much of this weekend is focused.

The longer you trawl the tracks at night, the greater the chance of bumping into a classy mammal. Roe and red deer are common; so too brown hare and red fox. The bandit-masked raccoon dog is frequently encountered. These descendants of fur-farm escapees typically trot along roads or trundle through adjacent fields. Keep alert for a lurking Eurasian elk, undulating pine marten, or, if you pass fallen trees crossing narrow drainage ditches, Eurasian beaver.

By day, wander the same forests looking for diurnal birds. First up, acquaint yourselves with local takes on familiar woodland birds. Willow tit, bullfinch, nuthatch and treecreeper all occur – but differ noticeably from birds in northwest Europe, most being suitably frostier in plumage tones, for a snowier climate. More obviously different is northern long-tailed tit. With a gleaming white head, this is more snowball than bird.

For woodpeckers – your daytime priorities – the best strategy is pull up every half-mile or so and listen. Forests are often mortally quiet, but every so often a woodpecker breaks the silence with its territorial yodel or drum. Moving stealthily, you can track them down – and usually enjoy good views.

Three-toed woodpecker takes top billing, with its yellow crown and faint white zigzags on jet-black wings. Latvia's old-growth forests have plenty of the dead wood demanded by white-backed woodpecker. You could happily admire this black, white and crimson cracker for hours. The dramatic black woodpecker – all staring eye and flaming skullcap – is fairly common.

The thick woods west of Druviena is not for middle spotted woodpeckers, however. You are more likely to see this red-crowned creature in trees back in the village. The same is true of the comparatively undemonstrative grey-headed woodpecker, which favours open woodland. Though not a woodpecker, spotted nutcracker is a local speciality. With fortune, you may bump into one of these piebald jay-like creatures.

Forests are not just about their trees, however, and consequently not only about arboreal life. The berry-rich understorey of Latvia's woodlands is the domain of two exciting, primarily terrestrial gamebirds – even if they do have a propensity to perch on branches too. For hazel grouse, try driving forest tracks north of Lubāna. This is another creature worth listening for – even if you could be forgiven for thinking that its weedy sibilance emanates from a small bird such as goldcrest. Near Balvi, try the same approach to encounter capercaillie. You are most likely to see this turkey-sized grouse fleeing into the trees. But this is the time of year when males defend display arenas. Encountering a 'rogue caper' is an experience like no other. Be sure to keep your distance to avoid being charged. Not only is it a waste of energy for a stressed-out bird, but it could be dangerous for you. Mind you, that *would* certainly be a European birding experience to remember…

" These descendants of fur-farm escapees typically trot along roads or trundle through adjacent fields "

STANISLAV DUBEN/S

▲ Although not native to Europe, raccoon dogs still thrill when you encounter one.

GETTING THERE Nearest airport is Riga, the Latvian capital (⊘ riga-airport.com). There are flights from several UK and European airports, including with low-cost airlines. It's 3 hours' (190km) drive northeast to Druviena, although crossing Riga to join the A2 may delay you.

WHERE TO GO For the best chance of seeing the target wildlife, I recommend using a local guide (see below). Should you travel independently, take care not to get lost along confusingly similar forest roads: making a GPS track of your route is sensible. For forests near **Druviena**, take the road northwest from the 'LaTS' shop (✸ 57.113988, 26.293231) in Druviena village. Follow this road for 5km, passing through Saltupes. Turn west at Ziemeļi (✸ 57.130417, 26.223746). At the fork after 200m, either turn right or veer left then take the first right. Both tracks lead to decent forest. Alternatively continue 1.8km north along the road beyond Ziemeļi. At Sproģi (✸ 57.146184, 26.220604), take the track west to reach forest. **Lubāna** is 40 minutes (40km) southeast of Druviena along the P83. To explore forests northeast of the village, take the minor road that connects the P36 and P83 then delve deeper along likely looking tracks on either side of the road (particularly to the north). Once you reach the P36 (✸ 57.025660, 26.992606), turn southeast to the junction with the P47 then head northeast along this road to **Balvi**. Follow the P35 eastnortheast for 10km to reach forest, then explore along tracks. From when you reach the P36, the journey takes 35 minutes (43km).

SUGGESTED BASES The nearest hotels to Druviena are in Cesvaine and Madona, both south along the P38/P37. Tour groups tend to stay at **Ezernieki** (⊘ celotajs.lv/en/e/ezernieki2; ✸ 56.812300, 26.566009), 15km southwest of Lubāna along the P82. There is top birding at this hotel, including three species of woodpecker, and in the vicinity (for other target species: simply drive forest tracks).

MAKE IT A WEEK Kemeri National Park excels for woodpeckers, if you don't see them all at Druviena. **Teiči Nature Reserve** is good for black grouse; Cape Kolka for parrot crossbill. **Parks in Riga** (eg: Kronvalda) are excellent for urban-breeding goshawk (as in Berlin: page 72). **Lake Lubāns**, Latvia's largest lake, is good for wildfowl and raptors. Otherwise, for birding inspiration check ⊘ ornitofaunistika.com/kur/wtw.htm, and, for up-to-date bird news, check ⊘ birdinglatvia.lv. Neighbouring Estonia offers three options. **Soomaa National Park** is a site for grey wolf – though you would need great fortune to encounter one. Visit **Saaremaa** island for hundreds of Steller's eider and ringed seal. Or try for Eurasian lynx (page 40)...

FLEXIBILITY All: year-round, but February–May best for birds, April–September for raccoon dog.

TITBITS Gaidis Grandāns (⊘ birdinglatvia.lv) is a well-known guide, usually working through the company **Dabas Tūres** (⊘ dabastures.lv); see ad, page 232.

JAMES LOWEN

Parrots of
the Arctic

WHERE Lapland, Finland
TARGETS Siberian jay, Siberian tit, pine grosbeak, red squirrel, aurora borealis
ACCESSIBILITY ⑤
CHILD-FRIENDLINESS ④ (snowballs!)

If bushes were visible here, rather than being buried beneath several feet of snow, we wouldn't beat about them. Finland north of the Arctic Circle, in early March, is bone-searingly cold. Yet without this boreal nip, you wouldn't be spending a weekend at this Lapland guesthouse. The freezing temperatures make it energy efficient for the few species of songbird hardy enough to endure the northern winter to congregate at the brilliant feeding station of Neljän Tuulen Tupa. Here these sought-after specialities have safe, constant access to an all-they-can-eat buffet of seeds, grain and fat. The resulting spectacle is a wildlife photographer's dream.

The most colourful protagonist is pine grosbeak, the 'parrot of the Arctic'. A finch the size of a song thrush, this heavily built, mammoth-billed seedeater comes in a varied palette. Females are greyish-yellow; young males, yellow-orange; and adult males, raspberry-pink. All glow against the snow – and there can easily be 50 fireballs burning brightly under Lapland's winter sun.

▲ An adult male pine grosbeak, the 'parrot of the Arctic'.

Extrovert and fearless, winter flocks grant access to within inches. An old Swedish name for pine grosbeak – 'silly fool' – rings true. Group members converse with one another, sometimes bursting into fast, undulating flight, long tails pulling behind them. They evaporate for 20 minutes or so, then return – as do all extroverts – to the stage.

The feeding station comprises a mound of snow into which photographers stick branches on which birds can perch. A vast, twittering gathering of a hundred redpolls makes good use of these, alighting momentarily before taking their place at the restaurant. Dainty white, brown and pink finches, redpolls are attractive birds, but confusing ones too. Ornithologists never seem to agree how many species there are, and some individuals are tricky to identify with certainty. The sunflower seeds here are gobbled by both Arctic and mealy redpolls, extreme examples of the former gleaming white, even against the snow.

> **" The Neljän Tuulen Tupa spectacle is a wildlife photographer's dream "**

Five species of tit flit hither and thither. Three are familiar – blue, great and coal – with the first two offering eyeball-searing splashes of colour. More special (if duller in plumage) are willow tits, a species that has declined dramatically in the UK. Top of this particular pops, however, is Siberian tit. As its name suggests, this bird just about nudges its way into northern Europe, where it frequents mature, undisturbed conifer forest. Subtly beautiful, its tonal palette comprises black, taupe, tawny, rusty-brown, and white.

JAMES LOWEN

Red squirrels in northern Finland are largely grey in colour. ▲

❝ As you approach the equinox, prospects of the world's best lightshow increase ❞

There are few finer natural sights than the aurora borealis. MARKUS KIILI/VISIT FINLAND

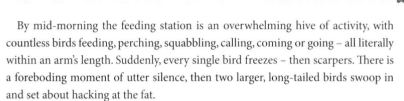

> ❝ **With dark masks and fiery flashes in both wings and tail, these pirates are Siberian jays – and they boss Neljän Tuulen Tupa** ❞

JAMES LOWEN

By mid-morning the feeding station is an overwhelming hive of activity, with countless birds feeding, perching, squabbling, calling, coming or going – all literally within an arm's length. Suddenly, every single bird freezes – then scarpers. There is a foreboding moment of utter silence, then two larger, long-tailed birds swoop in and set about hacking at the fat.

With dark masks and fiery flashes in both wings and tail, these pirates are Siberian jays – and they boss Neljän Tuulen Tupa. In summer, they plunder small birds' nests (hence the understandable fear displayed by redpolls, tits and grosbeaks). In winter, jays unearth edible treasure they have buried during times of plenty. Indifferent to human attention, they are big, bold and brilliant.

The same three adjectives apply to the red squirrels that live in the guesthouse roof. Greyer than individuals in Western Europe, these nimble, tufty rodents perform trapeze acts on feeders inches beyond the restaurant window.

Should you develop cabin fever despite the avian bounty, two options stand out for a shift of scenery. The first is the bird tower in Toivoniemi, 15km south. The second is simply to drive the E75 north towards Norway. Both approaches offer a decent shot at hawk owl. This diurnal predator is Europe's best-looking owl, despite its perpetual scowl. It is a resident of boreal forests, but shows a distinct preference for prominent perches near open or boggy terrain. As such, there is a very decent chance of spotting one. Should you fail, consolation will likely be provided by the odd reindeer (wild or Sámi-controlled? you wonder) and red fox.

Last, but very far from least: the northern lights or aurora borealis. As you approach the equinox, prospects of the world's best lightshow increase. You may need to stay up late to see it, but the near-absence of artificial light makes for suitably dark nights. Just pray for clear skies on at least one of the nights of your stay; cloud is a killer for aurora photography!

This weekend is a deep dive: an intense experience involving a few charismatic species at a single location, enriched by an amazing natural phenomenon. Should you wish it, there is no need to walk more than 10m from the guesthouse front door all weekend. Defrosting is but a few seconds away, which makes the cold eminently bearable. It is impossible not to take pleasing photographs with even the simplest of cameras. So relax, dress warmly, and enjoy.

▲ Siberian jay: demure in appearance but thuggish by nature.

GETTING THERE Nearest airport is Ivalo, to which Finnair flies daily from Helsinki. (Getting to Helsinki is simple from many European cities.) It is an easy 2-hour drive, north along the E75 via Inari, to Neljän Tuulen Tupa. In winter, hire cars are fitted with winter tyres.

WHERE TO GO Neljän Tuulen Tupa guesthouse (⌂ neljantuulentupa.com/en; ❄ 69.182141, 27.214341) is 5km north of the E75/92 junction. Feeders are at the side and rear of the main building. Just 15km south, the tower hide at **Toivoniemi** is 500m north along road 9710 from the E75 junction (❄ 69.055302, 27.082400).

SUGGESTED BASES Neljän Tuulen Tupa, no question! Wood-rich accommodation is warm and food hearty (reindeer stew!). Alternatively, you could stay in **Inari** (eg: ⌂ visitinari.fi) and visit for an hour or two (showing your gratitude by having your lunch at Tuulen Tupa).

MAKE IT A WEEK A perfect combination would be to explore **Varanger**, over the border in Norway (page 44). For something different, try a husky-dog safari or visit Sámi reindeer herders.

FLEXIBILITY Grosbeaks: late February into summer; squirrel, jay and tit: year-round; aurora: particularly September to April.

TITBITS Keep your eye out for the unusual: wolverine is sometimes seen here. Useful websites such as ⌂ aurora-service.eu predict the likelihood and intensity of the aurora weeks in advance, which can help you time a trip to maximise your chances.

JAMES LOWEN

Subtly beautiful, Siberian tit is a star performer at Neljän Tuulen Tupa. ▲

MIKE UNWIN

Lynxed in

WHERE Järva and Harju, central Estonia
TARGETS Eurasian lynx, Eurasian elk, hazel grouse, pygmy owl, three-toed woodpecker
ACCESSIBILITY ③
CHILD-FRIENDLINESS ①

I am viewing Estonia in greyscale. Winter is resolute here. Snow lies unrepentantly on the ground: a compact, white base layer. A generous band of pine trees triangulates skywards: spiky and unrelentingly black. Both elements of the monochrome – I hesitate to say both colours – are critical for this weekend. The snow enables us to clarify otherwise uncertain mammal movements, whilst the trees secrete sought-after owls and woodpeckers.

Our principal target is the most challenging in this book. Iberian lynx may scoop the dubious accolade of 'world's rarest cat', but it is disconcertingly straightforward to see (page 22). Eurasian lynx is a vastly different prospect. Although the species's range encompasses swathes of Europe and Asia, and although there are triple the number of Eurasians in Estonia *alone* as there are Iberians in the entire world, it is the more abundant, more widespread feline that represents the Holy Grail for European mammal-watchers.

Nevertheless, this weekend gives you a pretty good crack at this ultimate mammal. That it is possible at all is down to a hunter-turned-wildlife guide named

▲ Despite being more widespread than their Iberian relative, Eurasian lynx are more reclusive. This is a captive individual.

Aivo. For fear of reprisals within the hunting community, this giant of a man doesn't confess his surname – even preferring me to give him the moniker 'The Lynxman'. Nor does he welcome direct contact, instead requesting that people procure his services through Estonian Nature Tours, a local company. But he knows Kõrvemaa Landscape Protection Area – and its lynxes, its other mammals, its birds – like the back of his proverbial.

> **❝ Eurasian lynx represents the Holy Grail for European mammal-watchers ❞**

Kõrvemaa is barely an hour from the Estonian capital of Tallinn, but we could be in a different world. This old forest is dense and exciting, offering promise and whispering mystery. As Aivo's wheels crunch along snowy tracks, he indicates the prints of mammal after mammal. A badger went this way, a grey wolf that. A brown bear emerged from hibernation here, an otter crossed the road there. Every so often, Aivo halts the vehicle and gestures. A mountain hare – white upon white – freezes, ears erect. A young male Eurasian elk – a Hagrid amongst deer – fails to be dwarfed by the trees against which it lurks. Roe deer are commonplace, tufted white bottoms springing away for fear that we tote guns rather than binoculars.

The forest – matchstick-like birch, tense-shouldered larch and overladen spruce, mainly – broods in silence. Every so often a bird interrupts the stillness. Willow and crested tits usually, but black woodpeckers – ragamuffins with a piercing ivory eye and bill – frequently. Pygmy owls call in the morning; Ural owls at dusk. The former is particularly worth seeing; every bit as minute as its name suggests – barely larger

ONDREJ PROSICKY/D

'The Incredible Elk'? Male Eurasian elks are huge beasts. ▲

MARKUS VARESVUO/NPL

than its songbird prey. At ground level, a trio of gamebirds confesses its existence: a hazel grouse scuttles around (nervously), a black grouse perches atop an isolated spruce (defiantly), and a capercaillie guzzles grit from the road (needily).

All this is fabulous in itself, yet it is the pointy-eared feline that we crave. Aivo devotes days to fathoming the movements and home ranges of individual lynx. By checking snowy (or muddy) tracks, he knows when each has departed a particular forest block and entered the next one. Doing this every day gives him a decent idea of where we should position ourselves in the two hours before dusk, the period when lynx become particularly active. Wrapped up warm, and barely five minutes

GETTING THERE Nearest airport is Tallinn – served by regular flights from 30+ European cities – from where it is 75–90 minutes' drive (⊘ tallinn-airport.ee/en/).
WHERE TO GO Kõrvemaa Landscape Protection Area (⊘ korvemaa.ee/en/nature-and-history; ✳ 59.184360, 25.538519) is southeast of Tallinn. Drive via the E263 towards Ardu, then road 207 to Voose, 125 to Lehtmetsa and 141 to Albu. There are several entry points; the best area is bordered by roads 125, 12 and 13. A 4x4 is essential. Although access is unrestricted, I strongly recommend you only explore Kõrvemaa with a local guide, specifically Aivo (bookable through Estonian Nature Tours: ⊘ naturetours.ee). Without him, you may see birds and deer, but your chances of seeing lynx are zero. For **Lahemaa National Park** (⊘ tinyurl.com/lahemaa-np), take the E20 east from Tallinn, the 177 and 170 to Karula, then the 183 and 181 to Oandu. An excellent 4.7km long trail starts at the 187/188 junction (⊘ tinyurl.com/oandu-trail; ✳ 59.565661, 26.099849).
SUGGESTED BASES At Kõrvemaa, Albu is best: suitable accommodation is **Jäägri Villa** (⊘ jaagrivilla.ee/en; ✳ 59.154324, 25.656480). This smart lodge maxes out on Estonia's

▲ Hazel grouse is the smallest of three quality gamebirds inhabiting Estonia's forests.

into an anticipated evening-long vigil… boom! A female saunters across the track, followed obediently by her cub.

Clearly heftier than Iberian lynx, Eurasian lynx is built for stalking deer rather than rabbits. Its coat is greyer and more faintly marked than Iberian, its cheek jowls less exuberant, and it is shyer. And it stupefies. With a lingering look back at our open-mouthed faces, the female slopes into the brush. Her cub pads behind, innocently. They disapparate.

When you have seen the lynx – or when you have given up – head north to Lahemaa National Park for some comparative light relief. The drive is almost entirely agricultural. Hay bales pockmark landscape like Rolos in a saucer of custard. Occasional hooded crows and common buzzards contravene the desolate.

The glorious old forest of Lahemaa provides blessed contrast. The circular Oandu trail crinkles between great old trees and floats over mossy ground that blends wine-bottle greens with beer-bottle browns. A male hazel grouse seeks our attention with its oddly high-pitched, goldcrest-like whistle. A charismatic gamebird renowned for elusiveness, it is oddly conspicuous here. Nevertheless, it is merely Lahemaa's sideshow.

With dead wood everywhere, this forest is woodpecker heaven. In addition to numerous great spotted and black woodpeckers, the forest boasts 300 three-toed woodpecker territories, one-tenth of the Estonian total. Best of all, there are white-backed woodpeckers, an old-growth specialist. All four headbangers are garbed in black, three with white too. Essentially monochrome though they may be, the colour they grant to the Estonian winter is welcome.

hunting heritage: stuffed mammals (including Eurasian lynx!) decorate the shared areas, which takes some swallowing. Middle spotted woodpecker occurs in the park opposite. At Lahemaa, I highly recommend **Adami Country Guesthouse** on road 170 at Vainupea (adami.ee; ❀ 59.575108, 26.268729), with sensational food by celebrity chef Eva-Maria Liiv. Eva-Maria's brother is a birding guide: three-toed and white-backed woodpeckers occur on a trail leading west from road 170, 200m south of Adami. **MAKE IT A WEEK** Visit **Saaremaa** island for hundreds of Steller's eider and ringed seal. Watch white-tailed eagles along the Lahemaa coast, including at Vainupea. Overnight in **Biome Nature's hide** near Matsalu National Park (biomenature.com), where there is a fair chance of Eurasian lynx.
FLEXIBILITY Lynx: January to March is best (when snow is on the ground); owl and woodpecker: February to May; grouse and elk: year-round.

JUSSI MURTOSAARI/NPL

Lahemaa is one of the best places in Europe to spot three-toed woodpeckers. ▲

Northern delights

WHERE Varangerfjord, Finnmark, Norway
TARGETS Steller's eider, king eider, gyrfalcon, Brünnich's guillemot, hawk owl
ACCESSIBILITY ② (heavy snow may impede access on foot)
CHILD-FRIENDLINESS ③ (snowballs, but cold)

Varangerfjord's near-freezing sea is boiling. Off Vardø Island at the northeastern extremity of mainland Arctic Norway, the swell bubbles and fizzes – but with feathered activity. Both flickering black then white and flashing powder-blue then carrot-orange, thousands of seaduck and auks whirr frantically forward on hurried wings before plunging back on to the water surface. Each landing triggers the frenzied departure of another bird, so that the whole whirling flock flows forward. 'Welcome to what I call the king eider vortex,' grins Tormod Amundsen, a Varanger incomer and visionary architect who is on a mission to break down the barriers between birds and their watchers.

Running the architectural firm Biotope, Amundsen despairs at our disconnect from nature. He particularly dislikes the wooden-box approach to birdwatching hides that is ubiquitous on European wildlife reserves. Although Amundsen acknowledges that such structures minimise human disturbance to birdlife, he argues that they present both a physical and mental barrier between us and wildlife. He has dedicated his business to overcoming this disconnect.

▲ 'The king eider vortex': Varanger's seething mass of seaduck, here comprising common and king eiders.
HUGH HARROP/SHETLAND WILDLIFE

66 **Sheltered and shallow, Varangerfjord vibrates with life** 99

Accordingly, Biotope's open-sided 'hides' around Varanger (and beyond: five countries in addition to Norway have recently embraced Amundsen's architecture) let the outside in. 'They provide shelter for the watchers,' he says 'but also immerse you in the spectacle while maintaining a respectful distance'. To my eyes, they are works of art – sculptures that enhance the landscape rather than jarring with it. More importantly, they make us feel like *participants* in each wildlife spectacle.

Amundsen has chosen a mighty fine location to showcase his philosophy. Varanger is an intense experience: biting cold, reverential snowscapes, and torrents of birdlife. Europe may have no finer winter birdwatching experience. Sheltered and shallow, it is the only fjord in Norway that faces east. And it vibrates with life.

For close views of wildfowl, visit Vadsø harbour, where Amundsen's installation places you at eye level with groups of duck that characterise High Arctic seas. To get nearer still, enter Øyvind Arntzen's 'floating hide' – a refitted electric boat with windows inches above the water. Arntzen expertly steers the silent machine to within scant metres of these glorious creatures.

But which of Varanger's ducks (or, precisely, the drakes) is the most beautiful? Common eider is reassuringly familiar, with the male's largely white garb suffused with rose and mint. King eider is vaguely clown like, with the drake's blue head offset by a green face, orange shield and strawberry bill. Steller's eider (of which there are more at Vadsø than anywhere else in Europe) is less ostentatious, with peachy breast and flanks and bizarre green wattle on its nape. The innocent-looking long-tailed duck, meanwhile, does what it says on the tin.

From Vadsø, head northeast along the coast to Vardø. There's plenty of roadside excitement. Anywhere with trees, even in urban areas, you could encounter a hawk

JAMES LOWEN

owl surveying from upon high. Indeed, it would be an unlucky visit that does not produce one of these long-tailed predators. Talking of hunters, white-tailed eagles and red foxes are around too; neither is to be sniffed at.

Among the herbivores, reindeer and willow ptarmigan stands out. The latter, a grouse, should be starting to move from its wholly white winter plumage to the mottled chestnut-brown that affords camouflage amid tundra vegetation during summer. As you pass harbours, scan gull flocks: the hefty, icy-looking glaucous gulls should be present and glaring furiously. Offshore, look for harbour porpoise and Atlantic grey seal.

GETTING THERE The most suitable airport is Høybuktmoen at Kirkenes (⊘ tinyurl.com/ airport-kirkenes), flying via Oslo with SAS. The drive from Kirkenes to Varangerbotn takes 1½ hours. Varangerbotn to Vardø (non-stop) takes another 1½ hours.
WHERE TO GO The whole fjord east of **Varangerbotn** (✳ 70.173643, 28.566408) offers great birding (⊘ varanger.net). In **Vadsø** (✳ 70.073872, 29.746781), watch from the harbour, the Biotope hide immediately west of town, or the 'floating hide' operated by Øyvind Arntzen (⊘ varanger.info/?page_id=844). Outside April to August, when a daily ferry operates, getting to **Hornøya** island (⊘ hornoya.com ☉ 1 Mar– 1 Sep) involves booking a boat from Vardø Harbour KF (⊘ vardohavn.no). Should this prove impossible, you can watch auks and gyrfalcons distantly from Biotope's hide on Strandgata in northeast **Vardø** (✳ 70.379736, 31.118950). Book a boat (see page 45) to view Vardø's 'king eider vortex' from the water or view from shore at Batterigata (✳ 70.363745, 31.115857). Other good sites include **Kiberg** (✳ 70.283186, 31.001049) and **Svartnes** (⊘ 70.361987, 31.025136).

▲ Shark-like fins and a cornucopia of colour: the drake king eider.

Spend day two on the island of Vardø. As well as experiencing the 'king eider vortex' (ideally from a hired boat, but – failing that – from shore, through a telescope), join a trip to Hornøya. This islet hosts a spectacular seabird colony: teeming with 80,000 auks and kittiwakes (a small, cute gull with its wingtips dipped in ink).

> **Europe may have no finer winter birdwatching experience**

This deep into the Arctic, the breeding season is short, so every adult rushes to raise its young. The result is feathered bedlam. Five species of auk – notably Brünnich's, a northern breeder, but also including the irresistible Atlantic puffin – scorch past on urgent wings, heading to or returning from feeding grounds. But all are being watched. Above the mayhem circles the consummate boreal predator: the gyrfalcon. Females of this raptor are the size of a buzzard, yet nearly match a peregrine for speed. The combination adds up to unstoppable power. I watched a kittiwake circle blithely above the colony, only to be smashed by a plummeting 'gyr' that came out of the ether.

By the time of the spring equinox, the days are surprisingly long: almost 12 hours of light. There is no need to rush round trying to cram everything into a few short hours. This is just as well. Should the skies be clear, you may wish to stay up late into the night. March is a great month for observing the sky-dancing aurora borealis. The show of greens and reds, purples and pinks, blues and whites, is an integral part of Varanger's Arctic experience – northern lights among the northern delights.

SUGGESTED BASES Good hotels include **Vadsø Fjordhotell** (⌂ vadsoefjordhotell.no) and **Vardø Hotel** (⌂ vardohotel.no). Midway between the two is **Ekkerøy Feriehus** (great self-catering; ✳ 70.076914, 30.099386 ⌂ ekkeroy.net). An idiosyncratic lodging would be **Hornøya lighthouse** (⌂ vardoport.no).

MAKE IT A WEEK Combine with **Neljän Tuulen Tupa** in Finnish Lapland (page 34). Or stay in Norway, photographing seaduck from an electric photohide at **Båtsfjord** (⌂ arctictourist.no); the drive via Tana is good for hawk owl and gyrfalcon. Look for forest birds such as pine grosbeak around **Pasvik**, in south Varanger.

FLEXIBILITY Eiders: best February to March, but a few stay until May; gyrfalcon: year-round ; guillemot: March to August; owl: November to April; aurora: September to April.

TITBITS For **Biotope** architecture, see ⌂ biotope.no/p/architecture.html. Dress warmly: prepare for -20°C. Roads may be closed after snowfall; cars often convoy behind snowploughs!

Keep alert for hawk owls posing by the roadside. ▶

Giant transformers, phantom farters

WHERE Castro Verde, Alentejo, Portugal
TARGETS Great bustard, little bustard, black-bellied sandgrouse, Montagu's harrier, calandra lark
ACCESSIBILITY ⑤
CHILD-FRIENDLINESS ② (rather too much scanning for kids)

O n an upward inflection amidst undulating spring-green plains, a foaming car wash baffles. Rather than wheels, this frothy whiteness balances upon legs. That there are two limbs rather than four scuppers one explanation. This is no sheep. Then I click. After all, it is spring in the grasslands of southern Portugal. I must be watching a male great bustard's full-throttled display.

YOAV PERLMAN www.yoavperlman.com

▲ It's not a plane, but is it a bird? A displaying male great bustard astonishes.

This giant transformer is an Iberian beast like no other. Males are proud creatures, strutting with intent. An iron-grey head peeks over a flowing silvery moustache that threatens Salvador Dali's primacy. A fulsome auburn boa is echoed by griddled chestnut upperparts, largely ivory wings and a barred titian tail. At rest, the male great bustard impresses. But in display...?

Whether signalling dominance over rival males or in a no-holds-barred attempt to win over a choosy female, this bird puts on quite some performance. In the space of just five

> **66 The great bustards tussle, beak-to-beak in a push-of-war that defines the steppe hierarchy 99**

seconds, it flicks a ginger and white scarf from its tummy over its bill, riffles its bum and wing feathers into a huge snowball, then puffs out every conceivable chestnut plume to look like – let's be honest – nothing on Earth. If this performance inspires a contender to follow suit, the duo may tussle, beak-to-beak in a push-of-war that determines the steppe hierarchy.

Sadly – what an understatement – this battle is ever rarer in Iberia. Even in the three years since conservation scientist Yoav Perlman started investigating the decline of the region's grassland birds, one of Alentejo's few remaining great bustard populations has vanished. The habitat just isn't as good as it used to be – a result of recent and accelerating changes.

For centuries the western Mediterranean's 'pseudo-steppes' (or 'agro-steppes') – arid, stony treeless plains enduring cold winters and hot summers – have been gently cultivated. Weedy meadows have flourished alongside cereal fields, almond groves and lightly grazed pastures. Wildlife has had ample time to adjust to the gradual evolution in the use to which people put the land.

Such benign co-existence is no more. Radical, rapid intensification of land use (land abuse?), incentivised by the European Union's Common Agricultural Policy, is at fault. Once-diverse farmed landscapes – fallow fields, set-aside and flowering field margins – have reduced dramatically, replaced by insecticide-drenched monocultures. In consequence, the Iberian plains hold one of the highest proportions of declining 'priority' bird species in Europe. This area is a continent-scale conservation priority.

Castro Verde – which hosts you this weekend – is 'the most beautiful and biodiversity-rich agro-steppe remaining in southwest Iberia', says Perlman. Three-quarters of Portugal's great bustards thrive where spring riots with floral colour – purple viper's-bugloss, (scarlet) horned dock, (yellow) corn marigold and (white) chamomile. Castro Verde serves not merely as a superlative wildlife-watching destination, but also as a beacon for sensitive landscape management.

" Male little bustards communicate with one other – and with females – by blowing a raspberry. In the first two hours after dawn, they accompany the call with a brief display dance – their own salute to the sun "

A poised leap, flash of white wings and raspberry-like call: prerequisites for a male little bustard to attract a female. OSCAR DOMINGUEZ deepwildphoto.com

CARLOS N. G. BOCOS

Birdwatching here is simple. Drive roads north and east of the eponymous town – including along rougher tracks if access is permitted. Every half-mile or when something catches your eye, park carefully and scan from the car. Should you spot great bustards, give them wide berth to avoid disturbance. Local conservationists have been up in arms recently at blinkered birders venturing too near these sensitive birds.

Greats are not Alentejo's only bustard. Little bustards throng here at densities higher than anywhere else in their range. 'Iberia has lost half its little bustards in a

GETTING THERE Nearest airport is Faro (faro-airport.com), from where it is 1¼ hours' drive north (120km) to Castro Verde. Lisbon Portela airport would be 1 hour 50 minutes' drive (200km). Various airlines fly to both destinations from northern Europe, including UK.

WHERE TO GO Castro Verde is a Special Protection Area covering 60,000 ha of pseudo-steppe. In June 2017, it was designated a UNESCO Biosphere Reserve. A large area is brilliantly managed by Liga para a Protecão da Natura, a wildlife charity that operates **Vale Gonçalinho** environmental education centre 6km northeast of Castro Verde. From the firestation roundabout in town, follow signs (❋ 37.736237, -8.031570 tinyurl.com/castro-verde2 09.00–17.00 Tue–Sat). There is good birding (including bustards) here; friendly staff advise trails that you can walk without disturbing birds. Otherwise, explore the area by driving the N2, IP2 and N123 roads (respectively north, northeast and east of Castro Verde town) and tracks off these where access is allowed (with permission from LPN staff; see above). Two good such tracks lead south off the N123 at São Marcos do Ataboeira (❋ 37.705004, -7.937189; marked by a reserve sign) and southwest from the Entradas–Pocos road (❋ 37.790243, -8.049240).

▲ A male black-bellied sandgrouse watches warily, while a female pin-tailed sandgrouse loiters behind.

decade', says Yoav. 'Only in Castro Verde does it still thrive.' Nevertheless, given that little bustard is smaller than great bustard, prefers longer grass and doesn't gather in concentrated display arenas, it is harder to see. The best way to track one down is by listening… for a fart.

Male little bustards communicate with one other – and with females – by blowing a raspberry. In the first two hours after dawn, they accompany the call (I can't bring myself to refer to it as song) with a brief display dance – their own salute to the sun. Inflating black-and-white neck feathering into a cobra-like ruff, the male stomps his feet, thrusts back his head to call, then leaps into the air, flashing vividly white wings.

As you search for bustards, you will encounter bounteous wildlife. Larks – particularly calandra and crested – furnish the soundscape. Woodchat and southern grey shrikes perch prominently. An Iberian worm lizard – myopic and legless – skulks below a rock that is calling to be flipped. Skittish black-bellied sandgrouse arc over the plains before plummeting on to bare ground and melting away.

Large psammodramus lizards scuttle noisily through weedy verges where butterflies such as Iberian marbled white and red underwing skipper nuzzle flowers. A great spotted cuckoo – an avowed caterpillar-muncher – eyes their fluttering. A plethora of raptors surveys the rainbowed spring plains. Lesser kestrels and Montagu's harriers have freshly returned from Africa, the former breeding in noisy colonies that squat in old farm buildings. Black and red kites bounce through the air. Iberian imperial and booted eagles soar high, griffon and cinereous vultures loftier still. At Castro Verde, if no longer elsewhere, they are all safe – but for how long?

SUGGESTED BASES There are three accommodation options in Castro Verde and an attractive B&B in São Marcos do Ataboeira, **Abertarda** (⌗ abetarda.pt). Additional options are in **Almodôvar**, 30 minutes south along the N2 and **Mértola** in the heart of neighbouring Vale do Guadiana Natural Park (35 minutes east along the N123 and IC27).

MAKE IT A WEEK Go out at night, spotlighting for Egyptian mongoose (a mammal much sought-after in Europe given its otherwise African distribution) and eagle owl in **Vale do Guadiana Natural Park**. By day, this area is good for black-shouldered kite, Bonelli's eagle and other raptors. Exploring the **Algarve** (page 202) would be a good bet, seeking waterbirds, reptiles and amphibians. The hills of **Monchique** merit a visit for birds such as rock and cirl buntings, woodlark and crested tit. For inspiration see ⌗ tinyurl.com/alentejo1.

FLEXIBILITY Harrier: March to September; bustards and lark: resident, but best March to mid-April when displaying; sandgrouse: resident.

TITBITS A rash of local birding guides are keen to show you Castro Verde and beyond. These include ⌗ birdwatchinalentejo.com, ⌗ birdinginportugal.com, ⌗ algarvebirdman.com, ⌗ algarve-birdwatching.com and ⌗ birds.pt.

Costa del Chameleon

WHERE Nerja, Málaga province, Spain
TARGETS Spanish ibex, Mediterranean chameleon, mirror orchid, black wheatear, conehead mantis
ACCESSIBILITY ③
CHILD-FRIENDLINESS ⑤ (this suggestion is *all* about the family!)

It's the Easter holidays and the family needs a break in the sun. You're not flush with cash: the budget only stretches to the Costa del Sol. You're cringing at the prospect of a wildlife-free holiday amidt tourist hell. Don't. If you venture even a short way off the main drag, your beach holiday can nurture you with a raft of exquisite life forms. Even if you can only scrabble together a few hours in the wilds (the equivalent of a weekend, at most), the town of Nerja and its environs can afford ample natural joy – with Mediterranean orchids, mammals, birds, reptiles, and invertebrates all awaiting your perusal.

STUART A. REEVES

▲ Spotting a Mediterranean chameleon – a champion of camouflage – is no mean feat.

The first surprise comes under a dozen kilometres east of Nerja, at Cerro Gordo. As you park the car, your attention is manhandled by a group of goat-like creatures grazing quietly in the grassy hollow, a mere stony slope below you. Spanish ibex! True animals of the wild: nimble-hooved mountaineers that bring to mind rocky uplands, yet here browsing just a few score metres above sea level.

The path south dissects arid scrub. Scarce swallowtails grace past on wings of sexy underwear. Portuguese dappled, bath and green-striped whites extend the butterfly list. Where two paths scramble upwards towards a shrine, look for small, beautiful orchids sprouting from the bare earth.

> **Mirror orchid makes you swoon, its reflective lilac heart rimmed yellow and fringed burgundy**

Yellow ophrys beams like the Spanish sun, while mirror orchid makes you swoon, its reflective lilac heart rimmed yellow and fringed burgundy. Search the pine forest and you may spot sombre bee orchid – prettier than it sounds. For further delectable flowers, stop off at Torre de Maro as your return to Nerja. More mirror orchids sprout uphill of the car park, but the star is bug orchid. Quite which insect its pink-and-green flowers supposedly imitate is unclear. Answers on a postcard please.

If it's time for something touristy, you could do worse than head for the Cuevas de Nerja, the town's subterranean spectacle. As well as heading underground through the caves, spend time wandering trails on the adjacent hillside. Western Bonelli's warblers sing from pines that also harbour crested tit and common crossbill. More orchids delight here, including pink butterfly orchid if you walk far enough north. Best of all, this is a great area for wacky invertebrates such as conehead (praying) mantis: an extra-terrestrial on Earth.

Andalucía is renowned for gleaming hill villages, among which nearby Frigiliana sparkles particularly brightly. It was here, as a teenager on family holidays, that I first fell for Spain and its wildlife. Intervening decades have done nothing to dissipate that initial soft spot: Frigiliana offers fine Mediterranean birding in glorious surroundings.

Bee-eaters, red-rumped swallows, red-billed choughs, and short-toed eagles excite the skies. The tastiest treats, however, are nearer ground level. On the town's sheer edges, blue rock thrushes descant from roof tops and cliff faces. Walk north along the road, and rock buntings greet you while – best of all – black wheatears scorn claims that monochrome means dull.

A plant that reflects? The intensely beautiful mirror orchid. ▲

JAMES LOWEN

Birds might be fix enough for you, yet Frigiliana injects more wildlife into your day. If the kids spot the playground in the main square and fancy a clamber, consent readily. The flowering shrubs here attract butterflies such as African grass blue and Moroccan orange-tip. The walls are home to wall lizards, which peer out from cracks when nervous or, when relaxed, bask as benignly as tourists. Recent research has determined that what was once known as 'Iberian wall lizard' actually transpires to be a group of eight closely related and subtly different species. The one here is Vaucher's wall lizard.

As pallid and Alpine swifts seek to distract by zooming overhead, finish by deepening your interest in Nerja's life in cold blood. Pretty much any body of water – from a horticulturer's tank to a trickling stream – may hold Iberian water frog. These can be seen by day, but are more evident at night, when their cackling resounds over a kilometre. If you are staying in a villa, check its walls after dark, for Moorish and Turkish geckos can be impressively common. Up close, admire the former's spiny tail, bulging eyes and sucker toes.

Harder to spot – due to a combination of arboreal habits, scarcity and camouflage – is Nerja's herpetological star. You might associate chameleons with Africa (particularly Madagascar, which harbours half the world's 150 species), and rightly so. But we have them in Europe too. Admittedly, both 'our' two chameleons (African and Mediterranean) probably owe their presence here to ancient introductions.

Whatever its origin, Mediterranean chameleon is well established along the coast of southern Spain. Pressure from criminals collecting to supply the pet trade guards me against divulging precise sites. But if you go for a family walk along the Río Chillar, north of Nerja, or scrutinise trees in largely abandoned cultivations on hills northwest of the town – you never know your luck.

▲ Another cryptic denizen of the Costa del Sol – conehead mantis.

GETTING THERE Nearest airport is Málaga (⌀ tinyurl.com/airport-malaga), which is very well served by charter and scheduled flights from numerous European cities. Nerja is 1 hour 10 minutes' drive (80km) east along the A7.

WHERE TO GO Cerro Gordo is at km305 on the N340, east of Nerja. Park 50m south of the roundabout (✳ 36.749319, -3.783083) then explore southwards. On the same road, **Torre del Maro** is at km²97 (✳ 36.757793, -3.827979); walk east along the track to see orchids. Northeast of Nerja, **Cueva de Nerja** is signposted from the A7 motorway at km²95 (✳ 36.761730, -3.846017 ⌀ cuevadenerja.es); tracks head north into the foothills. **Frigiliana** is approximately 6km north of Nerja along the MA5105. Immediately north of town, a good area for black wheatear is ✳ 36.797546, -3.901748. You can walk along the **Río Chillar** northwards from Nerja itself (it gets interesting beyond the A7 motorway underpass), although many people start near the cement factory, then walk north from ✳ 36.771496, -3.879538.

SUGGESTED BASES Ample, varied accommodation in and around Nerja (⌀ nerjatoday. com) and – my personal preference – **Frigiliana** (⌀ frigiliana-rentals.com).

MAKE IT A WEEK If you are on a family holiday, your younger travellers will have opinions! Beaches aside, however, walking out from Nerja along any of the many footpaths should reveal interesting wildlife – from spotless starling to large psammodramus (a lizard). Hike along and around **Río Higueron** gorge east of Frigiliana for orchids, birds and butterflies. A few minutes from Málaga airport, **Río Guadalhorce Nature Reserve** (⌀ tinyurl.com/rio-guada) offers excellent birding, including the globally threatened white-headed duck.

FLEXIBILITY Orchids: March to April; ibex and wheatear: year-round; chameleon: February to November is best; mantis: spring–summer.

TITBITS A great resource for local walks is ⌀ axarquiaonfoot.com.

JONATHAN LETHBRIDGE www.justbirdphotos.com

Black wheatears often sing from prominent perches such as rocks. ▲

Conservation action in countries such as Spain is reversing population declines in European roller.
FRANZ CHRISTOPH ROBI/IMAGEBROKER/FLPA

April
May
June

Imperial cave salamander – European leaf-toed gecko – Bory's orchid
snake's-head iris – Corsican fire salamander – goshawk – Siberian flying
squirrel – brown bear – European roller – lesser kestrel – spring gentian
Alpine ibex – blue whale – harlequin duck – long-tailed mayfly
southern festoon – European pond terrapin – lilypad whiteface

Going underground

WHERE Northern Sardinia, Italy
TARGETS Supramonte cave salamander, imperial cave salamander, European leaf-toed gecko, lesser horseshoe bat, sawfly orchid
ACCESSIBILITY ②
CHILD-FRIENDLINESS ③

Our student naturalists' club used to meet every Thursday in a dank corner of a beer-soaked pub. Over draught Guinness, we chewed the fat about rare wildlife and rainforest expeditions. In the opposite corner, every Thursday, sat the student cavers' club. Over lukewarm ale, they chewed the fat about – I'm guessing here – precarious caves and potholing expeditions. The groups kept their distance, each giggling at the other. In retrospect, we weren't actually twain – and so should have met. Given this weekend's itinerary in Sardinia, that is a shame.

Cave salamanders are among Europe's wackiest animals. These long-tailed amphibians frequent caverns or cavities, emerging during cooler, wetter nights to explore their forested or rocky surroundings. Five of Europe's eight species are exclusive to the Mediterranean island of Sardinia. All have slender limbs with

66 Cave salamanders are among Europe's wackiest animals 99

FRANZ CHRISTOPH ROBI/IMAGEBROKER/FLPA

▲ Sardinia has an amazing diversity of troglodyte amphibians, such as this imperial cave salamander.

BOB GIBBONS/FLPA

stubby toes and bulging eyes. As they look pretty darn similar to one other, only keen 'herpers' – who were quite plausibly sat in a third corner of that student pub – bust a gut trying to see the whole quintet. For most of us, seeing one or two species is experience enough.

As their name suggests, seeing cave salamanders is no walk in the park. At the very least you will need to go underground, torch in hand or strapped to head. Most herpers who have seen these troglodytes recount tales of long hikes through barren karst before resorting to a GPS to pinpoint a narrow opening in a cliff face, through which they squeeze, squint and score. You may be relieved to hear that there will be no such adventuring today.

Cave-salamanders-made-easy starts near Sadali at the large tourist cavern of Grotta Is Janas. Here, amid stalactites and stalagmites, is the most accessible location to see imperial cave salamander. Walk slowly through the corridors and scan the cave 'walls' – particularly around the bat colony (the so-called 'guano room'; your nose will tell you when you reach this). Observe salamanders from a respectful distance: disturbance and habitat degradation by subterranean tourism is one of the reasons why Sardinia's whole quintet is of global conservation concern.

For your second crack at a cave salamander – this one the rarest of the lot – head to Valle di Lanaittu in a karst massif known as Supramonte. Grotta Sa Ohe (Oche) and Grotta Su Ventu (Bentu) are two caves connected by a natural siphon. During opening hours (which start in April, hence the timing of this weekend), you may pay to explore the caves. Su Ventu is the place for Supramonte cave salamander. Use the same tactics as at Is Janas – and marvel at the glorious weirdness that even student cavers and naturalists might have eulogised.

For some welcome fresh air, head to nearby Monte Albo. Leave the range's endemic cave salamander be and focus instead on orchids and birds. Monte Albo

Visit the famous ruin of Nuraghe Majori to see roosting lesser horseshoe bats – but take care not to disturb them. ▲

EMANUELE BIGGI/FLPA

> **❝** Diligent turning of rocks and perusal of walls should reveal reptiles such as European leaf-toed gecko **❞**

offers efficient birding, with a trio of sought-after species inhabiting maquis scrub below steepling cliffs. Park by the standing stones on the SP3, and explore the environs to see Barbary partridge (a Sardinian speciality), Marmora's warbler and Corsican finch.

This calcareous massif is a botanist's paradise. Orchids stubble colour against grey karst wherever you look, and you could easily rack up a dozen species even in random roadside stops. There are purples and pinks and yellows and violets and burgundys and magentas. There are blends of tongue orchids (two or more species, plus their hybrids), confusions of bee-type orchids of the genus *Ophrys* (including the gorgeous sawfly orchid), plus pink butterfly orchid, the endemic Sardinian orchid, Brancifort's orchid, three-toothed orchid, milky orchid…

GETTING THERE Nearest airports are Olbia (⊘ olbiaairport.com) and Cagliari (⊘ cagliari-airport.com). The former is closer to sites for the second day, the latter for first-day locations. **WHERE TO GO Grotta Is Janas**(✳ 39.845721, 9.266523; ⊘ tinyurl.com/is-janas) is 3.5km north of Sadali. In the **Supramonte**, make for **Grotta Sa Ohe** and **Su Ventu** (✳ 40.256847, 9.485516 ⊘ tinyurl.com/su-ventu), caves in the Valle de Lanaittu. Pay at the ticket office (✳ 40.256383, 9.486834 ☉ Apr–Sep 09.30–17.00) and walk west to the caves. Access to **Monte Albo** is along the SP3 southwest of Siniscola. A good area for birds is around the menhirs 4.2km south from the SP3/SP50 junction towards Lula (✳ 40.560348, 9.633454). **Santa Teresa Gallura** is at Sardinia's northern tip. **Capo Testa** lighthouse is 4km west of town (✳ 41.243581, 9.144333), **Punta Falcone** immediately north of town (✳ 41.243581, 9.144333) and **La Liccia campsite** 7km south (✳ 41.180936, 9.177873 ⊘ campinglaliccia. com). Two companies (Moby and BluNavy) operate four **ferries** daily from Santa Teresa Gallura to Bonifacio on Corsica (⊘ tinyurl.com/sardinia-ferry). **Nuraghe Majori** (✳ 40.917939, 9.096915 ⊘ gallurarcheologica.com) is signposted from the SS133 2km north of Tempio Pausania. **SUGGESTED BASES** Olbia (⊘ olbiaturismo.it) or Santa Teresa Gallura would be convenient. **MAKE IT A WEEK** In northeast Sardinia, look for mouflon on Figari Peninsula, east of Golfo Aranci. In the northwest, try **Cape Caccia** at dawn for Barbary partridge. Nearby **Lake Baratz** is outstanding for herptiles: look for Hermann's tortoise, European pond terrapin,

▲ Capo Testa lighthouse is a good place to look for European leaf-toed gecko.

If you need your fix of cold-blooded critter, drive 2 hours north to Santa Teresa Gallura. If you have energy, explore two or more of La Liccia campsite, Punta Falcone and Capo Testa by day and after nightfall. Tyrrhenian tree frogs – the smallest of their European ilk – call wherever there is standing water. Diligent turning of rocks and perusal of walls should reveal reptiles such as Moorish gecko, ocellated skink, pygmy algyroides and both Italian and Tyrrhenian wall lizards. European leaf-toed gecko – thick-tailed and secretive – lurks in dry-stone walls near Capo Testa lighthouse.

The following morning, take a half-day trip to France. Ferries from Santa Teresa take under an hour to reach Bonifacio on Corsica. An early morning (or evening) boat is a great way to garner fabulous views of three unusual seabirds: Scopoli's and Yelkouan shearwaters, and the Mediterranean variant of European storm-petrel. Travel as a foot passenger and return on the first available ferry.

Once back in Sardinia, drive west and inland to the famous ruin of Nuraghe Majori, near Tempio Pausania. Shine a torch into the darkest of the two chambers that shoulder the tower to see a colony of lesser horseshoe bats. The blackness may not be subterranean – so those student cavers may sneer – but Sardinia's wildlife experience is superb.

both wall lizards, Tyrrhenian tree frog, plus viperine and western whip snakes. Chance your arm at montane rivulets in **Sette Fratelli** for Sardinian brook newt and the more common Tyrrhenian painted frog.

FLEXIBILITY Salamanders and gecko: year-round, but February to May best; bat: March to October; orchid: March to May.

TITBITS Please do not disturb cave salamanders or bats; their welfare comes first. As an alternative to April, visit in June: although the orchids will be gone, rare dragonflies frequent west-coast lakes and Eleonora's falcon breeds on Isla San Pietro.

ARMANDO FRAZAO/S

Sardinia's throng of orchids includes sawfly. ▲

King of the gods – and orchids

WHERE Chania and Rethymno, Crete, Greece
TARGETS Bory's orchid, Cretan orchid, snake's-head iris, dragon arum, Balkan terrapin
ACCESSIBILITY ④
CHILD-FRIENDLINESS ⑤

'**E**ven if you think you're not that into plants, Spili Bumps is special', Philip Precey, tour leader at Wildlife Travel (see ad, page 236), had stressed before our visit. 'Don't miss it.' Precey was right. This limestone protrusion in western Crete – birthplace of Zeus, king of the Greek gods – is like nothing on Earth.

From the bustling town of Spili, the road winds through woodland and *garrigue* scrub before reaching the largely agricultural Gious–Kambos Plateau in the foothills of Mt Kedros. The 'Bumps' are well named; steep rocky hummocks shooting out of the flatness. Should spring be well advanced, your arrival should be greeted by fields splattered with blood. Fret not that these are the result of mythological battles. One of Zeus's sons, Ares, may well have been the god of war, but these scarlet tones are actually hundreds of Doerfler's tulips, one of many endemic (and thus special) plants for which Crete is renowned.

Although stunning, the tulip display is merely a botanical *hors d'oeuvre*. So walk through fields and across stream to reach the Bumps' stony ramparts. Orchids and other interesting plants flourish so thickly here that your progress will be slow.

" *Although stunning, the tulip display is merely a botanical hors d'oeuvre* "

▲ Spili Bumps is a botanist's nirvana.

JAMES LOWEN

Again, worry not. Crete's botanical kaleidoscope is best enjoyed at a leisurely pace. Take your time, descend to your knees and scrutinise every square metre of the hillocks. You will get a fine return on your investment of time.

The diversity of orchids is such that a field guide is essential to determine their identity. (Even then you may be bamboozled by some Doppelgänger plants.) Without one to hand, simply enjoy the different colours, patterns and shapes of more than 25 species that flower at any one moment – and perhaps take photographs to aid subsequent naming.

Groups of naked man orchid are conspicuous: aptly named, they have long slender limbs and are, shall we say, most definitely male. Theoretically closely related but very different in appearance is Bory's orchid. Slender and magenta, this rarity occurs only in southern Greece. Milky orchid is confusingly variable, ranging from dairy-white to foxglove-pink. Anatolian orchids may cling on, although these flower early. Sparse-flowered orchid is a primrose among the genus *Orchis*, its flowers being wan yellow with a sunnier core.

Spili's array of bee orchids (in the genus *Ophrys*, should that help you piece together the jigsaw) is astonishing. Heldreich's orchid is thought only to grow on Crete. Sombre bee orchids are undemonstrative, yellow bee orchids encircled with a golden halo. Then throw in toothed orchid, four-spotted orchid, various species of near-indistinguishable but undeniably sassy tongue orchids, and… and… and… You get the picture.

Spili is outstanding for orchids, but there is even more to overwhelm you here. Rock tulip abounds, while snake's-head iris – with rippling velvet flowers, lined with brilliant yellow – should make you go weak at the knees. Spili also excels for reptiles.

The lusciously velvet, if not overwhelmingly serpentine, snake's-head iris. ▲

“ **Balkan terrapins – miniature freshwater turtles – take star billing** ”

JAMES LOWEN

You should have no problems finding Balkan green lizard or the sublimely spotted ocellated skink. Carefully turn over some flat stones, particularly on the wall-like structures below the hill, and you may chance upon something truly thrilling such as leopard snake, which is generously blotched red.

Continue the reptilian theme the next day at Agia Lake. Balkan terrapins – miniature freshwater turtles – take star billing. Balkan green lizards keep them company. Both are easily seen along the western shore near Enasma Café. While rejuvenating with a steaming coffee, check the tiny ornamental pond inside the

GETTING THERE Nearest airport is Chania (⌀ chania-airport.com), which takes scheduled flights from Athens plus direct charters from North/West European cities.

WHERE TO GO From Chania, take the E75 east to Rethmyno, then road 97 south to Spili. In Spili, head northeast on the road to Gerakari. **Spili Bumps** is opposite an old taverna. Just beyond the wooded stream, park at ✳ 35.214111, 24.567214. Walk south along the track then west into the hillocks. Explore the whole area languidly. **Agia Lake** (⌀ crete-birding. co.uk/agialake.htm) is 7km southwest of Chania, north of Agia. Park by Enasma Café (✳ 35.477131, 23.931258) or Agia Lake restaurant (✳) 35.478974, 23.932513) and watch from the lakeside path. **Akotiri Peninsula** bulges northeast from Chania. Anywhere east of **Stavros** (✳ 35.589324, 24.098186) can be good. **Gouverneto monastery** is at ✳ 35.582229, 24.139572. Follow the gorge path northeast.

SUGGESTED BASES Chania has varied accommodation (⌀ tinyurl.com/chania-acc). An alternative would be Spili, where **Heracles Hotel** is recommended (⌀ heracles-hotel.eu).

MAKE IT A WEEK Greeks says that Crete is so diverse as to be an entire country; there's plenty

▲ Balkan terrapins are usually seen in or moving towards freshwater lakes.

café for common tree frog. This bright green, sucker-toed amphibian is most easily located at dusk, when it starts to call (surprisingly loudly!) but should be visible by day with a modicum of perusal.

Agia is also a great site for spring birdwatching. It is as reliable as anywhere for both little and Baillon's crakes, sparrow-sized rails that potter furtively in vegetation just off the lake bank. Raptors such as marsh harrier and booted eagle flap sedately past, whilst lethargic squacco and night herons laze in waterside vegetation. Overhead, bee-eaters rattle and Alpine swifts career.

For the remainder of the day, explore the rugged limestone protrusion that is Akrotiri Peninsula. Wandering the garrigue behind Stavros should produce several orchid species, notably Cretan orchid (a sublime endemic representative of the *Ophrys* bee orchid grouping) and the exuberant wild gladiolus. Akrotiri's monasteries – particularly Gouverneto – are worth exploring. Cretan wall lizards scamper around rocks separated by white turban buttercups, while black-eared wheatear and blue rock thrush are among birds lining the descent through a modest rocky gorge to the intensely blue Aegean Sea.

After you have refreshed yourself in the salty water, return uphill, this time humming to the weekend's botanical tune. New orchids may include Fleischmann's, eastern sawfly and pink butterfly, while larger plants may include the spectacular dragon arum. A metre tall, unabashedly phallic and velvety maroon, this is unmissable. If you're feeling brave, expand the experience by inhaling the arum's pungent aroma. Zeus would surely approve.

---

of natural interest to expand your trip. Hike into the **Levka Ori** (White Mountains) for ancient cypress trees and mountain birds. Look for Cretan wild goat and lammergeier around **Samariá Gorge** (page 184). Here, walk the steep path southwestwards up Gingilos for rare and endemic mountain plants. Giant orchid grows at **Armeni cemetery** (⊘ minoancrete.com/armeni). Take a shorter gorge walk at **Imbros**, with ample rock-adapted flowers. Admire abundant sand crocus on the **Omalos Plateau**, along with pink and silvery tulips, blue and purple crown anemones and yellow stars-of-Bethlehem. Check out **Katolikos Monastery** and surrounding caves on **Akrotiri Peninsula**: an amazing ten species of bats have been found roosting here. Wander between **Aptera** and its impressive hillfort for migrant birds, lizards, butterflies and orchids (including Robert's giant). Explore **Theriso Gorge** for Cretan turban and Cretan cyclamen. In the **Asterousia Mountains** south of Sternes, visit the eagle- and vulture-feeding station.

FLEXIBILITY Plants best end March to mid-April, but there is wider interest over a longer period; skink: February to September at least.

TITBITS Greenwings (⊘ greenwings.co.uk; see ad, page 233) run a fine botanical tour here.

DANIELE OCCHIATO/
MINDEN PICTURES/FLPA

Hide and seek

66 Cocking a snook at you, the Corsican nuthatch fizzes away into the forest **99**

WHERE Haut-Corse, Corsica, France
TARGETS Corsican nuthatch, Corsican finch, Marmora's warbler, Corsican fire salamander, Corsican crocus
ACCESSIBILITY ② (tough walks)
CHILD-FRIENDLINESS ② (ditto)

Y ou can hear it, but you just can't see it. Regardless of how intently you peer upwards through the branches lacing together this montane forest. From somewhere in the Corsican pine, a soft, scolding jay-like call issues. Occasionally a cadence bursts out: a slightly haunting, whistling rattle. The songster hides for a few more minutes – it's amazing how much concealment pine needles can offer – but you know that patience is paramount. Eventually it sidles into view, smart and skull-capped with a frowning white eyebrow and graphite back. With its upturned bill, it cocks a snook at you and fizzes away into the forest. A Corsican nuthatch – one of several creatures this weekend that occur nowhere else in the world but this rugged Mediterranean island.

With soaring granite peaks and parched maquis scrubland, damp beech woodlands and open pine forests, rushing rivers and bucolic meadows, Corsica offers variety in spades. Although distances are small, roads are narrow and dominated by switchbacks, so progress overland is slow. As such, a weekend visit needs careful prioritisation. Is it endemic birds you are after, or amphibians? Reptiles or flora? The answers – as well as your arrival point on the island – will determine the sites on which you focus.

Whatever your wildlife interests, though, questing for the nuthatch is a given. It occurs widely in upland pine forests such as Forêt d'Aïtone along the well-named Sentier de la Sittelle (French for 'Nuthatch Trail'), Haut Asco (along the orange trail from the car park) and Forêt de Bonifatu. Probably the most reliable place to track it down is Col de Sorba, southeast of the D69/T20 intersection. Here, above 1,100m

▲ Unique to Corsica, the Corsican nuthatch is a target for every birdwatcher visiting the island.

altitude, you can even see Corsican nuthatch in the car park – although a stroll is usually necessary.

As you search, you will surely see Corsican finch (a largely yellowy finch, recently 'split' from citril finch, that is shared with the neighbouring island of Sardinia) feeding on rocky ground decorated with the endemic Corsican hellebore. Here too are unique island races of common forest birds such as crossbill, jay, treecreeper, and great spotted woodpecker.

At the road junction itself, scrubby hillsides near Le Chalet restaurant enable a careful comparison of Marmora's warbler and the more familiar Dartford warbler. Both are punk-coiffed, graphite-blue birds; the former shares a distribution with Corsican finch. Among butterflies, Corsican wall browns flicker and an unexpectedly premature Corsican swallowtail powers through meadows behind the restaurant, which holds elder-flowered orchid amongst its botanical riches. Indeed orchids will riff through your visit; road verges tend to be where they grow best. Look for pink butterfly orchid, a confustication of tongue orchids (several bewilderingly similar species, which make things worse by apparently interbreeding), yellow ophrys, dark bee-orchid, and more besides. A little further north, at Belvédère de Pasciolo, Marmora's warbler occurs in the dry macquis and Moltoni's warbler in the lower, damper scrub.

Now head west to Col de Vergio, where a statue of Christ announces a popular car park. This offers second dibs at all three of this weekend's target birds: nuthatch in the forest below, warbler in the maquis scrub and finch anywhere rocky. But you're here for other fry. First up, Bedriaga's rock lizard. This hefty, agile, rock-climbing reptile occurs only on Sardinia and Corsica; look for it on expansive stony surfaces uphill from the car park. Second, flora. Among the prostrate juniper several

BOB GIBBONS/FLPA

Unique to the island, Corsican crocus flowers in montane pasture as snow melts. ▲

> 66 With soaring granite peaks and parched maquis scrubland, damp beech woodlands and open pine forests, rushing rivers and bucolic meadows, Corsica offers variety in spades 99

endemic plants grow, the most special of which is Corsican crocus. This beauty's bright lilac flowers are guarded by creamy outer petals that are feathered purple. Scan the mountaintops, and you could even see mouflon and golden eagle. No wonder Jesus chooses to stand vigil here.

Spend the remainder of your trip deepening your appreciation of Corsica's cold-blooded denizens. One way to do this is simply to take pot luck at any pristine forested stream in the mountains. By flipping stones, turning logs or peering into small basins of water in streamside rocks, you could conceivably encounter Corsican fire salamander, Corsican brook newt or Corsican painted frog.

As their name suggests, all three are special because they are endemic to the island. The salamander is the most attractive, its shiny black skin splodged egg-yolk yellow. The drab brown newt is the least demonstrative – but its rarity excites. The frog is the trickiest to identify, being frustratingly similar to Tyrrhenian painted frog, which occurs commonly across Corsica and Sardinia.

For the most efficient 'herping', perhaps make for Cascade des Anglais at Vizzavona. Bedriaga's rock lizard sprawls over rock faces near this forested waterfall, as does the locally common Tyrrhenian wall lizard. Examine puddles below boulders and trees – particularly after rain – to discover Corsican fire salamander. Seeing Corsican painted frog tadpoles simply involves checking quiet pools. Spotting an adult is much trickier. In Corsica, it's not only the birds that play hide and seek.

LEANDER KHIL www.leanderkhil.com

▲ Although not quite a single-island exclusive, Corsican finch is a treat for visitors interested in birds.

GETTING THERE Of Corsica's four airports, the most convenient for Haut-Corse are Bastia (⌂ bastia.aeroport.fr) and Ajaccio (⌂ tinyurl.com/airport-ajaccio). That said, the reality is that you'll take whatever flight you can get (probably via Paris or Nice) as April precedes Corsica's tourist season. This weekend's hub, Corte, lies a 1-hour drive (52km) from Bastia airport and 1½ hours (80km) from Ajaccio.

WHERE TO GO Leave **Vivario** west on the T20 (formerly N163). A good site for Marmora's and Moltoni's warblers is **Belvédère de Pasciolo** lay-by (✻ 42.175000, 9.163801). Continue south along the T20 to **Le Chalet restaurant** (✻ 42.169942, 9.165843), then head east on the D69. Nuthatch spots at **Col de Sorba** are 2.8–4km from the T20/D69 junction. A good track starts at ✻ 42.149992, 9.174943. The main car park is at ✻ 42.144224, 9.190352. From here, it is 2 hours' drive to Col de Vergio. Return to the T20, following it north to Corte. Take the D18 to Castirla, then the D84 west to **Col de Vergio** (✻ 42.290495, 8.878117). Parking by the statue, explore rocky areas and maquis to the north and south, and pine forests to the south. For **Cascade des Anglais** follow the T20 southwest of Vivario. Park at Col de Vizzavona (✻ 42.112309, 9.113182). Walk back east along the road to the tree adventure park (✻ 42.114917, 9.122153), where a trail heads north, zigzaging uphill to the waterfall area (✻ 42.117394, 9.109886). If you need it, another good site for both nuthatch and finch is along the D343 between Vivario and Col d'Erbajo (✻ 42.178694, 9.215806).

SUGGESTED BASES Corte has a dozen hotels. Even more convenient is Vivario, where **U Campanile** would be a good choice (⌂ hotel-restaurant-ucampanile.com).

MAKE IT A WEEK Assuming that the road to **Restonica Gorge** is eventually repaired (at the time of writing, it was closed 9km from the road head), explore the valley and do the tough walk to Lac de Melo for lammergeier, Alpine chough, Bedriaga's rock lizard, Corsican brook newt, and carpets of Corsican crocus. Another decent hike is **Haut Asco**, where you can see Corsican nuthatch, Alpine accentor and lammergeier. Col de Bavella is good for Hermann's tortoise, Corsican brook newt and Corsican crocus. The **Torre de Campomoro** holds European leaf-toed gecko; visit at night. Maquis west and east of Bonifacio excels for orchids, including dark early spider and mirror. Seawatch for Scopoli's and Yelkouan shearwaters from **Pertusato** lighthouse, southeast of Bonifacio, where Hermann's tortoise shuffles around and pygmy algyroides skulks in the scrub. **Cauria plateau** is excellent for tongue orchids and is a site for Corsican hare, which (despite its name) is introduced rather than endemic.

FLEXIBILITY Birds: can be found year-round; salamander: best March to October; crocus: March to May.

MARCO MAGGESI/S

Corsican fire salamander is a largely nocturnal amphibian best seen after rain. ▲

Berlin's dark grail

WHERE Berlin, Brandenburg, Germany
TARGETS Goshawk, great bustard, mandarin, wild boar, northern raccoon
ACCESSIBILITY ⑤
CHILD-FRIENDLINESS ③

A thin spring morning filters through central Berlin's most famous park, the Tiergarten. An uncertain sun toils to dissipate the early chill. Many of the towering trees have fulsome crowns, splaying green. Great tits are calling, incessantly discordant. Hooded crows are cawing, intensely conversational. Then a muscular streak of white, a rapid complication of grey. A blithely unaware woodpigeon cascades downy feathers. It now exists solely as a goshawk's breakfast.

Don't dismiss a goshawk as being merely a big sparrowhawk, and thus unworthy of attention. Goshawk is to sparrowhawk what leopard is to tabby. The biggest female sparrowhawk is barely half the weight of the titchiest male goshawk. Goshawks eat sparrowhawks. They are terrifyingly competent avian predators.

Little wonder that goshawks have so bewitched writers. Novelist T H White, who wrote fantasy novels that influenced J K Rowling's *Harry Potter* series, was bewitched by a goshawk that he sought to tame. He described the tug-and-war of spirit in *The Goshawk*. White's struggle inspired Helen Macdonald, whose *H is for Hawk* became a huge hit. Intent on assuaging grief, she purchased and trained her own goshawk. Conor Jameson was mesmerised by a stuffed 'gos' in a glass case. *Looking for the goshawk* recounts his journey to unravel the mysteries of this rapacious raptor. Jameson's travels take him beyond Britain, to Berlin. The German capital harbours an astonishing 100-odd goshawk pairs – Europe's highest density. In the whole of Britain, in piddling contrast, there are 400 pairs.

> **Goshawks eat sparrowhawks. They are terrifyingly competent avian predators.**

My first experience of Berlin came in early 1990, scant months after the fall of the Wall that divided countries, political philosophies and families. I gawped before the Brandenburg Gate, reflecting on revolution. Goshawks were neither on Berlin's agenda nor mine. By the time of my second visit a decade later, unbeknownst to me, they were all over Europe's third-most wooded city. Wandering from Brandenburg

OLIVER SMART/RSPB

Goshawks have long bewitched writers, starting with novelist T H White. ▲

into Tiergarten, my jaw hit the concrete path when a female gos powered through the canopy. The encounter overturned the applecart containing my preconceptions of urban wildlife.

Tiergarten is as good a place as any to admire Berlin's goshawks. Three pairs breed here and they are unexpectedly easy to see. In Britain, this raptor is confined to remote, dense woodlands – and is rarely seen except in late-winter display flight. Helen Macdonald calls it the birdwatcher's 'dark grail'. In Berlin, goshawks pose on open branches in the biggest trees, fixing observers with a steely stare. In Berlin, gos is boss.

Several other interesting creatures are making a fist of things in Berlin's parks, woodlands and gardens. Since being introduced in the 1920s, mandarin ducks have lived freely in Tiergarten and have spread to other lakes in Brandenburg state. The thousand ducks now inhabiting the German capital have become the second-largest population outside this stunning duck's native range in East Asia, where it symbolises fidelity.

There are city-dwelling mammals as well as birds. Red squirrels are common. Herds of wild boar now slink around Berlin's green spaces. Jungfernheide Park and Tegeler Forest, near Berlin Tegel airport, are good places to search, particularly either side of dusk. Northern raccoon – a species native to North America that escaped from German fur farms in the 1930s – is now a regular sight in Berlin parks and suburbs, particularly when raiding dustbins after dark. Indeed, the adaptable omnivore's population has exploded. Numbers killed by hunters in Brandenburg

GETTING THERE Berlin has two airports: Schönefeld and Tegel (⌀ berlin-airport.de). If staying within the city, it is worth buying a Berlin Welcome card giving unlimited travel on public transport (⌀ berlin-welcomecard.de). Be sure to validate the ticket upon first use to avoid *schwarzfahren* (riding illegally).

WHERE TO GO Berlin's **Tiergarten** (✺ 52.514280, 13.361484 ⌀ tinyurl.com/tiergarten-web ☉ always) stretches for roughly 3km by 1km; Brandenburg Gate lies at its eastern end (✺ 52.514280, 13.361484). Goshawks breed widely in Berlin's parks and cemeteries, the latter including Dorotheenstadt (✺ 52.562450, 13.332734). **Jungfernheide Park** (✺ 52.565477, 13.262187) and **Tegeler Forest** (✺ 52.589574, 13.246652) are both close to Berlin–Tegel airport. In the former site, little bittern breeds on Flughafensee (a lake). Another good area is **Tempelhofer Feld** (✺ 52.474084, 13.404811), a park on the site of the old Tempelhof airfield. Centered on Garlitz (✺ 52.560372, 12.570733), **Havelländisches Luch** lies 70km (1½ hours' drive) west of Berlin, between the towns of Nauen and Rathenow. The best area is bordered by the L982 (to the west), railway (north), Garlitz–Barnewitz road (south) and have increased 140-fold in 25 years. Some 600 groups of these *Waschbären* ('wash bears') now roam the city; one has even denned in a hotel on Alexanderplatz, among Berlin's most famous squares. Berliners have developed polarised attitudes to the bandit-masked interlopers. Some have taken the mammals to their hearts, caring for them. Others treat them as vermin.

If your city-break itinerary permits, sidle outside Berlin, heading 70km into western Brandenburg. The grasslands of Havelländisches Luch, a protected haven amidst endless agricultural fields, hold Europe's northernmost population of great bustard. Thanks to conservation action, numbers here have doubled in the past two decades. Watch from tower hides as the birds stride majestically, fly languidly or display ludicrously.

Back in Berlin, you have time for another stroll around a city-centre park before the return home. Last night's clubbers laze, on the comedown. Parents heave overladen prams towards playgrounds. But your eyes are upon a jumbled stick-nest occupied by a female goshawk.

The sight prompts contemplation. Why are goshawks secretive in Britain yet extrovert in Berlin? Why is the raptor a bird of dense, rural woodland in UK, yet open, urban parkland in Berlin? Why are they apparently not shot in Germany, yet remain persecuted in the UK? At a deeper level, what does the hawks' abundance in this European capital say about the relationship between Germans and nature – and what might other nationalities learn from this? Like White, Macdonald and Jameson before you, the goshawk's talons are now firmly embedded in your soul.

L99 (east). View from the two tower hides. A little further north, **Gülper See** (✳ 52.733624, 12.276858) offers good birding.

SUGGESTED BASES Berlin (⊘ visitberlin.de) has ample accommodation.

MAKE IT A WEEK On the outskirts of Berlin, there are some great walks in **Grunewald/ Teufelssee**: moor frog and sand lizard occur, plus there is good birding too. Once you're done with Berlin, explore Brandenburg state (and possibly western Poland). **Karower Teiche** holds breeding red-necked grebe. **Randow Bruch** (✳ 53.198734,14.10082) has lesser spotted and white-tailed eagles. **Blumberger Mühle** (⊘ blumberger-muehle.nabu.de) is another good site for the latter, and you should see 'herptiles' such as fire-bellied toad, pool frog, eastern grass snake, and European pond terrapin.

FLEXIBILITY Goshawk: year-round but best January to June; raccoon: most active April to October; others: year-round.

TITBITS Experienced local guide **Rolf Nessing** offers birding tours in and around Berlin (⊘ birdingberlin.com; see ad, page 232).

Delta force

WHERE Danube Delta, Dobrogea, Romania
TARGETS White pelican, ferruginous duck, Pallas's gull,
dice snake, steppe runner
ACCESSIBILITY ⑤
CHILD-FRIENDLINESS ④

Half-an-hour before dawn, our small motorboat glides onto the water. A youthful mist embraces the channel and caresses the marsh. A kingfisher pierces the fug with a strident *cheeek*, flashing neon as it hurtles by. Where trees arch overhead, our passing explodes scores of roosting herons from banks and branches. Night herons: hunched veteran brasserie waiters. Squacco herons: Essex girls with strawberry-blond locks, white blouse, pink boots. Purple herons: flowing with serpentine grace.

The size of the UK county of Northumberland, the Danube Delta spreads itself between Romania and Ukraine as the 2,840km-long river feeds the Black Sea. Long famed for its wildlife importance, the delta is the European Union's largest, and the only one in the world designated as a UNESCO Biosphere Reserve. Its 30 distinct ecosystems – collectively housing 5,000 species of plant and animal – include the planet's largest reedbed.

Regrettably, the Delta has gone awry. Its litany of pressures is harrowing: overfishing, illicit trade in sturgeon (for caviar), uncontrolled hunting, unregulated tourism, pollution, and disturbance from speedboats. The Danube remains magical – but how long can it withstand human abuse?

We emerge on to Isac Lake just as the sun squints over a sea of reeds. Our horizons expand, enabling us to scan water and sky for early risers. We are not disappointed. There are birds everywhere. Grebes abound, mostly great crested but with red-necked and black-necked favouring a secluded, well-vegetated bay. Here too a pair of ferruginous duck, the male startlingly white eyed. Nearly two-thirds of this duck's European population breeds in Romania. Flocks of terns swarm like midges as they dip over the lake surface. We discern three approaches to black, white and

▲ With the longest wings of any European bird, white pelicans are truly gargantuan. RICHARD STEEL

grey garb, pertaining to black, whiskered and white-winged black terns.

Overhead, the Delta's skies are congested with avian traffic. Glossy ibises, pointed at both ends, needle the air. Earnest groups of great cormorants rush to their treetop colony before hooded crows snatch their chicks. Stunted versions – pygmy cormorants – ache along with arthritic wingbeats. Pelicans plane past with languid flaps of rectangular wings. Among the many white pelicans, we discern the odd Dalmatian – a punk-haired waterbird threatened with global extinction and heavily dependent on a healthy Delta.

The River Danube itself is for making up time, rather than spending it. Wildlife shuns this main drag, instead spreading throughout forested backwaters and willow-fringed channels. You should spend the weekend similarly. These are waterways to dispense with the engine and drift at nature's pace. Now only the Danube's avian choir deranges the tranquility. Reedbeds harbour an identity parade of brownish warblers: reed and great reed, sedge and Savi's. All chunter without pause, espousing territorial claims. The cacophony is enhanced by the fluting of a golden oriole and the throbbing tones of a thrush nightingale. A penduline tit whistles sadly before resuming construction of its hanging nest.

Secluded under a shady bank we watch red-footed falcons mate at their canopy colony. Great bitterns boom unseen, but a little bittern teeters above a reedy

> **The Danube remains magical – but how long can it withstand human abuse?**

Ferruginous duck: one of Europe's most-threatened waterbirds. ▲

PHILIP PRECEY wildlife-travel.co.uk

channel, clasping one of the firmer stems. Marsh frogs cackle energetically. A musk rat paddles past, oblivious to our presence. A European pond terrapin plops from lilypad to water. A dice snake – the most aquatic of Europe's serpents – weaves through the channel, tracking fish. A myriad of dragonflies and damselflies dazzle us. A beautiful demoiselle helicopters as a hairy dragonfly harries a four-spotted chaser into the sky… where a hobby handbrake-turns into its next meal.

GETTING THERE Nearest airport is Bucharest (bucharestairports.ro/en), which takes flights from many European cities. You can also reach the Romanian capital from rail hubs including Vienna. It is then 4 hours' drive to Tulcea.

WHERE TO GO For a proper **Danube Delta** experience, you really should explore by boat. This means putting your itinerary largely in the hands of a local operators. (The few roads make for a less satisfactory experience, in my view.) Wildlife-tour groups typically use pontons (floating hotels), but there are alternatives. Passenger boats leave **Tulcea** (45.180454, 28.800964) daily for communities such as **Crişan** (45.174295, 29.385541), from where you can rent a motorboat plus driver-guide. You can do the same from Tulcea (eg: through Ibis Tours ibis-tours.ro) or **Murighiol** (45.039762, 29.166855). The main area to explore is the sheltered bays and lakes north of **Sulina Channel** (45.176105, 29.315153). Lakes along the **Sontea Channel** (eg: Nebunu 45.247902, 29.006054 and Ligheanca 45.231566, 29.213652) are good. Other fine areas include **Isac Lake** (45.106119, 29.270178), **Letea island** (45.295325, 29.515285), the **Mila 23 lakes** (45.228599, 29.246832), the labyrinth of channels near **Caroarman** (45.085396, 29.407697) and the port of **Sfântu Gheorghe** (44.895403, 29.588242).

▲ Chuntering along a quiet backwater offers the best way to see Danube Delta wildlife.

The longer you spend mooching around the watery quietness, the greater your chance of an unexpected encounter with something like wildcat or golden jackal or of being serenaded by eastern tree frogs. Should you wish a change of scenery, however, two options stand out – both enabling some leg-stretching.

Throttle east to the Black Sea port of Sfântu Gheorghe. A shallow bay teems with pelicans, egrets and terns. White-tailed eagles laze overhead. Pallas's gulls patrol, confident that they are Europe's best-looking gull. A muddy lagoon oozes with passage waders, notably thousands of ruff, the males garbed like Elizabethan fops. If you can find a quiet sandy beach, you might encounter steppe runner, a lizard that basks below small shrubs and whose European range is restricted to Romania's Black Sea coast.

Alternatively, make for Letea island, where shells infiltrating the sandy substrate demonstrate that this land was once sea. Rolling dunes interpolate airy woodlands of gnarled oaks ribboned with silk-vine lianas. A collared flycatcher sings sporadically. A black woodpecker bounces past like an enormous dusky butterfly. There are real lepidopterans too, and in abundance: the eye-searing large copper and the seductive lacework that marks out a scarce swallowtail. But even on this almost exclusively arid island, it is the water that mesmerises. In small pools and ditches, common spadefoot toads seek to avoid the attention of a hungry grass snake. They all demand that the Danube Delta retain its force.

SUGGESTED BASES Crişan, in the heart of the delta, makes an excellent base. A recommended operator here, also offering rooms, is **Pension Vasiliu** (⌂ ecoturismdelta.ro). Staying in Tulcea (eg: at Ibis Tours' guesthouse) makes sense for exploring Sontea Channel. Murighiol is better for reaching Sfântu Gheorghe.

MAKE IT A WEEK Babadag Forest for lesser-spotted and eastern imperial eagles. The rolling steppes of **Dobrogea** for golden jackal, European souslik, saker falcon and isabelline wheatear. Roman ruins at **Histria** hold reptiles such as Caspian whip snake, spur-thighed tortoise and Balkan wall lizard. **Vadu** beach excels for steppe runner, European pond terrapin and spur-thighed tortoise. **Lake Sinoe** holds abundant birdlife, including paddyfield warbler. Alternatively, head west into Transylvania's **Carpathian Mountains** for brown bear near Zărneşti (try Carpathian Nature Tours ⌂ cntours.ro or Sakertour ⌂ sakertour.com; see ad, page 234) or Braşov (⌂ absolute-nature.ro/bear-hide-transylvania-romania) and for Carpathian blue slug (much cooler than it sounds).

FLEXIBILITY April to October for all although the Delta is most vibrant in spring.

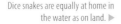
Dice snakes are equally at home in the water as on land. ▶

" Siberian flying squirrel is pin-up material: impossibly bushy-tailed, unsurpassably bright-eyed "

NATURE PRODUCTION/NPL

Estonian nightlife

WHERE Ida-Viru, northeast Estonia
TARGETS Siberian flying squirrel, brown bear, raccoon dog, pine marten, capercaillie
ACCESSIBILITY ④
CHILD-FRIENDLINESS ① (late nights)

Birch trees quill skywards. Spruce stand tall, defiantly draping overcoats. Muscular aspen shun leaves for trunks as grey as the Soviet-era housing estates that Uudo Timm and I passed as we crossed Estonia eastwards. Even amidt forest that has towered since Lenin's Bolshevik revolution exactly 100 years ago, I cannot shed thought of Estonia's reluctant history.

Our journey witnesses Estonia's rejection of its Soviet past. We pass derelict cooperative farms and abandoned schools. Villages seared of their heart. Once-mighty forests plundered for timber. A few kilometres shy of the Russian border, we arrive. Uudo guides me into one of Estonia's finest woodlands, Muraka. Spongy moss trampolines our footfall. Uudo points to a discreet hole midway up a mighty aspen – a small circular entry and exit point.

▲ Venture out with an expert if you want to see a Siberian flying squirrel.

Our quarry – arguably Europe's cutest mammal – lives inside the cavity. The Siberian flying squirrel is pin-up material: impossibly bushy-tailed, unsurpassably bright-eyed – and it flies (well, glides)! Its elusiveness, however, is legendary. It took Uudo, an Estonian scientist and conservationist studying the squirrel since the 1980s, seven tantalising years to spot his first.

Three decades on, visiting wildlife-watchers should have no such bother. Uudo and colleagues have fitted a number of animals with radio transmitters so they can understand their movements and habitat needs. Provided the transmitter remains functional and the squirrel remains broadly faithful to its expected home range, Uudo can lead you to the precise tree in which it is slumbering the day away.

Then all you have to do is wait until dusk, whereupon a pair of huge, peaty-pooled eyes should squint out from the animal's chosen cavity. Once it is happy that all is well, the squirrel emerges fully and – typically – takes things slowly for a few minutes before gliding and scampering into the darkness.

Even the wait is eminently pleasurable, with a host of exciting birds and mammals confessing their presence. Capercaillies grovel on the dirt track, gathering grit to aid their digestive travails. Hazel grouse scamper around, testing ageing ears with their high-pitched whistles. A black woodpecker giggles nearby. Common cranes yodel from their roost. A roe deer regards us nervously. A couple of male woodcocks – pot-bellied and long-billed – parabola overhead, calling attention with their lisping, twiggy call: *tswiick!* A pine marten undulates past then pauses, thick-tailed and creamy-breasted. As the gloaming thickens, a pygmy owl pipes – a call that is neither (precisely) mellow nor (quite) melancholy. Barely larger than a chaffinch, the owl heralds the night. And night means Siberian flying squirrel…

ROBIN CHITTENDEN www.robinchittenden.co.uk

Estonia is one of several countries with brown bear hides, where you can watch ursines without disturbing them. ▲

" A pine marten undulates past
then pauses, thick tailed and
creamy breasted "

Charismatic and with chestnut tones to the fur – encounters with pine martens are always worth treasuring.
IAIN H LEACH

JONATHAN LETHBRIDGE www.justbirdphotos.com

Actually night means a number of exciting mammals. Just as well you have another dusk-till-dawn session available in your weekend. So – if you can resist the temptation to look for lesser spotted eagle, black grouse and grey-headed woodpecker – spend the day resting in preparation for an all-night vigil in Alutaguse Forest.

Arriving late afternoon, you meet a guide from NaTurEst, the company that operates hides which offer a very good chance indeed of seeing brown bear. 'I have only failed once in more than 30 visits,' said Tarvo Walker, who guides for Estonian Nature Tours, 'and that was when the army was on operations nearby'.

GETTING THERE Tallinn is the nearest airport (⊘ tallinn-airport.ee). It's about 1¾ hours' drive (175km) from here to the bear and squirrel areas.

WHERE TO GO Siberian flying squirrel currently occurs at 44 sites in extreme northeast Estonia, mostly in mixed aspen and birch woodland, including in **Muraka forest** north of **Tudulinna** (❊ 59.036697, 27.081069). Finding one on your own is impossible so you need to contract an expert guide. I recommend contacting Uudo Timm via Estonian Nature Tours (⊘ naturetours. ee). The brown bear hide in **Alutaguse Forest** is 2km northwest of Piilse (❊ 59.253300, 26.977505 but park at ❊ 59.258396, 26.972694). Reserve through NaTurEst (⊘ natourest. ee/brown-bear-2). The hide is moderately comfortable, with bunk beds and a dry toilet; photo hatches enable the use of protruding telephoto lenses. Other mammals that might make an appearance include red fox, pine marten, badger and even wolverine.

SUGGESTED BASES The most convenient accommodation is **Matsu Talu guesthouse** (❊ 59.046956, 27.035462 ⊘ matsutalu.eu) along road 88 northwest of Tudulinna. This is

▲ Male capercaillies are even bigger than you expect. Swarthy forest turkeys!

It is a short walk through mixed forest to two hides that overlook a clearing. In a single spindly birch, a willow warbler cascades while a pair of waxwing trills. Nearby, a pied flycatcher rejoices but jays bicker. Each hide is equipped with bunks and sleeping bags – although any time spent in the Land of Nod risks missing an ursine arrival. Your call… your risk…

As light is sucked from the evening, so your brain and retina combine to bewitch you. Was that a movement, a shadow, an animal, a mythical beast? Looking through binoculars to enhance your visual powers, you determine that the flickering shape belongs to a real-life raccoon dog. Stocky, short-legged and furry-tailed, this is a striking mammal. A black face mask is offset by a white ring around a sooty nose, and most of the pelage is attractively grizzled. In short time, four others appear.

Attractive though this canid clearly is, raccoon dog is a controversial animal. Native to Asia, but not Europe, this is an 'invasive alien species' in Estonia and other European countries. Introduced to the former Soviet Union to increase the number of fur-producing game species, it is now a major menace to rare ground-nesting birds such as great bittern, and amphibians like great crested newt. Many conservationists would dearly love to eradicate raccoon dogs.

Much bigger and much less contentious is the brown bear. At some point during your vigil, one or more animals should pad through. You may hear the crunch of foot upon twigs before the giant materialises. The raccoon dogs slink into the shadows, while the bear sniffs until it finds the cached bait. It prods the offering and takes a nibble. Seemingly unimpressed, it huffs away eastwards in the vague direction of the Russian border. The symbolism does not escape me.

close to both sites. Classier, but more distant accommodation is at **Art Café** in Rakvere (artcafe.ee).

MAKE IT A WEEK Visit a great snipe lek near **Kärevere** with Estonian Nature Tours (naturetours.ee/?page=3498), then track down breeding woodpeckers and red-breasted flycatcher. Book a bat tour with NaTurEst to see northern and pond bats (tinyurl.com/bat-estonia). In western Estonia, watch migrating Arctic waterfowl at **Haapsalu** and **Matsalu National Park**. Try ponds north of **Haversi** for migrating waders including broad-billed sandpiper. Watch dragonflies and woodpeckers along the boardwalk in **Nigula Bog**, southwest Estonia (tinyurlcom/nigula-bog).

FLEXIBILITY Squirrel: April to June; bear: late April to September; pine marten, raccoon dog and capercaillie: most of the year.

TITBITS Flying squirrels often reveal their presence by depositing pyramids of golden, rice-grain-shaped droppings at the base of aspen trees. Flying squirrel can also be seen in Finland, including with the company **Taiga Spirit** (tinyurl.com/finland-squirrel).

Lesser
is lovelier

WHERE Extremadura, Cáceres province, central-west Spain
TARGETS Lesser kestrel, white-rumped swift, European roller, Spanish terrapin, Schreiber's green lizard
ACCESSIBILITY ②
CHILD-FRIENDLINESS ④

Taut and urgent, the powder-blue and terracotta falcon scorches through the intense evening sky before alighting atop the gleaming white circle of a building. A giant centipede – caught but not yet dispatched – squirms leggily in the predator's bill. With growing youngsters to nourish, the male lesser kestrel shuffles towards its nest, a cavity beneath the roof tiles of Trujillo's eerily quiet bullring. You watch, mesmerised, from the adjacent road.

This walled city is the finest in Extremadura, perhaps in Spain overall. It is also the most birdy urban area I have ever visited. Some 130 pairs of lesser kestrels – smaller than their more widespread cousin, common kestrel, but undeniably lovelier – breed on 29 Trujillo buildings, prompting designation of the town as a 'Special Protection Area' under EU legislation. Around ten pairs nest on the Plaza de Toros. To avoid disturbing these rare birds, the bullring is closed on all bar one day between February and July.

A walk through the town combines admiration of both built and natural heritage. Crag martins rest on ledges, white storks raise young on artificial promontories, and subalpine warblers scratch away vocally in scrub beside the ramparts. Common butterflies include the subtly beautiful mallow skipper, while hummingbird hawk-moths blister past in a fiery blur. Geniez's wall lizards peer out of holes in – you guessed it – walls, while western psammodromus, a heftier cousin, sprawls motionless on the ground. *Hombre* and *natura*, cheek by jowl.

End your first day at Trujillo, but start it on the steppe nearer Cáceres. Even this late in spring, dawn on the grassy plains is magical, with calandra and thekla larks cheering the rising sun. Your target is European roller, a cobalt-coloured, crow-like bird that profits from nest-boxes carefully

▶ The roller's powerful bill swiftly dispatches insect prey such as this katydid, a relative of the grasshopper.
OLIVER SMART www.smartimages.co.uk

FABIO PUPIN/FLPA

"Schreiber's green lizard is arguably Europe's most stunning reptile"

sited beneath roadside telegraph poles. This invertebrate-muncher's populations are dwindling as agriculture intensifies, so enjoy this beauty now lest it disappear. There's plenty else to enjoy. With luck, you should locate great bustard, black-winged kite and Iberian imperial eagle – though easier delights will be Montagu's harrier and Iberian hare.

For the middle tranche of this first day, head an hour east into the 'geopark' of Sierra de Las Villuercas – rugged, tranquil mountains oddly snubbed by tourists. If the day is hot, seek shady solace in a marvellous walk just south of Castañar de Ibor. Amid chestnut-dominated copses, several species of orchid may still be flowering along the trailside banks. Look for narrow-leaved helleborine, plus Lange's and dense-flowered orchids.

Common goldenring – a mean-looking dragonfly if ever there was one – patrols the trickling streams, and you may encounter other species of dragon and damsel. Butterflies are abundant, particularly in sunny glades. Knapweed fritillary and cardinal jostle with clouded yellow and Cleopatra. A swallowtail dwarfs a long-tailed blue, Spanish gatekeeper outnumbers southern white admiral. Large tortoiseshells inflame the ground by your feet.

The lepidopteran diversity may be overwhelming, yet the main reason for visiting Ibor is cold-blooded. Schreiber's green lizard is arguably Europe's most stunning reptile: large, bright blue and vivid green. Occurring only in Iberia and generally rare, it is surprisingly common in Villuercas. Look for it basking on rocks alongside streams.

Few reptiles are as brightly coloured as Schreiber's green lizard. A stunner. ▲

Devote day two to Monfragüe National Park, a natural marvel that you could happily spend a week exploring (page 7). *En route* from Trujillo peer over the bridge at the Río Almonte to admire the rare Spanish terrapin swimming in the shallows. Then make for Monfragüe Castle, and limber up for a half- or full-day hike, packed full of wildlife.

> **❝ Is there no limit on Extremadura's bounteous wildlife? ❞**

Crag martins, rock buntings and red-rumped swallows accompany your climb through stony, prickly terrain, stippled with holm oaks and wild olive trees. *En route*, watch out for horseshoe whip snake winding through trees and ocellated lizard basking atop rocks. Adults of the latter hefty reptile are bright green with eye-catching blue flank-spots: glorious! As you near the castle, a red deer forages, unperturbed by your arrival.

At the summit, make for the protruding platform. Never-ending griffon and cinereous vultures cruise past, seemingly within touching distance. Also look to the skies for white-rumped swift: old red-rumped swallow nests near the castle provide one of its few European breeding sites. Then descend the northern slope, through moist woodland dominated by strawberry trees. Here your goal comprises two sumptuous, multicoloured and dramatically patterned butterflies: two-tailed pasha and Spanish festoon.

GETTING THERE Nearest airports are Seville (⊘ sevilla-airport.com) and Madrid (⊘ aeropuertomadrid-barajas.com), from each of which it is 275km (2–3 hours' drive) to Trujillo in Cáceres.

WHERE TO GO Trujillo lies just off the A-5 Madrid–Badajoz motorway; the bullring is at ✳ 39.456733, -5.872662. The best area of **Cáceres plains** is along the CC99, between km35 of the A58 Trujillo–Cáceres motorway and Santa Marta de Magasca. In Sierra de Las Villuercas, take EX386 south from **Castañar de Ibor** and park at the hairpin by the restaurant (✳ 39.624137, -5.413534). Walk the signposted trail east, uphill towards the Fuente Fría. For **Monfragüe National Park** (⊘ parquedemonfrague.com) follow the EX208 northwest from Trujillo, pausing at the Río Almonte bridge near km53. **Monfragüe Castle** car park is at ✳ 39.822441, -6.047264 (follow the 'red' walk up and over the cliff), **Salto del Gitano** at ✳ 39.828526, -6.057419 and **Villarreal de San Carlos** at ✳ 39.847095, -6.029737.

SUGGESTED BASES Centrally located for sites covered, Trujillo (⊘ trujillo.es) has ample accommodation options. Some 11km east is the excellent **Casa Rural El Recuerdo** (⊘ casaruralelrecuerdo.com). Villarreal de San Carlos in Monfragüe has holiday flats.

BERT WILLAERT/NPL

Below one pathside cliff face lies a cool pool. Finches gather to drink here, and the dark waters harbour Bosca's and southern marbled newts, plus Iberian water frog. Further along the trail, stone basins with drinking water sometimes host newts – and even fire salamander. Reaching the road, pause at the bridge over the reservoir, where Alpine swifts and house martins hurtle around.

Then follow the road west back to the castle car park. Take an hour or so at the Salto del Gitano viewpoint, where you can admire Egyptian vulture amongst its numerous (griffon and cinereous) cousins, nesting black storks, displaying blue rock thrush and purring crested tit. With birds, mammals, reptiles, amphibians and butterflies, is there no limit on Extremadura's bounteous wildlife?

Also in the national park, **Casa Babel** is an attractive *casa rural* (casababel.es) and the **Hospedería Parque de Monfragüe** is large but stylish (hospederiasdeextremadura.com). **MAKE IT A WEEK** Explore Monfragüe fully. There are plenty of walks around Villarreal de San Carlos, plus lesser-visited areas such as Portilla del Tiétar, where Iberian imperial eagles often nest. Near Almaraz, visit **Arrocampo Reservoir**, which is excellent for little bittern and purple heron. Nearby, the **Orchydarium** (orchydarium.es) can update you on whether local specialities such as the *almaracencis* variant of bee orchid are still flowering. The private reserve of **Finca La Parrilla** – part of the INNATE network – offers exclusive wildlife-watching and nature photography, with specialities including common genet and various amphibians (innatenetwork.com/parrilla_eng.html).
FLEXIBILITY Kestrel/roller: April to July; swift: May to October; lizard/terrapin: February to November. Note that steppe wildlife overall is best February to April.
TITBITS A network of individual wildlife guides operates through **Extremadura Birding** (birdinginextremadura.com); in a cool spring, it should still be in flower – and is a joy to behold, so cross fingers!

Spanish terrapin populations have slumped in recent decades, and the reptile is now globally threatened. ▲

Melting pot

WHERE The Burren, County Clare, Ireland
TARGETS Dense-flowered orchid, mountain avens, spring gentian, large-flowered butterwort, transparent burnet
ACCESSIBILITY ②
CHILD-FRIENDLINESS ④

'The Burren is a botanical wonderland', enthuses Jon Dunn, author of *Orchid Summer*. Dunn's admiration for Ireland's vast swathe of limestone is echoed by botanists continent-wide. The Burren, they concur, is unprecedented. Its uniqueness lies not in plants that occur nowhere else in Europe, but in being a botanical melting pot. This natural rock garden (*boireann* means 'big rocky area') is where plants from north, south and east meet and greet – in jaw-dropping abundance, variety and palette.

Within a single square metre, you could find flowers from three distant compass points mingling. Spring gentian is an Alpine that grows in montane Europe; mountain avens a plant of Scandinavian tundra. Dense-flowered orchid and large-flowered butterwort are otherwise strictly Mediterranean flowers. Three-quarters of Ireland's flora grows here in 1% of its land area. No other wildflower wonder *anywhere* offers such fascinating juxtaposition.

And there's more floral wackiness shredding the botanical rulebook. Plants that are associated with acidic soil, such as heathers, that somehow grow on The

DR CHRIS GIBSON chrisgibsonwildlife.co.uk

▲ Spring gentian: one of The Burren's floral delights.

BOB GIBBONS/FLPA

Burren's (alkaline) limestone. Plants of shady woodland flourish in open areas. Montane plants thrive at sea level. The Burren oozes oddity and drips with contradictions. This land of anomaly beseeches exploration.

The Burren's tapestry is best known for austere-looking limestone plateaus, with deep fissures (grykes or *scailps*) secreting entire worlds of green. Many carboniferous pavements are lightly turfed, the thin soil granting colonisation by drifts of plants – pinks and blues and whites and yellows punctuating the green. There are valleys too, and hazel woodlands and sea cliffs, chalky grasslands and marshy fens, lochs and turloughs (ephemeral waterbodies). The entire landscape is traversed by droves (ancient roadways, now grassed and florally enhanced).

Following the final retreat of the glaciers, Arctic plants rushed to take root in The Burren. Over time, milder climes enabled Alpines from continental Europe to move in, followed by Mediterranean plants. The warming – a combination of the Gulf Stream and the radiator-like limestone, which absorbs

> 66 Botanists continent-wide concur: The Burren is unprecedented 99

heat in summer then releases it in winter – had its downside. Tundra plants could barely stand the heat and, with exceptions such as mountain avens, died out.

Let's take a closer look at this weekend's botanical stars. Explosions of spring gentian – with their intense blue, trumpet-shaped flowers – weaken your knees.

Irish saxifrage blooming where limestone meets coast on The Burren. ▲

The carpet-forming mountain avens is like a glamorous daisy, its golden core ringed by ivory petals. For a group of plants renowned for ostentation, dense-flowered orchid is understated. Its creamy-white flowers top a simple, slender stem. The yellow suns of shrubby cinquefoil bush outwards from grykes and above turloughs. Deep purple, star-shaped and unremittingly carnivorous, large-flowered butterwort hails from the mountains of southwest Europe; The Burren forms its sole northern outpost.

You could wander pretty much anywhere in The Burren and encounter clusters, clumps and carpets of exciting, beautiful flowers. But in a mere weekend, choose wisely. Spend one day along Clare's coast, the other inland.

Above the sea, start at Abbey Hill. Spring gentian and mountain avens rub shoulders. You may find your first dense-flowered orchid and common spotted orchid of the white-flowered variety *okellyi* – interspersed with early purple and fly orchids. 'For me', says Dunn, 'early purple orchids actually steal The Burren's show. In places you feel like you've stepped into an Impressionist painting, they carpet the landscape so thickly in every shade from snow white to deepest, royal purple.'

Moving west, Cappanawalla is an outstanding shattered pavement that rewards your breathy climb. Orchids abound; so too mountain everlasting and mountain avens. But the star is large-flowered butterwort, which flowers in a flush. At Black Head, explore eastwards for interesting plants – including maidenhair fern and Burren saxifrage – on the shady, north-facing escarpment.

GETTING THERE Ferry routes between the UK and Ireland – enabling you to take your own car – are Dublin–Holyhead, Fishguard–Rosslare, Pembroke–Rosslare and Liverpool–Dublin (⌂ directferries.ie). Nearest airport is Shannon (⌂ shannonairport.ie), which takes flights from several UK cities. From Shannon, it is a 1-hour drive (65km) to Doolin, along the M18, N85 and N67. A free national park bus service operates from Corofin (⌂ burrennationalpark.ie/visit/bus-service; ⊙ May–Sep).
WHERE TO GO The Burren (⌂ burren.ie) covers at least 250 km². It is roughly bordered by Ballyvaughan, Kinvara, Tubber, Corovinand Lisdoonvarna. In the north, **Abbey Hill** is at ❋ 53.138558, -9.045704 and **Cappanawalla** at ❋ 53.122621, -9.195960. Park at **Black Head** lighthouse (❋ 53.153525, -9.264754) then explore eastwards. Park at ❋ 53.117352, -9.286919 for **Fanore dunes**. The **Khyber Pass** leads east from ❋ 53.124173, -9.277525, with **Formoyle** at ❋ 53.116070, -9.247052. Access **Poulsallagh** (**Poll Sallach**) from the R477 at ❋ 53.060727, -9.362414. **Burren National Park** (⌂ burrennationalpark.ie) lies in the southeast of the area. In Killinaboy, leave the R476 east on to the L1112, which you follow for 5km to Gortlecka crossroads. Park in the lay-by (❋ 52.996558, -9.037868). This is the starting point for a 1.5km nature trail and four hiking routes, three of which lead northeast

Further south, Fanore dunes are splattered with spring gentian. Head inland along a deep cleft (the 'Khyber Pass') that shelters the River Caher. Hillsides beyond Formoyle chapel are superbly flowery, abounding with mountain avens and spring gentian. Further south still, a great limestone pavement gushes into the sea at Poulsallagh (Poll Sallach). New plants include thrift, hoary rock-rose, bloody cranesbill, spring sandwort, and Irish marsh-orchid.

Spend day two walking the national park nature trail at Mullaghmor, and exploring Kellhilla (Slieve Carron) reserve. Both areas – blissfully quiet, excitingly remote – excel for dense-flowered and fly orchids. Nearby Lough Gealàin, a turlough, is shrouded with various marsh- and spotted orchids and harbours shrubby cinquefoil.

Despite the botanical paradise, don't assume that The Burren has exclusively floral attractions. There is exciting fauna too. Irish hare (a subspecies of mountain hare) is frequently seen. A semi-tame common bottlenose dolphin known as Dusty often frequents Doolin or Fanore. Among butterflies, wall browns flit energetically on limestone, while wood whites shelter in grasslands fringing serene woodlands. Transparent burnet – scarlet and black – is a readily seen day-flying moth, its local abundance belying its national status of rare and localised. Another rare day-flyer is dew moth, a deliciously caramel-coloured insect. But let's – ahem – not beat about the bush. Botany is what The Burren is about.

via **Lough Gealáin** (❋ 52.999216, -9.020995) to **Mullagh mor** (❋ 53.007222, -9.002761). For **Kellhilla (Slieve Carron)**, leave the L1014 at Carran, heading northeast for 9km to the car park (❋ 53.076403, -8.998930). Dusty the common bottlenose dolphin (⌀ dustythedolphin.com) frequents **Doolin** and **Fanore**.
SUGGESTED BASES Accommodation suggestions are at ⌀ burren.ie/where-to-stay. In Lisdoonvarna, **Sheedys Hotel** (⌀ sheedys.com) neighbours a fen rich in marsh orchids.
MAKE IT A WEEK Visit the **Aran islands** for (wilder!) common bottlenose dolphin, common and Atlantic grey seals, Irish saxifrage and Babington's leek. The **Cliffs of Moher** are Europe's second-highest sea cliffs and harbour seabirds including Atlantic puffin and kittiwake. Enjoy marsh orchids by Sheedy's Hotel in **Lisdoonvarna**. Look for Réal's wood white at **Ballydoogan Bog**, Galway.
FLEXIBILITY Plants: May to June; burnet: late May to July.
TITBITS Wildlife Travel (⌀ wildlife-travel.co.uk; see ad, page 236) are among companies offering botanical tours of The Burren.

A rose chafer beetle ascends the stem of a dense-flowered orchid. ▶
JON DUNN www.jondunn.com

FABIO LIVERANI/NPL

City-break falcons

WHERE Matera, Basilicata, southern Italy
TARGETS Lesser kestrel, lanner falcon, Egyptian vulture
ACCESSIBILITY ②
CHILD-FRIENDLINESS ④

The delicate, invertebrate-munching falcon has no knowledge that its home will become the European Capital of Culture in 2019. The elegant, pastel-toned male is unaware that its summertime lodging is a UNESCO World Heritage Site. All that it – and the two thousand-plus other lesser kestrels that aggregate into the continent's largest breeding colony – knows is that this cave-hollowed, hilltop town in southern Italy offers safe places to nest. This may help to reverse the heinous population declines that its kind have suffered. The human occupants of Matera – troglodytes past, present and transitory – seem happy to help. Just.

Basilicata partitions the stiletto heel of Italy (Puglia) from the country's toes (Calabria). Matera is the region's most famous, indeed formerly infamous,

▲ Lesser kestrels are part and parcel of a visit to the Italian hill town of Matera.

town. Sprawling across slopes of Gravin Gorge alongside the modern town and glowing golden in evening light, I Sassi (literally, 'The Rocks') comprises a large area of remarkable dwellings. All are half-carved into and half-built from the surrounding *tufo* – tuff, a light, porous rock of volcanic origin. First inhabited in Palaeolithic times, these cave homes continued to accommodate Materaís until the 1950s. By then, the Italian authorities had been scandalised by the troglodytes' insanitary living conditions and high infant-mortality rates – and forcibly moved the residents into modern lodgings.

> **66** Since 1950, Western Europe's lesser kestrel population has disintegrated. Just 5% remains **99**

Within a generation, the malaria-ridden squalor was vanquished. Savvy, well-to-do residents reoccupied the caves. The UNESCO accolade followed in 1993, recognising Matera as 'the most outstanding, intact example of a troglodyte settlement in the Mediterranean'. Two decades later, ever-more cavehouses have been converted into hotels, restaurants and private residences. Matera is booming.

And so are its avian stars. The town's Lego-like construct, perched at the tip of a plateau with insect-rich valleys below, is precisely what suits this rare and elegant raptor. Since 1950, Western Europe's lesser kestrel population has disintegrated. Just 5% remains across the region as a whole, although Italy – largely thanks to Matera – is bucking the trend. As such, there is no better place to watch this delicate bird of prey go about its business.

With its higgledy-piggledy architecture and rich cultural heritage, Matera is an ideal location to weave wildlife into a city break (or, depending on your priorities, vice versa). Wiggle through alleys and snake down cobbled stairways to both explore the town and locate its kestrels – which are seemingly everywhere.

The falcons nest on window ledges and in flower boxes. They create homes on urban parapets and under roofs. They tuck their young amid statues and – in tacit acceptance of a brasher culture – in the lee of satellite dishes. Particularly before the breeding season ramps up, 3,000 birds may roost communally in a single large pine tree in the town centre, unfazed by traffic.

No other European bird of prey nests in such close association with people, nor in such tightly woven colonies. In Matera, its numbers have been boosted through the provision of nestboxes. In 2016, kestrels occupied 70% of these purpose-built homes. The local community increasingly takes pride in its feathered residents. There are guided walks to see them, and residents hand-rear chicks that have toppled from ledges. One local restaurant even honours the falcon through its name (Al Falco Grillaio).

DR CHRIS GIBSON chrisgibsonwildlife.co.uk

GETTING THERE The nearest airport is Bari (⊘ bari-airport.com, ⊘ aeroportidipuglia.it/homepagebari), which is served by low-cost and other airlines from cities including London Stansted. From here it is a 1-hour drive (70km) to Matera. Alternatively, if you are staying in Matera all weekend, a more environmentally friendly option would be to take the 'Pugliairbus' from the airport to Matera (⊘ aeroportidipuglia.it/bus1).

WHERE TO GO The town of **Matera** (old town at ✻ 40.666092, 16.612701) is small enough to simply walk around. It won't take long to spot lesser kestrels – but you may need height to optimise views. With a weekend at your disposal, you have time to discover the best spots. Given all Matera's caves, bats should be commonplace. To date, Soprano pipistrelle and Geoffroy's bat are known to occur, but other species may also be present. **Oasi San Giuliano Nature Reserve** (✻ 40.600933, 16.542701 ⊘ tinyurl.com/wwf-sangiuliano) is 20km southwest of Matera, mainly along the SS7.

SUGGESTED BASES Where else but **Matera** (⊘ visitmatera.it)? Perhaps stay in a cave-hotel, the plushest including **Sextantio Le Grotte della Civita** (⊘ legrottedellacivita.sextantio.it).

▲ Even without lesser kestrels sailing overhead, the spectacular town of Matera demands a visit.

It wasn't always so. Residents of Basilicata formerly had a taste for eggs and chicks. A recent programme reconstructing Matera's buildings paid scant demand to kestrel needs, demolishing many breeding sites. Even now, side-effects of human habitation such as cats constrain the falcons' breeding success. And the birds don't do themselves favours by excreting waste over lines of laundry.

But this should not worry a casual visitor such as yourself. There are more than enough lesser kestrels – streetwise and sociable – to enjoy. Spot a male nipping through the air in pursuit of an errant dragonfly. Witness a female plummeting to the ground outside the town to grab a cricket that it somehow spotted from height. Watch recently fledged kestrels twist through their urban, limestone canopy as they get to grips with an aerial future. Or, as we approach the end of the breeding season, admire flocks of the delicate sky-dancers; slaloming and sashaying in concert.

Should you need an escape from Matera's maze-like confines, you could head east, down into the Parco della Murgia Materana. Here look for another rare falcon – lanner – or the similarly scarce Egyptian vulture, both of which have benefited from EU-funded conservation action. Search diligently for reptiles such as western whip, four-lined and Italian aesculapian snakes. Or, if you crave water in these arid hills, venture to Lago di San Giuliano. Here the World Wildlife Fund runs a wetland reserve that harbours little bittern, night heron and black-winged stilt.

San Giuliano makes a pleasant change from Matera's bustle. Nevertheless, I wager that the town will have got its claws into you as cleanly as a lesser kestrel into a grasshopper, and that you'll be itching to return.

MAKE IT A WEEK Shared between Basilicata and Calabria, **Pollino National Park** (⊘ parcopollino.it) is a good bet. Here there are high peaks and lava flows, open meadows and vast forests, limestone formations and rocky ravines. You could hike all week without risking boredom. Mammals known to occur include Apennine grey wolf, otter and wildcat. A good option to try for them would be to take a night-drive along the **Strada Colle San Martino–Piano Ruggio road**, which starts at ✽ 39.8945N 16.049E. One diligent observer has found forest dormouse in the **Bocca del Forna** (39.894N 16.088E). For a better shot at Apennine wolf, plus specialities such as black stork, Egyptian vulture and spectacled salamander, try the privately owned **Wild Lucania reserve** (⊘ skuanature.com/wild_lucania_eng.html), which is particularly well set up for wildlife photographers.
FLEXIBILITY Kestrels: April to September, but May to August best; others: year-round.

ALICK SIMMONS

The European Union has funded conservation of Egyptian vultures around Matera. ▲

66 In early summer, before the merino-wool-clad crowds descend, the three target mammals are hard to miss. **99**

BLICKWINKEL/A

Nimble as a mountain goat

WHERE Gran Paradiso, Piedmont and Aosta Valley, Italy
TARGETS Alpine ibex, Alpine chamois, Alpine marmot, owly sulphur, nine-spotted
ACCESSIBILITY ①
CHILD-FRIENDLINESS ④

The call is insistent, enjoining attention. A shrill, emphatic whistle literally screaming alarm. It comes from the ground yet you sense that the danger emanates from the sky. Do you look up (for predator) or down (for nervous potential victim)? Scanning rocky turf carpeting the south-facing slope in Italy's Gran Paradiso, you spot the watchdog standing erect on its hindlegs – a fluffy bear, in miniature. Within seconds, the threat – perceived or real – has expired. Again silent, the Alpine marmot reverts to an unperturbed, horizontal position, shape-shifting into a creature somewhere between a chipmunk and a beaver – but with a squirrel's bushy tail. There may be no more endearing animal in this book.

▲ Alpine ibex and snow-splattered rocky mountains: quintessential Gran Paradiso.

No prizes for guessing where the Alpine marmot lives. Although it has been introduced to the Pyrenees (page 122), the Alps are its true home. And this guide would be incomplete without a weekend exploring Europe's mightiest mountain range, replete with flowery meadows, gushing rivers, serene forests, rocky plateaus, and ultimate peaks.

One problem with foreign mini-breaks is that mountains do not lend themselves easily to a mere weekend. Proper montane hikes involve a night or two in a high-altitude *refugio*. Aching limbs demand a rest day between adventures. And there is always another peak to ascend. Mountains perpetually leave you wanting more. But this no excuse not to visit for a mere weekend. Choose a decent base – in the case of Italy's oldest national park, I suggest Valsavarenche – and even a couple of short walks is way better than couch-potatoing all weekend. Glass half-full, always.

The particular joy of Gran Paradiso – at least around Valsavarenche – is that interesting animals and plants are widespread. Accordingly, almost *any* walk from the village or from the head of the valley at Pont will bring wildlife joy. In early summer, before the merino-wool-clad crowds descend, the three target mammals are hard to miss. The marmot is common everywhere. Alpine chamois is all over the place, from low down to high up. You will see Alpine ibex from pretty much any path straining above 1,500m. During the evening, some even frequent Tighet village car park and roadside fields at Pont – so even if you're too tired to lace up the walking boots, you can still see it.

So what of these latter two target mammals? Both are mountaineering goats and distinct species from their Iberian equivalents (see pages 157 and 55). Females and kids live in herds, joined by males only during the rut. The ibex is stocky, thick-necked and big-bottomed. Males are double the weight of females, with long, thick boomerangs for horns. The chamois is slighter, with short horns and a raccoon-like facemask. It is remarkable that the ibex is still with us: it was hunted to near-extinction in the 19th century. Every single animal alive today is descended from the few hundred individuals that survived solely in – wait for it – Gran Paradiso.

As you look for mammals, you'll see plenty of other fabulously Alpine stuff. Widespread butterflies include Glanville fritillary, black-veined white, green hairstreak and small blue. Less frequently, you will encounter swallowtail and scarce swallowtail. The top prizes are Apollo – a butterfly that will buckle your knees – and almond-eyed ringlet. Keep a similar search image for day-flying moths, and you should see the spectacular nine-spotted. With long black wings blotched white,

JOVANA BILA DUBAIC/S

Should you think moths are boring and brown, the nine-spotted demands you reconsider. ▲

and body generously banded black and yellow, this insect does its bit to correct any assumption that all moths are small, brown and nondescript.

Among more unusual insects, the undeniable star is owly sulphur – a huge, brightly coloured insect that looks like a dragonfly. Another headliner is the superbly named wartbiter, a hefty green bush-cricket. Look for both in meadows, the former particularly just south of Vers-le-Bois. Rocky areas, meanwhile, are the place to look for lizards. Gran Paradiso's common reptiles include the sizeable western green lizard and the slimmer Italian wall lizard.

Exciting, luscious plants are commonplace. You shouldn't have much problem seeing the deep-blue spring gentian, here in the core of its range, rather than the anomalous population on The Burren (page 90). The same applies to the ragged, lilac Alpine snowbell, the searingly pink Piedmont primrose and others such as dark columbine, Liotard's star-of-Bethlehem and St Bernard's lily. Jaw-droppingly beautiful, all of them.

In competition with all this wilderness wealth, birds somewhat take a back seat. Which is frankly bizarre, given that their quality is high enough to justify a weekend in their own right. Wherever you walk through pine forests, listen out for the rolling, throaty call of spotted nutcracker. A wallcreeper butterflies past a sheer cliff on wings of wonder. A rock bunting twitters below. A metallic twinkling is your cue to look up for a flyover citril finch. And as you peer upwards into the heavens, you spot a golden eagle soaring malevolantly. Perhaps the danger to which the Alpine marmot alerted its brethren was real after all.

GETTING THERE Nearest airport is Turin (⌖ aeroportoditorino.it), from where it is 1 hour 50 minutes (150km) to Valsavarenche. Milan airport (⌖ milanomalpensa-airport.com) is not a bad option either, being 2½ hours (225km) away by car.

WHERE TO GO Gran Paradiso National Park (⌖ pngp.it/en) straddles the boundary between Aosta Valley and Piedmont in northwest Italy. There are numerous hiking trails, many strenuous. These are collated on ⌖ pngp.it/en/sentieri/ and some feature in Gillian Price's Cicerone Guide to *Gran Paradiso*. To reach **Valsavarenche (Dégioz)**, leave the E25 at exit Aosta–Ovest St Pierre. Take the SR47 to join the SS26, then head west to the SR23. Follow this 19km south to the village (✹ 45.585129, 7.211418). Pretty much any path you spot (⌖ tinyurl. com/valsavarenche-walk) will be worth walking. Several options stand out; none are hugely taxing. One is the mule-track (trail 8) leading to **Orvieille refuge and the Djouan lakes** (⌖ tinyurl.com/orvieille-walk; starts at ✹ 45.566562, 7.207915). A second is trail 5 from Pont to Vittorio Emanuele II refuge (⌖ tinyurl.com/pont-trail5; start from the Hotel Gran Paradiso Trekking car park at ✹ 45.524536, 7.200798). A third is the relatively flat trail 3 from Pont

(⌂ tinyurl.com/pont-trail3), which excels for ibex. **Vers-le-Bois** is on the west bank of the River Savana, opposite Valsavarenche. The meadows are slightly south at ✳ 45.591196, 7.206546. One valley east of Valsavarenche is **Valnontey** (✳ 45.586729, 7.340698). A simple riverside walk here can garner you observations of special flowers as well as the three target mammals. Perfect!

SUGGESTED BASES This early in the season before all accommodation is open, a good base is the enchanting village of **Valsavarenche** (⌂ www.comune.valsavarenche.ao.it/it/turismo). Places to stay across the national park are brigaded at ⌂ tinyurl.com/gp-accommodation.

MAKE IT A WEEK Hike all week, choosing from the selection in the Cicerone Guide or at ⌂ pngp.it/en/sentieri.

FLEXIBILITY Ibex and chamois: year-round but they go (too) high July to August; marmot: May to September (otherwise hibernating); owly sulphur: May to August; nine-spotted: May to July.

TITBITS It is worth getting the Kompass walking map to the national park.

An agile goat with the face of a badger, Alpine chamois. ▲

66 The blue whale is the mightiest creature ever to have graced Earth 99

Perfect blues

WHERE Lake Mývatn and Húsavík, Northeastern Region, Iceland
TARGETS Blue whale, humpback whale, harlequin duck, Barrow's goldeneye, red-necked phalarope
ACCESSIBILITY ⑤
CHILD-FRIENDLINESS ⑤

Nearing the culmination of its journey to Iceland's northern coast, the River Laxá silvers as it flurries through underwater channels and sparkles over rocks. A vision is stationed atop a throne of the darkest, wettest boulders. The world's most swoonsome duck – the harlequin – is fully aware that this domain is his. And cares not a jot for your admiration. Clad in deep, dense blue with vigorous snowy paint splashes and fiery flanks, the drake harlequin is named after Arlecchino, a colourfully attired character in the *commedia dell'arte*, the Italian theatre.

Iceland. This country of fire and ice, this nation of sagas and geysers, is also among Europe's most special wildlife-watching destinations. Like the infamous Eyjafjallajökull volcano in 2010, tourism here has erupted. Between when I first visited (2000) and 2014, the total number of overnight stays in the country has increased seven-fold.

▲ Nothing can prepare you for your first encounter with the vastness of a blue whale.
MARK CARWARDINE/MINDEN PICTURES/FLPA

Lest you diss the island as overcrowded, the good news for wildlife-watchers is that virtually all tourism is concentrated in the capital of Reykjavík and the (relatively) nearby 'Golden Circle' that comprises Þingvellir (Thingvellir) National Park, Geysir geothermal area and Gullfoss waterfall. The remainder of Iceland – including this weekend's locus – remains blissfully undervisited. You will meet orders of magnitude more Arctic terns (and other birds) than people.

Spend one day around Lake Mývatn, the 'lake of midges'. Rather than feared, Mývatn's non-biting flying insects (chironimids) should be celebrated. They largely explain why northern Iceland is dripping with waders: they constitute bountiful food. Snipe, common redshank, whimbrel and golden plover seemingly abound. Black-tailed godwits are scarcer, but also smarter in their toffee-toned nuptial finery.

The shorebird star, however, is red-necked phalarope. As well as being tiny and tame, swimming buoyantly and spinning unendingly, this delicate midge-muncher offers a fascinating backstory. Bucking nature's usual trend, females are the Lotharios. The *femmes fatales* seduce multiple males, each of which assume sole responsibility for raising a brood of chicks. Many of north Iceland's tiny pools and roadside ditches harbour phalaropes – but nowhere more so than around Lake Mývatn.

Created by a basaltic lava eruption just 2,000 years ago, Mývatn's wetlands have become Europe's most important location for breeding wildfowl, with 13 species of duck alone. Harlequin takes pride of place, but Barrow's goldeneye lags by a mere neck. This duck breeds in no other European country, the remainder of its range lying across the Atlantic. It is known locally as *húsönd* (house-duck), on account of its habit of nesting in boxes at farmhouses. Drakes are strikingly pied with outsized heads – well worth a look. Females (also cute) will be occupied with young. This congregation of duck and waders presumably accounts for the area being Europe's best for gyrfalcon, the world's largest *Falco*.

A particular joy of visiting Iceland is simply driving around, pulling up when something catches your eye. Many of the country's interesting birds facilitate such an approach by keeping a lookout from prominent perches such as lava outcrops. Rock ptarmigan (a grouse) and waders are cases in point. Scanning waterbodies is another good ploy. It shouldn't take long to find lakes that are home to such stunners as breeding Slavonian grebe, red-throated diver or – the sexiest of them all – great northern diver. The latter, known in North America as common loon, will be familiar should you hear one. Its eerie wailing is the go-to soundscape for (rather too) many a spooky film scene.

A fine place to see great northern diver is Kaldbakstjarnir, southwest of Húsavík. Which is convenient since this fishing village happens to be Iceland's whale-watching capital. It is well known that the country has a rather contradictory attitude to whales. Successive Icelandic governments have opposed a ban on commercial whaling, and minke whales continue to be 'harvested' here. Yet four-fifths of Icelanders never buy whale meat and just one in 75 inhabitants regularly consumes it.

Fortunately, one aspect of whales on which all Icelanders appear to agree is that whale-watching tourism is a good thing. Several Húsavík-based companies run

GETTING THERE Airlines, notably WOW Air and Icelandair, run from many European cities to Keflavík (⟡ kefairport.is). Taxi to Reykjavík domestic airport (45 minutes) and fly to Húsavík on Eagle Air (45 minutes; ⟡ eagleair.is). Alternatively, drive 6 hours (longer if you stop to watch wildlife, which will be hard to resist!) from Keflavík to Mývatn, along roads 41 and 1. With care, roads are passable without a 4x4.

WHERE TO GO Lake Mývatn (✹ 65.617939, -16.969981) is south of the junction of roads 1/87. Roads 1 and 48 encircle the lake; check the birding route at ⟡ birdingtrail.is. Notable spots are Hotel Reykjahlíð (✹ 65.642462, -16.913636), Neslandavík (✹ 65.631096, -17.012856), Álar (✹ 65.616720, -17.048760) and Álftavogur bay (✹ 65.569531, -17.046180). On road 848, park by the River Laxá bridge (✹ 65.571231, -17.072883) for harlequin duck and Barrow's goldeneye. Alternatively, walk downstream where road 1 crosses River Laxá (✹ 65.586114, -17.133998). **Húsavík** (✹ 66.045802, -17.344745), 45 minutes north, hosts several whale-watching operators. Choose a member of the Icelandic Whale Watching Association (⟡ icewhale.is) such as North Sailing (⟡ northsailing.is). **Kaldbakstjarnir** Lake is at ✹ 66.021358, -17.363354.

WANG LIQIANG/S

boat trips into Skjálfandi Bay from March to October, and success rates are very high. Humpback whale is the most commonly seen ocean giant, being encountered on nine trips out of ten. Also frequently seen is minke whale, ostensibly cocking a snook at those humans who claim to be sustainably harvesting the whales' *compadres* in waters off Reykjavík.

But it is the second of Iceland's 'perfect blues' that everyone yearns to see when cruising Skjálfandi Bay. The blue whale is the mightiest creature ever to have graced Earth. To watch this leviathan surface, its back rolling… and rolling… and rolling before its excuse for a dorsal fin eventually heaves into view, is to realise a dream. Chances may seem slight – perhaps just 10% over the season as a whole – but from May to July, prospects leap. Perfect.

SUGGESTED BASES Accommodation is generally pricey. Minimise costs by using hostels (hostel.is); Berg and Árbót are convenient.

MAKE IT A WEEK From Húsavík, visit **Flatey Island** for possible red and numerous red-necked phalaropes. **Snæfellsnes Peninsula** is good for Arctic fox, particularly near Látrabjarg's exhilarating seabird colony (tame Atlantic puffin plus Brünnich's guillemot). Nearby **Rif** has a huge Arctic tern colony plus numerous red-necked phalarope. On the tourist route, **Þingvellir** excels for great northern diver, **Geysir** and **Skaftafell Glacier** harbour northern green and frog orchids, while white-beaked dolphins leap off **Reykjavík**. Birding suggestions are on northiceland.is/birding and birdingtrail.is. An excellent Crossbill Guide (see ad, inside-back cover) advises on wildlife-watching across the whole of Iceland.

FLEXIBILITY Blue whale: May to June, fewer in July; humpback: April to October; ducks: year-round, but best April to June and September to November; phalarope: May to July.

TITBITS Put your money where your mouth is. Demonstrate that you prefer your wildlife to be alive by supporting Iceland's growing movement of whale-friendly eateries: icewhale.is/whale-friendly-restaurants.

When you're bored of harlequin ducks, you're bored of life. What stunners. ▲

Tisza, in bloom

WHERE Jász-Nagykun-Szolnok and Hajdú-Bihar, Hungary
TARGETS Long-tailed mayfly, southern festoon, red-footed falcon, European pond terrapin, common tree frog
ACCESSIBILITY ③
CHILD-FRIENDLINESS ④

> **❝ The long-tailed mayflies' race against time – their race for life – is on ❞**

SOLVIN ZANKL/NPL

It is 16.00 on a stubbornly sultry mid-June afternoon in central Hungary. The River Tisza drifts reluctantly past tree-heavy banks. The flow is bloated, viscous, opaque and apparently lifeless. But at 17.00, something truly remarkable occurs. The river starts to literally burst with life.

After two years living underwater as crustacean-like larvae, male long-tailed mayflies pop through the meniscus. The emergence attracts the attention of white wagtails, which twist black and white over the water surface, nabbing impromptu meals. Fish become airborne as they too leap for food. But soon the swarms become so dense that neither predator makes much impact. The mayflies' race against time – their race for life – is on.

By 17.30, the males seek safety in riverside vegetation, hanging like bonsai bats from trunk, branch, twig or even stationary human. Once air-dried, they undertake one final transformation. Wings that were transparent become a handsome royal blue. Dual filaments at the abdomen tip (the 'tail') extend remarkably, tripling the insect's length. With neither mouth nor stomach, Europe's largest mayflies are unable to feed. They have sufficient fat reserves to fuel just 30 minutes of flight time – so they must judge their procreationary quest to perfection.

At 18.00, the first female emerges. The males are on her instantaneously. They tussle to mate with her and with every other female that transitions between the elements. As the sun contemplates its evening descent, so the air thickens and goldens. Above the Tisza – still bloated, viscous and opaque – the invertebrate glitterstorm enraptures. The only sound is the whistling of millions of paired wings.

▲ Long-tailed mayfly, the star of the Tisza's show.

The libidinal efforts and power struggles take their toll. By 18.30, the first males run out of puff. Their fluttering becomes flopping. Dying bodies litter the water surface with chitin. The females devote their remaining energies to winging their way upstream, where they gauge river depth and current before laying their fertilised eggs.

By 20.30, they too expire. The event that locals call Tiszavirágzás ('the blooming of the Tisza') is over after a few abrupt, intense hours.

Your mayfly experience is the culmination of a weekend otherwise spent 150km upstream, either side of the River Tisza in Hortobágy. Hungary's first national park, pronounced 'Hort-o-budjz', was designated during the year of my birth, 1973. Half the size of Greater London, Hortobágy protects the second-largest swathe of *puszta* (steppe) west of the Urals plus expansive wetlands and snaking riverine forest.

Hortobágy is dichotomous. Its romance lies in vast empty expanses, yet the apparent voids are actually full of wildlife, if you know where to look. Its *puszta* is critical to the sense of national identity, yet nowadays next-to-nobody actually lives here. The national park is justly revered for protecting the environment, yet much is not available for first-hand appreciation, being off-limits without the company of a guide.

With just a day and a half at your disposal, prioritise your attention wherever you find water. Small puddles – even wheel ruts in tracks – are the haunt of fire-bellied toads, which abound at Hortobágy. Floating on the water surface, the male of this charismatic small amphibian expands its body then, with chest sac inflated, utters a rhythmic, melancholic *woop*. Ephemeral water sources are also the haunt of unusual dragonflies such as dark spreadwing (a local speciality, particularly frequenting brackish waterbodies), southern skimmer and broad scarlet. Common tree frog – Hortobágy's other ubiquitous amphibian – is less tied to water. It can be found adorning grasses, crouching on shrubs and belting out from trees.

ROBIN CHITTENDEN www.robinchittenden.co.uk

Common tree frogs crouch on vegetation over much of Hortobágy. ▲

The River Tisza, 'blooming' with millions of mayflies.
OLIVER SMART www.smartimages.co.uk

" As the sun contemplates its evening descent, so the air thickens and goldens. Above the Tisza the invertebrate glitterstorm enraptures "

MICHAEL SOUTHCOTT

GETTING THERE Numerous airlines (including low-cost companies) fly to Budapest airport (⌀ bud.hu), where European sousliks – a type of ground-squirrel – huddle by the taxi rank. From here, the River Tisza at Tiszakürt is 1¼ hours' (115km) drive southeast and Hortobágy village is 2 hours (188km) northeast.

WHERE TO GO Well-known sites for the **River Tisza mayflies** are **Tiszakürt** (✻ 46.886469, 20.107337) and adjacent **Tiszainoka** (✻ 46.907399, 20.133769), plus **Nagykörű** (✻ 47.267373, 20.456006). The latter is roughly halfway to **Hortobágy National Park** (⌀ hnp.hu/en/szervezeti-egyseg/tourism; buy permits from the visitor centre at ✻ 47.582515, 21.151473). **Halastó fishponds** are accessed from Hortobágy–Halastó. Turn north off the N33 near km67, cross the narrow-gauge railway line and park at ✻ 47.604587, 21.071132. You can take the train 4km to Kondás Pond and walk back. Near **Fényes-tó** (a lake) on the N33, red-footed falcon breeds at ✻ 47.581642, 21.002720 and European bee-eater at ✻ 47.587426, 21.010326. Another falcon site is **Kócsújfalu** (✻ 47.548064, 20.928580), 20km southwest of Hortobágy along the N33. For **Little Hortobágy**, continue 28km west along the N33 to

▲ Europe's most sumptuous falcon, the red-footed (here a male).

Halastó fishponds are a must-visit. There are plenty of dragonflies and amphibians here too. But this area stands out for larger water-dwelling creatures. European pond terrapin favours channels just east of Halastó village. The ponds themselves are splattered with long-necked waterbirds: spoonbill, pygmy cormorant and an octet comprising herons, bitterns and egrets. The reedbeds host an array of brown warblers, notably moustached, which skulks in edge vegetation and glowers from beneath its white eyebrow.

A short way southwest along the N33 brings you to a real treat – a breeding colony of red-footed falcon, an aeronaut that nabs and scoffs dragonflies. Males are sumptuously dark blue, as if summer sky and smoke have defied the laws of physics to merge. Females, meanwhile, have glowing embers for underparts. Stunners.

Finally, Little Hortobágy, northwest of the River Tisza. A good area is the plains northwest of Tiszabábolna, where access is comparatively unfettered. Rare raptors such as saker and eastern imperial eagle perch on pylons and trees. Channels and rivers sport dragonflies. Wet grasslands are riddled with fire-bellied toads and common tree frogs. Flowering meadows nourish citron billows of eastern pale clouded yellows and other butterflies such as the sensational southern festoon, with its crazy-paving wings of custard-cream and black. The village also provides access to the Tisza's riverine forests, where black stork nests and lesser purple emperor swoops. From here, if you drift downriver far enough, you might just catch those mayflies…

RORUE/S

Poroszló, then go north to Borsodivánka and east to Tiszabábolna (✳ 47.696223, 20.815484). Head northwest across plains towards Szentistván.

SUGGESTED BASES Hortobágy village is the usual nature-watcher's base, offering several accommodation options. Szolnok (✳ 47.168648, 20.178171) is close to the mayfly sites.

MAKE IT A WEEK At the **visitor centre**, book a national park guide to explore Hortobágy's otherwise off-limits areas. Ask to see the reintroduced Przewalski's horse. Visit a colony of European souslik 4km northeast of **Cserepfalu** (✳ 47.964401, 20.557329). **Bükk Hills** and **Aggtelek** are brilliant for butterflies and bats; Sakertour (⬧ sakertour.com; see ad, page 234) offer several birding tours in Hortobágy and more widely in Hungary.

FLEXIBILITY Mayfly: mid-June most reliable, but emergence can be late May to late June; falcon: May to July; amphibians: April to August; festoon: May to June.

TITBITS The excellent Crossbill Guide *Hortobágy* (see ad, inside-back cover) suggests several routes to follow and additional sites to visit.

The wing pattern of the southern festoon is thought to mimic that of a swallowtail. ▲

Lakeland

WHERE La Brenne, Indre, Centre-Val de Loire, France
TARGETS Lilypad whiteface, yellow-spotted emerald, Brenne marsh-orchid, whiskered tern, viperine snake
ACCESSIBILITY ③
CHILD-FRIENDLINESS ③

Hundreds of lime-green lily pads – ovals with a snip from one tip to core – swell timidly atop the dense, dark pond. One of the many resident fish has doubtless provoked the undulation. A whiskered tern smokes past, searching for smaller aquatic prey. Atop one of the closest floating leaves sits a most distinctive dragonfly. Short, squat and wide winged, with a narrow waist and bulging abdomen tip, it can only be a lilypad whiteface – a well-named 'dragon', and a rare one to boot this far west.

This pond is one of thousands of waterbodies that qualify La Brenne as a waterworld. From the air, this region – slightly north of France's midpoint – resembles a shattered mirror, the glistening fragments aggregating into one of Europe's most vital wetlands. Go higher still, and you perceive La Brenne, together with its sister lakeland of the Sologne, to be an anomaly in the Gallic landscape. From a wildlife perspective, the wider Loire region is an agriculture-driven desert. Huge, monotonous grey fields furnish the country with its essential bread and wine but deprive nature of all but token existence. Such context renders La Brenne all the more special.

Barely two hours from Paris, La Brenne has long been a haunt of birdwatchers. More recently, those enthused by dragonflies, butterflies and orchids have come to cherish the area's wealth of biodiversity. With such wildlife riches, it shocks to learn that La Brenne is anything but natural. Every single étang (lake) is manmade, the output of a massive drainage programme dating back to the Middle Ages. The ponds now serve as commercial fisheries, restricting wildlife to the more sensitively managed examples.

Start your exploration at Étang de Bellebouche, site of a famous heronry. Like much of La Brenne, this is private. But unlike almost all such locations here, the landowners generously grant public access. View nesting purple and night herons from either of two hides, and watch the gawky youngsters of little and cattle egrets being fed by their parents. Watch out for dragonflies; this is a cracking site for yellow-spotted emerald, a sought-after creature with green eyes and golden dots the length of its jet abdomen.

A few kilometres north, the chalk marsh of Étang Vieux could not be more different to Bellebouche's peaty lake. Walk the trail through wet meadows dominated by great fen sedge and black bog-rush, watching butterflies such as wood white and short-tailed blue. With luck you may chance upon a tardy marsh fritillary or an early-emerging dryad, the latter's expansive wings eyed four times with neon. Along the road to Saulnay, look for Brenne marsh-orchid, a pink flower that is endemic to the region. Late June is at the end of its blooming period, so check shady verges for longer-lasting plants.

> " From the air, La Brenne resembles a shattered mirror, the glistening fragments aggregating into one of Europe's most vital wetlands "

OLIVER SMART/RSPB

Whiskered terns are delicate 'marsh terns' that nest on floating vegetation. ▲

WILL LANGDON

Spend the rest of the day at La Chérine National Nature Reserve. Interrogate the protected area along its footpaths and from its four hides. Look for lilypad whiteface along the boardwalk to the hide at Étang Cistude – and on the floating oval leaves in front of it. At Étang de la Sous, watch black-necked grebe and whiskered tern nesting among the floating vegetation, and keep an eye out for local scarcities such

GETTING THERE From the UK, take the Eurostar (⌀ eurostar.com) to Lille then the TGV (⌀ sncf.com/en/trains/tgv) to Poitiers. Then drive 80km (1¼ hours) east along the D591 to La Brenne. Alternatively, fly to Poitiers airport from London Stansted or Edinburgh.

WHERE TO GO Bellebouche is 10km east of Mezières-en-Brenne along the D21 (✳ 46.784279, 1.310213). Footpaths west and east of the lake lead to hides. Étang Vieux is 9km northeast of Mezières along the D926. Park by the D58 at ✳ 46.846321, 1.307623 and follow the nature trail. Brenne marsh-orchids grow on the northern verge of the D58 as it leads west to the D148. **La Chérine National Nature Reserve** (⌀ reserve-cherine.fr) is 7km south of Mezières, west of the D6A/D17 junction. There are car parks for hides at Étang Cistude/ Maison de la Nature (✳ 46.789631, 1.200978), Étang des Essarts (✳ 46.794991, 1.190988) and Étang de la Sous (✳ 46.795916, 1.173122). **La Brenne Regional Nature Park** (⌀ parc-naturel-brenne.fr) visitor centre is at **Maison du Parc** in Le Bouchet (✳ 46.720914,

▲ Yellow-spotted emerald: a target dragonfly for a visit to La Brenne.

as great reed warbler and little bittern. European pond terrapin – an ever-rarer reptile – basks on logs in front of Ricot hide and frequents the ditch left of the bridge leading to Essarts hide. The latter site also harbours western green lizards that are unusually showy for this typically skittish species.

Start day two in the southern Brenne. The hides at Foucault Reserve offer a decent prospect of black-winged stilt, black-necked grebe and whiskered tern. European pond terrapin lounges in the pond by the car park for the northernmost hide. Wooded verges along the D32 north of Maison du Parc visitor centre at Le Bouchet boast woodland brown, an unambitiously named but rare butterfly. Scrutinise the visitor centre étang for dragonflies such as broad scarlet and dainty bluet, plus the water-loving viperine snake. Sharp eyes may detect common tree frog – but you must visit at night to hear its cacophonous call. Scrubby areas throng with western green and common wall lizards.

For the final roll of the weekend dice, exit La Brenne westwards for Le Pinail. Cessation of quarrying at this peat-bog reserve left thousands of mini craters. Over time, these have filled with water; acidic pools now pockmark the tall heathland. Sheltered and warm, with ample waterbodies and secluded perches, Le Pinail comprises sensational dragonfly habitat. Your target species – yellow-spotted whiteface – is a blood-red, black and cream rock-star of an insect.

A rich supporting cast features a trio of emeralds – downy, orange-spotted and yellow-spotted – plus green-eyed (aka Norfolk) hawker. Among butterflies, large chequered skippers yo-yo through the purple moor-grass, whilst pearly heaths repay close inspection. This lakeland osmoses wildlife-rich tranquility. Little wonder that the French call the area *la douce France* – gentle France.

1.173329). **Foucault** reserve car park is at ✳ 46.726635, 1.235816, with the pond terrapin pool on the D17 at ✳ 46.733055, 1.233027. **Le Pinail Reserve** (⊘ reserve-pinail.org; ✳ 46.710115, 0.517168) is west of La Brenne, 2km southwest of Vouneuil-sur-Vienne.

SUGGESTED BASES Mezières-en-Brenne (⊘ tourisme-mezieres-en-brenne.fr/en) or Rosnay are logical bases.

MAKE IT A WEEK Watch dragonflies (including orange featherleg, western clubtail and white-tailed skimmer, goblet-marked damselfly and green-eyed hooktail) around the étang just north of **Persac**. Enjoy orchids including red helleborine and violet bird's-nest in limestone woods along the River Anglin either side of **Rives**. Watch butterflies including lesser purple emperor in tracts of oak woodland at **Forêt de Lancosme**.

FLEXIBILITY Mid-May to early July is best.

TITBITS Seek inspiration from the excellent Crossbill Guide to the Loire Valley.

JAMES LOWEN

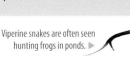

Viperine snakes are often seen hunting frogs in ponds. ▶

Europe's mightiest seal, the walrus. In our region, a speciality of Svalbard (weekend trip)

THEO ALLOFS/MINDEN PICTURES/FLPA

July
August
September

Wolverine – grey wolf – lammergeier – Arctic fox – walrus – Apollo
musk ox – Zino's petrel – Bryde's whale – black-bellied hamster
European souslik – Cuvier's beaked whale – Cantabrian brown bear
wildcat – Barbary macaque – two-tailed pasha
Apennine grey wolf – olm – nose-horned viper

66 **Mean-looking and formerly mythical, the wolverine is more villain than super-hero** 99

CHRIS TOWNEND/WISE BIRDING HOLIDAYS

Ultimate meat-eaters

WHERE Kainuu and North Karelia, Finland
TARGETS Wolverine, grey wolf, brown bear
ACCESSIBILITY ⑤
CHILD-FRIENDLINESS ① (all-night vigils)

Slaloming between pipe-cleaner pine trees, a shaggy shadow is undulating through the bilberry-rich understorey. The mammal's bounding gait is neither clumsy nor fluid, but is certainly flexible of spine. Stocky and shaggy, it reminds you of badger, stoat and hyena in similar measure. Pausing, forelimbs cresting fallen log, the creature turns its short-snouted face your way. It is! It is, it is, it is! Mean-looking and formerly mythical, the wolverine issues a soulless glare – more villain than super-hero. A stab of nerves pollutes your exhilaration. You are slightly relieved to be concealed within a log-lined hide.

Prior to the mid-noughties, seeing wolverine was a pipe dream. Even in places – across North America and boreal Europe – where they were known to occur, this ultimate carnivore was glimpsed annually at best. Since then, hides in eastern Finland designed to enable people to photograph brown bears have managed to consistently attract wolverines. As a result, the procession of wildlife-watchers to privately run locations in eastern Finland is lengthening year on year.

▲ A worthy member of the *X-men*, the wolverine bristles with muscly intent.

The procedure at each site follows a broadly similar pattern. After an early, communal dinner, visitors head towards a series of hides. These range from spartan, box-like constructs housing a single photographer to expansive units with plush seating. All come with bunks, dry-toilets and snacks to keep you going through the night, which is when mammals are most active. Ah, yes, the night. You weren't anticipating sleeping this weekend, were you? Once you have been dropped off, you stay put until around 08.00 when you are whisked off to breakfast. And no nodding off on the job.

This far north, just after the summer solstice, sleep is admittedly a relative term. The air will thicken for a couple of hours but there will remain sufficient light to watch a succession of thrilling creatures come for a free meal. Ah yes, a free meal. You didn't think these top carnivores wandered past the hides of their own accord, did you? They are on a mission – always hungry, usually tentative, sometimes relaxed – to gnaw the preferred pig, cow or fish.

Ah yes, *they*. Whilst wolverine is unequivocally the highlight, you should see brown bear *and* have a fair chance of grey wolf too. Quite the Triple Crown. In mid-summer, ursines are done with mating so are cramming in the calories before autumn temperatures stipulate hibernation. Grey wolves have no such time constraints, being active year-round. But they are also more elusive, the small packs ranging widely.

> 66 Joyously, you may even see the carnivores interacting. Should a bear return to 'its' bait, woe betide any interloping lone canid. 99

Interactions between grey wolf and brown bear are a USP of Kuikka Base Camp.

119

LR

That's the what, when and how. But what of the where? The simplest approach is to spend the whole weekend at a single location, swapping hides on the second night. The adventurous strategy – maximising chances of a clean sweep of the carnivore Classics – would be to try one operator each night. If your energy levels will take it, do the latter.

This means starting at Erä-Eero near Lieksa, the world's best site for wolverine. Two comfortable hides – one geared towards photographers – survey either lake and forest edge, or a clearing. Most people enjoy prolonged views of several different wolverines in a 'night' – although they often appear during daytime too. The odd bear is regularly seen at close quarters in the forest, while wolves are occasional visitors. Birds typically wait until mammals have disappeared before attending to

GETTING THERE For Erä-Eero, nearest airport is Joensuu (↺ finavia.fi/en/joensuu). From here it is 1½ hours' drive (110km) northeast to the lodge, via Uimaharju. If you visit two or more lodges, the best airport is Kajaani (↺ finavia.fi/en/kajaani). From here it is 2¼ hours' drive (168km) to Kuikka Base Camp, 1½ hours' drive (130km) to Wild Brown Bear Centre, and 2½ hours' drive (205km) to Erä-Eero.

WHERE TO GO **Erä-Eero** is 27km southeast of Lieksa, along road 522 then off to the south (↺ eraeero.com). You meet at Keljänpuro Lodge (❂ 63.212800, 30.389050) before moving 7km to the hides. The drive north to the other two lodges takes 2¼–½ hours (155–190km). **Kuikka Base Camp**, run by Wildlife Safaris Finland (↺ wildfinland.org; ❂ 64.109543, 30.401109; see ad, page 230) is 58km east of Kuhmo, mostly along road 9121. **Wild Brown Bear Centre** (↺ wildbrownbear.fi; ❂ 64.506989, 29.973173) is 2km east of road 89, 21km east of Iivantiira.

SUGGESTED BASES All three operations offer accommodation at an additional cost. Given the limited hours for sleeping (generally only between 10.00 and 15.00), it makes sense to use these.

△ Ghost wolf. A genetic quirk accounts for Kuikka's unusually pale grey wolf.

their hunger. Ravens are particularly prominent, groups blackening the ground as they squabble about leftovers. Gulls, woodpeckers and tits also ensure that you will rarely get bored in Erä-Eero's hides.

Once you have recharged batteries, drive 2½ hours north to the Kuhmo area. Here the best choices are Wild Brown Bear Centre and Kuikka Base Camp. The former is a sophisticated operation, with 20-odd hides scattered around large clearings, forest and woodland edge. The latter is run by the Godfather of Finnish Bear Tourism, Lassi Rautiainen, with at least 14 hides spread across forest, clearing and swamp. Both offer outstanding encounters with bears (photographers challenge themselves to capture images of multiple individuals in a variety of scenery). Kuikka edges it for wolf sightings, thanks to Lassi's years-long study of the packs frequenting his region.

Joyously, you may even see the carnivores interacting. Bears are the kings of the boreal 'jungle', but even they may are wary about straying from the forest while the sun remains high. Ongoing hunting pressure means that wolves are even more clandestine. They lurk in shadows, will-o'-the-wisping their presence between the pines. Only when the coast is clear of both bears and humans will they venture out. Should a bear return to 'its' bait, woe betide any interloping lone canid. If there is a pack, however, the situation may reverse. Normally wolves boss it over wolverines (which often hang back in the treeline). Nevertheless, every so often a feisty mustelid turns tables, forcing the former's retreat. In this contest between ultimate meat-eaters, nothing is ever certain.

MAKE IT A WEEK The obvious option is to spend a couple of nights in each set of hides – thereby getting the best of all worlds. But a few alternatives or complements stand out. Kuhmo is good for the forest subspecies of reindeer. **Kuusamo** offers great birding, including black-throated diver, red-necked grebe and red-flanked bluetail. Further north, calypso orchid will probably be over at **Oulanka National Park**, but lady's slipper should be in full bloom. Although late in the season, you could hire a guide to show you breeding owls (Tengmalm's, Ural, pygmy, hawk and great grey). There are options around **Oulu** and in **Patvinsuo National Park**. To the south, **Linnansaari National Park** holds 'Saimaa' ringed seal – an isolated, threatened subspecies.

FLEXIBILITY Wolverine: year-round, best April to July; wolf: year-round; bear: April to October.

TITBITS If you come in May, a logical extension would be to see Finland's owls, for which it is the peak month. The Wild Brown Bear Centre website offers useful advice on how the wildlife experience evolves through the season. UK operator **Wise Birding** (⌨ wisebirding.co.uk; see ad, page 230) runs wolverine-focused tours.

Top of the world

FRANZ CHRISTOPH ROBILER/IMAGEBROKER/FLPA

> **66** Overhead, a lammergeier follows a single-minded path through the air, sniffing for another bone to break **99**

WHERE Ordesa, Pyrenees, Aragón, Spain
TARGETS Lammergeier, Alpine marmot, Pyrenean rock lizard, Pyrenean brook newt, Pyrenean saxifrage
ACCESSIBILITY ①
CHILD-FRIENDLINESS ② – ④ (depends on route chosen)

It is hard to avoid feeling insignificant in the Pyrenees. Yomping along a glaciated valley that unfolds for 20km, you look up, and up some more, at the vertical cliffs encasing you. Their limestone top steeples 400m above you – akin to stacking London's Stock Exchange Tower above The Shard, the capital's loftiest building. 'Awesome' – inspiring overwhelming wonder – is an overused and consequently devalued adjective. But as a descriptor of Ordesa Valley, it is justified – for its wildlife as well as the scenery.

Atop a rocky platter straining above a whiffling river, a Pyrenean rock lizard services its solar addiction. Under a stone sheltering the bed of a sparkling sidestream lurks a Pyrenean brook newt. At your flank, a cornucopia of montane flowers kaleidoscopes your vision. An Alpine marmot slouches in the sun, wantonly. Overhead, a lammergeier follows a single-minded path through the air, sniffing for another bone to break. Such an intense juxtaposition of exciting wildlife justifies the lactic acid dominating your climb-weary legs.

The great mountain chain of the Pyrenees offers choice wildlife walks. But where? Its embarrassment of riches provokes a hesitant response to even the most fundamental question. Hike the Spanish side or the French? So why prioritise Ordesa above all other possibilities?

Three singular reasons stand out. First, Ordesa is the benchmark against which all Pyrenean hikes are rated. Second, 2018 – when this book hits the shelves –

⏶ The bone breaker in action. An adult lammergeier, bearded and beady-eyed.

marks the centenary of Ordesa's ordination as a national park. Third, Ordesa is the Pyrenees' most poignant location given its association with the first great extinction of Europe's Millennium.

Having reserved your overnight berth at Refugio de Góriz, above the valley head of Circo de Soaso, pack for a two-day excursion. The candidate hikes (*fajas*) share a starting point (Pradera car park) and destination (Góriz). The most modest climb follows the valley floor, north of the River Arazas. Winding through beech and fir forests, slipping past frothing waterfalls, you emerge into flower-filled alpine meadows. The Senda de Cazadores is tougher – but more rewarding for wildlife – thanks to its initial steep ascent, which takes 2 hours. The hard work done while you are fresh, the remaining length contours easily along the southern cliffs to the Circo.

Assuming you follow the Senda de Cazadores, your first steps traverse a willowy wood. Then comes the climb. On balance, skip looking for wildlife during this section, focusing instead on regularising step and conserving stamina. That said, when a large cliff looms into view, treat yourself to a break in a small clearing where plants such as Alpine pasqueflower and Thore's buttercup grow. At the top, you reach a viewpoint (*mirador*). As you rehydrate, scan the skies for your first golden eagle, griffon vulture and Alpine swift.

STEFAN HUWILER/IMAGEBROKER/FLPA

Although introduced to the Pyrenees, Alpine marmots are a highlight of the Ordesa hike.

> **" Steep limestone slopes are curtained in pink rock roses, plus various saxifrages including the drooping spikes of Pyrenean saxifrage "**

The walking becomes easier now, enabling you to revel in the landscape and snoop around rocks for lovely flowers such as Pyrenean avens, large-flowered meadow-rue, purple columbines, rampions, Alpine bartsia and much more besides. As you press towards the rocky ampitheatre of Circo de Soaso, your chances of being scrutinised by a lammergeier (aka bearded vulture) increase.

Rocky grassland at the segue between pines and meadows marks a good area for citril finch (a buzzy yellow and green seedeater) and Pyrenean chamois, an attractive herbivore with a badger-patterned face. A related mammal that you will sadly not encounter is Pyrenean ibex. The very last example of this subspecies was found dead in Ordesa on 6 January 2000. Extinction, lest one forget, is forever.

Wildflowers dazzle around the Circo itself. Steep limestone slopes are curtained in pink rock roses, plus various saxifrages including the drooping spikes of Pyrenean saxifrage. This area also excels for high-altitude butterflies such as purple-edged copper and Spanish Argus. Don't let your eye stray too far from the vertical cliff faces, however, lest you miss an avian echo of these winged insects, the wallcreeper. There's little chance that you will miss Alpine marmot, at least. Chunky-headed and impossibly furry, these delightful mammals were reintroduced by hunters to the Pyrenees in the 1960s – and have spread rapidly. Their apparent sunbathing is actually designed to lose heat.

GETTING THERE Nearest airport is Zaragoza (⊘ tinyurl.com/airport-zaragoza), served by Air Europa and Ryanair. From here it is 2 hours to Torla (the gateway to Ordesa) along the A23 and N260. **WHERE TO GO Ordesa y Monte Perdido National Park** (⊘ ordesa.net) is 8km northeast by road from **Torla**. Parking is normally at Pradera de Ordesa (✴ 42.649381, -0.061665) but cars are banned during holiday periods (Easter, Jul–Sep, mid-Oct). So take a shuttle bus that departs Torla's National Park visitor centre (⊘ ordesa.net/parque-nacional/autobuses ⊙ 06.00–22.00 daily, every 20 mins; €4.50 return). From Pradera, access is solely on foot. The easiest walk to **Circo de Soaso** and Cola de Caballo waterfall (✴ 42.649981, 0.015862) follows the river valley throughout (8km; 3.5 hours one-way); it is well signposted. My suggested route returns along this path, but takes the **Senda de Cazadores/Faja de Pelay** on the way out (11km; 4.5 hours one-way). **Refugio de Góriz** (✴ 42.662997, 0.015141; ⊘ goriz.es) is 1.5km further on (and up!) along trail GR-11. It offers basic accommodation and ample food; booking essential.

FABIO PUPIN/FLPA

From Circo de Soaso, it is a steep climb to the refuge at Góriz. This gives access to the Pyrenees' finest alpine meadows – with mats of purple saxifrage, and the vibrant blue of spring gentian. The next morning, reward your earlier endeavours by returning at a leisurely pace along the path north of the river. Pause wherever flowers splash the route, looking for the yellow spheres of globeflower or the sky-blue bells of Pyrenean hyacinth. Spend time ferreting around the river too. Even if you can't find the target reptile or amphibian, you will need only the slightest sun to reveal the more abundant Catalonian wall lizard. This is one Pyrenean creature that we surely cannot drive to extinction.

SUGGESTED BASES Torla (ordesa.net/alojamiento-y-servicios) for the night before the walk, and Refugio de Goríz for the overnight.

MAKE IT A WEEK The issue is keeping it to a week! Both sides of the Pyrenees are filled with locations to explore. On the Spanish side, outstanding locations nearby include Bujaruelo and the Otal Valley, and the Pineta Valley. Garganta de Escuaín below Revilla (42.598863, 0.146106) has a feeding station attended by lammergeier. In France, why not try for the mythical Pyrenean desman at an exciting new site between Refuge Ayous and Lac Bersau (tinyurl.com/desman1)?

FLEXIBILITY June to September for all targets (and snow-free paths). Rock lizard needs sun – but not too much of it!

TITBITS This is a popular, sometimes crowded, route. Perhaps choose weekdays rather than weekends. Buy your bus ticket the previous day and queue before 08.00.

Ordesa: brilliant wildlife (here a Pyrenean rock lizard, on the left) amid brilliant scenery.

Angel of the north

WHERE Spitsbergen, Svalbard, Norway
TARGETS Arctic fox, bearded seal, walrus, ivory gull, little auk
ACCESSIBILITY ②
CHILD-FRIENDLINESS ⑤ (though most boats operate minimum-age limits)

O pening your eyes, you find yourself in heaven. A few metres above your head, against an unending sun, an angel is floating through the air. Its whiteness is of a purity that makes snow look sullied. Its flight is uncontaminated grace. This ethereal wonder is an ivory gull, and it is a High Arctic exclusive – wholly in its icy element.

This beauty is a paradigm-busting gull. You need endure neither intimidatory behaviour nor infuriating screaming from this species. Instead, it is tranquility, beauty and harmony in a single weep-inducing avian form. Ignoring lost vagrants that end up on the shores of Western Europe, the Norwegian island of Spitsbergen (part of the Svalbard complex) offers your only chance of seeing it. Fortunately the insular capital of Longyearbyen is easily accessible and acceptably affordable – and offers a mouth-watering list of other wildlife specialities.

JAMES LOWEN

The highlight of land-based mammal-watching around Longyearbyen: Arctic fox.

66 *Ivory gull: tranquility, beauty and harmony in a single weep-inducing avian form* **99**

KEVIN ELSBY/FLPA

Europe's most northerly town (78°N) is a functional little place, but that comes with advantages. It is easy to get around the vicinity and to see ample Arctic wildlife whilst remaining on dry land. Even better, there are all-day boat trips that head a fair way northwest to the research station of Ny-Ålesund, west along Isfjorden towards the Russian settlement of Barentsburg or northeast across the same fjord to the former mining community of Pyramiden.

Although tour operators shy away from claiming it (and thus it doesn't feature among the five formal targets for this weekend), these waterborne excursions offer a fair chance of encountering the world's most poignant mammal among other fabulous northern fauna. Polar bear in a weekend? That's got to be worth a crack!

But why poignant? The answer is simple. There can be no animal for which context is more integral – and more symbolic. As our obsession with fossil fuels refuses to abate, so Arctic ice melts ever more rapidly. With it disappears the summer habitat and feeding grounds of the world's largest ursine. Unsurprisingly, it is globally threatened.

To maximise your chances, spend successive days on all-day boat trips to Ny-Ålesund (or Forlandet) then to Pyramiden (or around the Isfjorden). Should you encounter either extensive ice or a shoreline carcass of a seal or whale, you are in with a shout. Should you see a white shape swimming in the water, however, it is more likely to be a beluga – a melon-headed, sociable whale that is as quintessentially Arctic as the bear and the avian angel of the north. Even if you fail – and you should prepare for that as the best chance of seeing both white mammals would demand a trip of several days – you should spot some exciting marine creatures.

Minke and fin whales are to be expected. The latter, should you need reminding, is the second-largest creature ever to have lived on Earth. Several species of Arctic seal should be on your radar. Bearded seal – replete with extended whiskers – is the most likely, but ringed is feasible. Moving up an order of magnitude in size, most trips to Ny-Ålesund take in the walrus colony on Forlandet. If weather permits, you can go ashore and observe these one-tonne, heavily tusked mammals at close range. For their sake (and yours) never get between a walrus and water…

Birds complement the mammals. You should see hundreds of kittiwakes and fulmars, many of the latter being smoky-plumaged northern birds. An ivory gull should make a transcendental appearance at some point. Ghostly glaucous gulls

An adult ivory gull, all icy plumage and angelic demeanour.

> **The longer you watch, the greater your chances of seeing something excitingly white…**

are regular. Numerous auks include Brünnich's and black guillemots, plus whirring buzzballs that are little auks (more of which later).

Although the boat trips last most of the day, the 'white nights' of the Arctic summer enable you to explore around Longyearbyen between excursions. Hire a car, neck a double espresso and get out there! Reindeer is common – even around the town itself. Although confiding, these are entirely wild creatures – and comprise a small subspecies unique to Svalbard. Look out for agitated pairs of barnacle goose, pink-footed goose or Arctic tern. This often means that an Arctic fox is on the prowl. These are gorgeous canids, with a chocolate and caramel coat in summer.

Heading west from Longyearbyen, make for the little auk colony near Bjørndalen. Thousands breed below boulders on the steepling cliff. The air thickens with adults hurrying between feeding grounds and hungry chicks. Inevitably, Arctic foxes often snoop around here too, sniffing out unattended nests. Then return to Longyearbyen and continue into Adventalen Valley. Two feathered attractions – rock ptarmigan (a grouse) and snow bunting – scuttle across the stony ground. From vantage points such as Kloakken, scan for three stunning birds – king eider, long-tailed duck and red phalarope – that inhabit Adventfjorden or adjacent waterbodies. The longer you watch, the greater your chances of seeing something excitingly white…

GETTING THERE In season, there are daily flights from Tromsø (1½ hours) and Oslo (3 hours) to Svalbard airport (tinyurl.com/airport-svalbard), 5km northwest of Longyearbyen. There are scheduled flights to Tromsø from Oslo (and other Norwegian airports), Stockholm and Copenhagen plus charters from cities including Amsterdam and Paris. There is a weekly ferry to/from Tromsø.

WHERE TO GO Ships depart from **Longyearbyen harbour** (78.228804, 15.600584; portlongyear.no). As well as longer cruises, day trips head west to **Barentsburg** (78.075308, 14.183521), northwest to **Ny-Ålesund** (78.918223, 11.967721) and northeast to **Pyramiden** (78.632472, 16.346902). The main tour operators are Spitsbergen Travel (spitsbergentravel.no) and Svalbard Wildlife Expeditions (wildlife.no). Arguably more suitable, Better Moments (bettermoments.no/boat-trips/) offers RIB trips to see walrus at **Poolepynten** headland on Forlandet (78.4448, 11.8937) and to explore Isfjorden for whales and bears. On land, Kloakken (78.226037, 15.651441), north of the university, offers good views over **Adventfjorden**. Ponds by the dog cages 1km further east are good for

DAVID FISHER

king eider and long-tailed duck (✳ 78.218629, 15.694516). The road through **Adventvalen** continues east to the radar station/Mine 7 (✳ 78.148898, 16.026587).

SUGGESTED BASES Longyearbyen is the only option (⌂ visitsvalbard.com/en/). Hotels (eg: the atmospheric **Basecamp Spitsbergen** ⌂ basecampexplorer.com) are pricy. Cheaper are guesthouses such as **Gjestehus Nybyen** (⌂ gjestehuset102.no/en.html) and **Mary-Ann's Polarrigg** (⌂ polarriggen.com).

MAKE IT A WEEK Take a five-night cruise to northwest Spitsbergen or a ten-night circumnavigation of the island. You should encounter polar bear, beluga, harp seal *et al*. UK companies offering cruises include **Wildlife Travel** (⌂ wildlife-travel.co.uk; see ad, page 236).

FLEXIBILITY Longyearbyen harbour operates when ice free. This restricts the tourist cruise season to June–early September. In other months, intrepid folk can explore by skidoo: polar bears are active April to October at least.

TITBITS Polar bears are potentially dangerous. On ground-based excursions outside Longyearbyen, stay in your vehicle unless with an armed guide.

You don't need to spend a week circumnavigating Spitsbergen to see walrus. ◃

Butterfly nirvana

WHERE Picos de Europa, Cantabria and Castilla y León, Spain
TARGETS Apollo, dusky large blue, split-eyed owl-fly, wallcreeper, snow vole
ACCESSIBILITY ① (this is effectively a walking holiday)
CHILD-FRIENDLINESS ⑤ (my daughter loved it!)

The cable car scythes through the dense cloud that smothers life several hundred metres below and emerges into unblemished skies. Stepping out of the *teleférico* that transports you to the plateau of Fuente Dé in the Picos de Europa, you enter a brave new world of heady mountain peaks, butterflies and birds that look like butterflies.

A childhood friend, Matt Hobbs, had long extolled the virtues of this montane national park in northern Spain: 'the Picos is my favourite place on Earth'. Matt led wildlife tours to 'the Picos' in his twenties, and got married there in his thirties. I finally whisked my family there in my forties. And fell utterly, irreversibly in love. Make no mistake: the Picos de Europa is a gem.

Alpine choughs – scraggy-looking crows with yellow bills – drape in the air above your head, scrutinising your passage northwards. Even along the main track, which may throng with day-trippers, fellow high-altitude birds such as Alpine accentor and snow finch catch your eye as they forage unabashedly. A snow vole scurries between boulders, pausing briefly to assess your threat. A puddle attracts the first butterflies, each a different shade of blue. Chalk-hill blue is the palest (and most common), Escher's blue eye-searingly neon. An intermediate tone is grabbed by Gavarnie blue, an unremittingly montane butterfly that is named after the famous cirque in the French Pyrenees.

Pressing on, a soaring cliff (Peña Olvidada) commands the landscape. Griffon vultures and ravens encircle its crags, doing the cliff's bidding. A lammergeier, the bone-breaking vulture with a Hulk Hogan moustache, stays aloof. Scanning the rocky slopes, you should see Pyrenean chamois (aka isard). Long-legged, chestnut-coated and badger-faced, this montane goat issues distinctive short horns that inflect backwards.

Where the path splits, bear left towards La Vueltona, keeping Peña Olvidada to your right. This is prime real estate for one of Europe's most endearing birds. Should you spot a wallcreeper shuffling like a grey mouse between crevices in the boulder scree, you may be non-plussed by my enthusiasm. But once it flicks open its wings or takes flight, you will comprehend. Flopping butterfly-like, the wallcreeper dazzles with its white-spotted, scarlet and black wings. There is nothing on Earth remotely like it.

As you search, or on your way back from a successful sighting, check the numerous butterflies that flit past. Spot an apparently all-black one and you may have chanced upon Lefèbvre's ringlet – another butterfly restricted to scant mountains in northern Spain and southern France.

A more striking sight will be the marvellously named Apollo. One of Europe's largest and most sumptuous butterflies, this deity's ivory, tissue-paper wings are smudged black and eyed crimson. Inhabiting montane meadows with rocky outcrops, Apollo is considered globally threatened thanks to forestry and climate change. The Greek god of truth would not be impressed.

WILL LANGDON

❝ One of Europe's largest and most sumptuous butterflies, this deity's ivory, tissue-paper wings are smudged black and eyed crimson ❞

You could see 60 types of butterfly in a Picos weekend, of which Apollo is the most jaw-dropping. ▲

JAMES LOWEN

Also take a scrambly path downslope to any of the ponds that hold water. Alpine newts float in the shallows, flashing their burnt-orange bellies as they rise for air. Spiny toads are common around the shoreline, and you may encounter common midwife toad – an amphibian whose males carry the eggs until they hatch.

Deciding where to complement your Fuente day is tricky, thanks to the stupefying choice in and around the Picos. On balance, start at the pass of Puerto San Glorio then head lower towards Embalse de Besande. The pass must be the easiest site anywhere to see citril finch, another high-altitude specialist. Water is scarce in these arid mountains, so the lemon-and-lime birds quench their thirst in the quagmire neighbouring the car park.

GETTING THERE Nearest airports are Santander (⊘ tinyurl.com/airport-sant) and Bilbao (⊘ tinyurl.com/airport-bilbao), from which low-cost airlines serve London and other destinations. Alternatively travel by ferry from the UK (Plymouth–Santander or Portsmouth–Bilbao; page 155). The Picos is a 3-hour drive from Bilbao (Santander, 2 hours).
WHERE TO GO **Fuente Dé** (✳ 43.144256,-4.811261) is 25 minutes' drive west of Potes, along the CA185. Arrive by 08.30 to take the cable car (⊘ cantur.com/instalaciones/5-teleferico-de-fuente-de) to the top, then explore the area north and west towards La Vueltona. With time and energy, descend east via Hotel Áliva, then south into Espinama for a sumptuous butterfly-rich hike. **Puerto San Glorio** (✳ 43.052568, -4.796656) is the mountain pass on the N621 heading south out of the Picos. Stay around the car park to see citril finch. **Embalse de Besande** lies east of the P215, 2.5km south of Besande. Park at ✳ 42.874657,-4.879746, then explore meadows alongside the track and east to the reservoir. Dusky large blue favours the flush at ✳ 42.876646, -4.876999.

⊲ Split-eyed owl-flies are an unexpected highlight of a trip to the Picos de Europa.

And then there's Besande itself. As you enter meadows besides the reservoir (*embalse*), numerous electrically charged grasshoppers gust up at your tread. The identity of most may befuddle, so marvel instead at the stunning, well-named blue-winged and red-winged grasshoppers. These are great, but it is for butterflies that Besande overwhelms. Seeing 50 species – almost as many as breed in the entire UK – in a morning is straightforward.

And in what numbers! You can justifiably feel short-changed should your collective total not enter the thousands.

And still the quality somehow outstrips quantity. If you didn't see Apollo at Fuente Dé, you should do so here. Expect to see a size-spectrum of blazing fritillaries, clouds of yellows, lingerie racks of marbled whites, smouldering scores of coppers, and skies of blues. The latter include a scarce and localised treat, dusky large blue. It favours damp, low-lying meadows where great burnet thrives.

> This bizarre and impressively sized creature possesses enormous eyes, stalked antennae and sulphur-yellow garb

Above a drier grassland, another winged insect demands your attention. It also baffles you. It behaves rather like a dragonfly, hawking with predatory intent a few metres above ground. It also looks rather like a dragonfly, with partly translucent wings divided into discrete cells. Yet this bizarre and impressively sized creature possesses stalked antennae and sulphur-yellow garb. This split-eyed owl-fly is yet another remarkable gift from a peerless region. Entranced by the Picos, my family and I plan to return again, and again, and…

SUGGESTED BASES The town of **Potes** (⊘ tinyurl.com/potes-web), or villages nearby such as Cosgaya and Tudes, are ideal. Check out ⊘ thepicosdeeuropa.com.

MAKE IT A WEEK Where to start? Wildlife-rich walks *abound* throughout the Picos. Three excellent, contrasting locations would be **Arroyo de Mostajar** (✳ 43.095233,-4.850968), **Cosgaya** (✳ 43.110472, -4.729662) and **Covadonga** (✳ 43.274845, -4.992087), all of which feature in the excellent Sunflower guide *Walking in Picos de Europa*, written by local nature expert Teresa Farino. Mostajar excels for butterflies including Chapman's ringlet, Apollo and dusky large blue. Cosgaya offers a beautiful walk by a wooded river, with ample common butterflies plus Seone's viper. Covadonga is a honeypot site, but flee the crowds and you should see Iberian rock lizard, rufous-tailed rock thrush, Lefèbvre's ringlet and common hawker. Finally, look for wildcat in roadside meadows between Besande and Boca de Huérgano (page 158). August is better, but July possible…

FLEXIBILITY June to August gives a decent crack at all targets.

" Two metres long and thickset, with heavy shoulders and a bulging upper back, this is a mighty beast "

Strong as an ox

WHERE Dovrefjell National Park, Oppland, Norway
TARGETS Musk ox, Eurasian elk, reindeer, Norway lemming, bluethroat
ACCESSIBILITY ②
CHILD-FRIENDLINESS ④

A stiff breeze crackles over the Norwegian fell. Tufts of coarse copper vegetation merge into tree-frog-green grass before the ground bronzes once more. To your left [50] shades of grey betray boulders, scree and other rocky formations. At your right and some way downslope, a crystalline river sparkles in descent. Ahead of you, Kolla Mountain domes towards a hazy blue sky. And on its slopes, the world's largest goat – a contemporary of the woolly mammoth, no less – stands immense and insouciant.

With a name like musk ox (muskox, if you prefer), and a thickset appearance more reminiscent of a buffalo than a Billy Goat Gruff, you would be forgiven for assuming that this huge herbivore is a type of cattle. This is not quite right, though. Musk oxen are housed in the Bovidae family. But within that grouping, their subfamily is not Bovinae (cattle and allies), but Caprinae – sheep and goats. The musk ox hulks in their midst.

⛰ Mighty and montane: musk ox are once again thriving in Norway. JUAN CARLOS MUNOZ/NPL

Two metres long and thickset, with heavy shoulders and a bulging upper back, this is a mighty beast. Atop a neck that would make Mike Tyson proud, hooked horns almost merge to form a thick central boss. The shaggiest, most chocolatey fur – think shagpile carpet and curtain combined – drapes over sturdy, musclebound legs. This is not a goat with which to mess. Unless you are a rival bull.

July heralds the rut. Male oxen seek to exert their dominance – and thereby gain 'rights' to a harem of half-a-dozen females – by pawing the ground, swinging their head and roaring. Should that not resolve the hierarchy, the incumbent or contender may kick out or emphasise the might of its horns. If things remain even-stevens, battle ensues. Each half-tonne battering ram backs up the length of a cricket pitch, then charges head-on – repeatedly – until one concedes the contest.

Musk ox went extinct in Europe 3–4,000 years ago, its native range now restricted to the Arctic New World. Eighty years ago, the species was returned to the Old World at Dovrefjell National Park in central Norway. The introduction programme has proved successful, with perhaps 260 animals now sweeping the mountains, usually in groups of up to a dozen. Admiring them is relatively straightforward, with access from a main road through the park. Diligent scanning, particularly of Kolla's slopes, should reveal a group of massive, unkempt boulders-on-legs. Then it's a matter of hiking closer. Remain downwind and stay a respectful distance from these potentially grumpy, volatile animals. They can easily outrun you…

Wandering the *fjell* is worth a full day in its own right. Redshank chitter anxiously and golden plover whistle plaintively. Rock and willow ptarmigan both breed in the tundra. The cryptic camouflage of these grouse makes it tricky to spot the birds until you are upon them. Mountain hare is similarly difficult to detect. Principally nocturnal, this herbivore hunkers down by day in a secluded, sunny hollow. Should it spot you first – and it surely will – it flees in a broad arc, fluffy white bottom yo-yoing through the heather.

More easily spotted are reindeer, concerted lichen-grazers. This is the only deer in which both sexes grow antlers, although the males' bony protrusions are double the height and might of the females'. You may also chance upon a Norway lemming (or potentially many, should it be a 'lemming year' when breeding success is high). These rotund, short-tailed rodents are worth admiring. Their pelage comprises childish squiggles of black, yellow and buff. A smart creature.

And one that provides sustenance for a carnivore that should also be in your bank of Dovrefjell search images. You will surely see short-eared owl, an unashamedly diurnal predator. Mightier, and with a taste for mountain hare, is rough-legged buzzard. Top of the hook-billed wish list – for it occurs at low density and is an avian bodybuilder – is gyrfalcon. A swish of sharp wings angling through the sky, and you may well have jammed the gold.

Where you encounter scrub and trees, look for smaller birds. Two northern thrushes – redwing and fieldfare – breed here. So too, particularly around vegetated flushes, is the robin-like bluethroat. Males are spectacular creatures, their red-centered, russet-rimmed blue throat leaving no doubt as to their identity.

Finish the weekend by joining an evening guided walk to see Eurasian elk (as they are known in Europe; North Americans call them 'moose'). Males are taller

GETTING THERE Nearest airport is Trondheim (⊘ tinyurl.com/airport-trondheim), which takes direct flights from a score of European cities including London Gatwick and Amsterdam. From here it is 3 hours (135km) to Dovrefjell. Or fly to Oslo (⊘ tinyurl.com/airport-oslo) then drive 5 hours (360km). Train travel is a viable alternative: the Dovre Railway connects Oslo and Trondheim. Helpfully, there are stations at key sites such as Dombås, Fokstua, Hjerkinn, Kongsvoll, and Oppdal. **WHERE TO GO Dovrefjell–Sunndalsfjella National Park** (⊘ tinyurl.com/dovrefjell) is bisected by the E6 which follows Drivdalen Valley between the towns of Oppdal and Dombås. The best area for musk ox is around **Kolla** Mountain (✳ 62.290258, 9.486382). Scan from the E6 to locate animals. A good car park lies 1km west of the E6/29 road junction at Hjerkinn (✳ 62.226309, 9.519005). Kolla is 5km northwest along obvious tracks. You can work the area independently or go with a guided group (see page 137).
SUGGESTED BASES Oppdal (⊘ tinyurl.com/oppdal2) and Dombås are sensible options. **Fokstumyra Fjellstue**, 1km northeast of Dombås, offers tranquil lodging (⊘ fokstugu.no).

RICHARD STEEL

than you are, and as long as a musk ox, with legs a supermodel would crave. Massive though the world's largest deer are, Eurasian elk are also shy creatures that tend to hide away until colour drains from the day. Males will soon start shedding the velvet from their spatulate antlers, ahead of the autumn rut. For now they are solitary animals, browsing nervously at the end of their strangely horse-like snouts. Enjoy its oddness, gasp at its immensity, until obscurity takes control and draws your Norwegian weekend to a close.

MAKE IT A WEEK Go birding. The wider you explore, the more you will find. Lakes hold breeding waterbirds such as red-throated and black-throated divers, scaup and velvet scoter. Red-necked phalaropes pirouette on tiny pools, where other nesting waders may include Temminck's stint and wood sandpiper. Good sites are **Orkelsjoen Lake** (❋ 62.501210, 9.868846) and, particularly, **Fokstumyra reserve** (⬨ tinyurl.com/fokstumyra). Park by the railway station 600m northwest of Fokstumyra Fjellstue at ❋ 62.119032, 9.279736). Follow the trail 7km through varied tundra habitats.

FLEXIBILITY Mammals: year-round (though mid-June to late August best); bluethroat: May to August.

TITBITS Two companies offer daily departures from late June to late August (less frequently at other times): **Oppdal Safari** (⬨ moskussafari.no) and **Moskusopplevelse** (⬨ moskusopplevelse. no/#moskussafari). Oppdal Safari also offers elk-viewing. If you're adventurous, try seeing musk ox, when winter snow covers Dovrefjell. Harder work but more evocative.

Knees may buckle upon a close encounter with a male bluethroat. ◣

KJERSTI JOERGENSEN/D

Moby-Dick under the midnight sun

WHERE Andøya, Vesterålen, Norway
TARGETS Sperm whale, long-finned pilot whale, harbour seal, white-tailed eagle, Atlantic puffin
ACCESSIBILITY ④
CHILD-FRIENDLINESS ⑤ (children under 12 wear life jackets)

Arrowing above springy vegetation, row upon row of wooden chevrons sculpt the village edge. From each *hjell* (rack) dangle hundreds upon hundreds of headless cod. Each fish desiccates and stiffens in the surprisingly soft Arctic breeze. Life in the Norwegian archipelago of Vesterålen is, we surmise, intimate with the sea.

This supposition proves as true for wildlife as it does for humans. Here it is to the sea that nature ultimately cleaves. As wildlife-watchers, we follow. The fishing village of Andenes, at the northern extremity of Andøya Island, serves as your departure point. As you huddle with three-score passengers along 30 metres of boat, you determine that your ticker is not alone in pummelling with anticipation. Will this be the day that you finally look a whale in the eye?

⬧ Snow-capped mountains provide a mighty hinterland for a great creature of the deep: sperm whale.

Not just any whale either, but sperm whale, the leviathan that gave rise to Hermann Melville's 'Great American Novel', *Moby-Dick; or, The Whale*. Unlike Ahab, the story's protagonist (and, indeed, unlike those employed in the Norwegian whaling industry whose immortality baffles and dismays), your quest involves celebrating the live whale. Some might argue that wildlife-watchers should boycott Norway on grounds that it has scorned the worldwide whaling ban. I counter that rewarding sensitive whale-based tourism with our *krone* foments a valuable economic alternative to whaling.

> **❝ The giant rolls smoothly then bids farewell with its slender tail flukes ❞**

But let us not rush to the gargantuan. Start your Vesterålen weekend with smaller marine denizens before ascending the size spectrum. First, take a short boat trip to the islet of Bleiksøya. Another triangular form, Bleiksøya is a chunk of rocky Toblerone rising from the sea a mile off Andøya's coastline.

As you approach, rotund waiters whirr through the air, black above, white below and boasting one of the heftiest and most exuberant bills in the entire avian world. The jagged rock is home to 75,000 pairs of Atlantic puffin – one of Europe's biggest colonies. The puffin's bigger relatives – razorbill and guillemot – also beaver past, while kittiwakes bounce through the air nonchalantly, adults' wingtips dipped in ink. Confusingly similar-looking shags and cormorants hustle past. A white-tailed eagle muscles a warning to inattentive seabirds. As the RIB completes its circumnavigation of Bleiksøya, it powers towards a neighbouring rugged outcrop – Forøy – where shockingly white gannets urgently forsake their breeding colony to spear the swell for sustenance.

JAMES LOWEN

With a whoosh of wings, the white-tailed eagle swoops to grab an unsuspecting fish. ▲

ESPEN BERGERSEN/NPL

Trips depart daily in summer – but there are two twists on the typical excursion that merit particular consideration. Given that you are in the land of the insomniac sun, it would be rude not to profit from a new trip running at 22.00. Midnight birding: what's not to like? And how about snorkelling with puffins? Snug in a drysuit, peer through diamond-clear water at the auks as they plumb the depths for fish or paddle furiously with fluorescent amber legs. Again, what's not to like?

Bleiksøya shares a name with the Bleiks Canyon, a deep-sea trench that explains why Andøya is synonymous with the ocean's champion freediver. Most sperm-whale trips start by cruising near Anda lighthouse, where you may spot harbour seal and otter. After this agreeable introduction, the boat chugs westwards for an hour to reach the continental shelf – the prime area for whales.

GETTING THERE Nearest airport is Andøya at Andenes (⌀ avinor.no/en/airport/andoya-airport). In summer, Norwegian (⌀ norwegian.com) flies daily from Oslo. Widerøe (⌀ wideroe.no) flies daily from Bodø and Tromsø (which have connections to Oslo and other Norwegian cities). From Tromsø, it takes 5 hours to reach Andenes via the Gryllefjord ferry (⌀ www.senjafergene.no; three times daily). Driving from Bodø takes 6¾ hours (390km). Either set of land travel is longer than the norm for this book – but the trip is worth it.

WHERE TO GO Established **whale-watching operators in Andenes** are Hvalsafari AS (⌀ whalesafari.com), which operates two large boats and offers four trips daily in peak season, and Sea Safari Andenes (⌀ seasafariandenes.no), which operates RIBs. The former, long-established company is so confident that you will see whales that it offers a free trip should you fail. Sea Safari runs the **seabird trips** to Bleiksøya and Forøy.

SUGGESTED BASES For an overview of Andøya see ⌀ visitandoy.info/en. The logical base is Andenes (✳ 69.324167, 16.1325), where **Andrikken Hotell** (⌀ andrikkenhotell.no) offers

⬧ Long-finned pilot whales are curious, gregarious types.

Making time may be the primary objective at this point, but Andøya's marine wildlife doesn't know that. Seabirds such as fulmars provide constant accompaniment. Sharp eyes may pick out a European storm-petrel tiptoeing above the undulations, or discern the elegance of a long-tailed skua among the commoner Arctic skuas. Should someone spot a harbour porpoise or a pod of long-finned pilot whales, glistening blackly as they huddle close together, the skipper will slow for you to admire them.

Weathered of face and wild of hair, the man at the helm may keep his azure gaze firmly on the swell, but his ears are gathering information from the boat's hydrophone. Andøya's wildlife guides no longer rely solely on vision to deliver their clients' wishes. Nowadays underwater microphones capture the echolocatory clicks made by whales as they communicate, navigate and hunt. Astute interpretation of the cetacean sonar enables the captain to position the boat precisely to optimise views of the surfacing sperm whales while minimising disturbance.

Your first sight is likely a vast bushy exhalation or 'blow'. The animal itself then emerges, blowhole first. It rests a while, 'logging' at the surface like a floating tree trunk. A huge head emerges – one-third the whale's length and housing the heaviest brain of any animal – and you take the opportunity for an eyeball encounter. A triangular dorsal fin breaks the swell as the whale enriches its blood with oxygen. Then the steeply arched back thickens as the giant rolls smoothly, flirting its knobbly spine before bidding farewell with the underside of its slender tail flukes. This particular whale is gone, for now, but thanks to your support for Norway's whale-watching economy, it will return many more times yet.

JAMES LOWEN

cabins as well as the hotel. Both operators listed in *Where to go* also offer accommodation. **Stave Camping** is a decent alternative and offers varied accommodation (⊘ stavecamping. no). It even has hot pools opening in 2018!

MAKE IT A WEEK Drive Andøya's **National Tourist Route** (⊘ nasjonaleturistveger. no/en/routes/andøya), looking for whales, seals and eagles from shore. Explore the next island chain south, the **Lofotens** (⊘ lofoten.info). So scenic is this archipelago that seemingly every twist in the road produces a new subject for a postcard. Look for red-throated divers and scaup on lakes, and bluethroats in scrubby areas. And visit the world's most efficiently named village – Å – at the Lofotens' southern tip.

FLEXIBILITY The main whale-watching season is May to September (although there is also whale-watching for orca, in particular, from December to March; page 210). Seabird trips run May to August.

The rocky island of Bleiksøya is home to 75,000 pairs of Atlantic puffin.

> **People used to believe the Zino's petrel's calls to be the suffering souls of long-dead shepherds**

Zino moonwalk

WHERE Madeira, Portugal
TARGETS Zino's petrel, Madeiran firecrest, Bryde's whale, Madeiran pipistrelle, Madeiran wall lizard
ACCESSIBILITY ②
CHILD-FRIENDLINESS ④

Angular pinnacles thrust upwards, ripping the crimson sunset. Madeira's second-tallest mountain, Pico do Areeiro – 1,800 metres worth of rock on a volcanic island that looms out of the Atlantic – is blackening by the minute. Adrenalin propels you up the steep, narrow path. You are dimly aware of precipitous drop-offs at each flank. Aided by guide and headtorch, you ascend the knife-edge for 30 minutes. As you break through the cloud, the moon startles, silvering the landscape. Arriving at Miradouro Ninho da Manta, you kill the light and listen to the bizarre nocturnal serenades of Europe's rarest bird – the most magical experience in this book.

Fewer than 200 Zino's petrels exist worldwide. The seabird's entire population breeds on just six inaccessible ledges of a single massif in central Madeira. It is known locally as *freira* (nun) as its grey-and-white plumage recalls the habits of 16th-century nuns that hid from pirates in these mountains.

Zino's petrels forage at sea by day, returning to their breeding colony under the cover of darkness in order to avoid predators. Pairs reunite with eerie calls that recall a rasping tawny owl or a tremulous terrier. So mysterious are these sounds that people used to believe they were the suffering souls of long-dead shepherds. Moonlight illuminates these long-winged marvels as they hurtle below twinkling stars, whoosh between sooty peaks and disappear into indistinct valleys.

Most birdwatchers who have revered Areeiro's nocturnal spirits regard the trip as a 'top ten' life experience. Yet Madeira – the largest island in a small archipelago 630km west of Morocco – offers more besides. Conveniently, its highlights can be easily woven into a family holiday.

▲ One of the world's rarest birds, Zino's petrel breeds solely on Madeira.

Celebrate the arrival of daylight by wandering along a *levada* (irrigation channel) amid the laurel forest that spans the north of the island. In this lush, botanically effervescent woodland, palms and cycads proliferate, succulents and agaves abound.

Ribeiro Frio is probably the best area to explore, particularly around Balcões mirador. Endemic subspecies of chaffinch and blackbird greet you fearlessly. Madeiran firecrest is common if hyperactive. Seen well, this podium-hogger dazzles with bronze, silver and gold. Observe the canopy for a while and you should spot Madeiran laurel-pigeon (aka trocaz pigeon), another bird that occurs nowhere else in the world.

Several of Madeira's butterflies are geographically special too. In the forests, Madeiran speckled wood swoops low and Madeiran cleopatra flies high. Revisit Areeiro by day for plentiful Madeiran small copper and Madeiran grayling. The island's sole native reptile – endemic, of course – abounds here. Wall lizards *per se* are typically skittish, but Madeiran wall lizard is an extrovert – and one that is partial to pears, bananas and other fruit proffered by walkers.

The return to Areeiro will get you thinking about seabirds, which reminds you to descend to sea level and join a boat trip from Machico. Here in the mid-Atlantic, pelagics are notoriously fickle. Wind blows seabirds close to the coast, but excessive wind cancels excursions. Calm days optimise viewing conditions for whales and dolphins, but are pointless for seabirds, which mooch on the surface of waters far offshore.

JONATHAN LETHBRIDGE www.justbirdphotos.com

Superbly striped and flame-crowned, Madeiran firecrest is a local speciality.

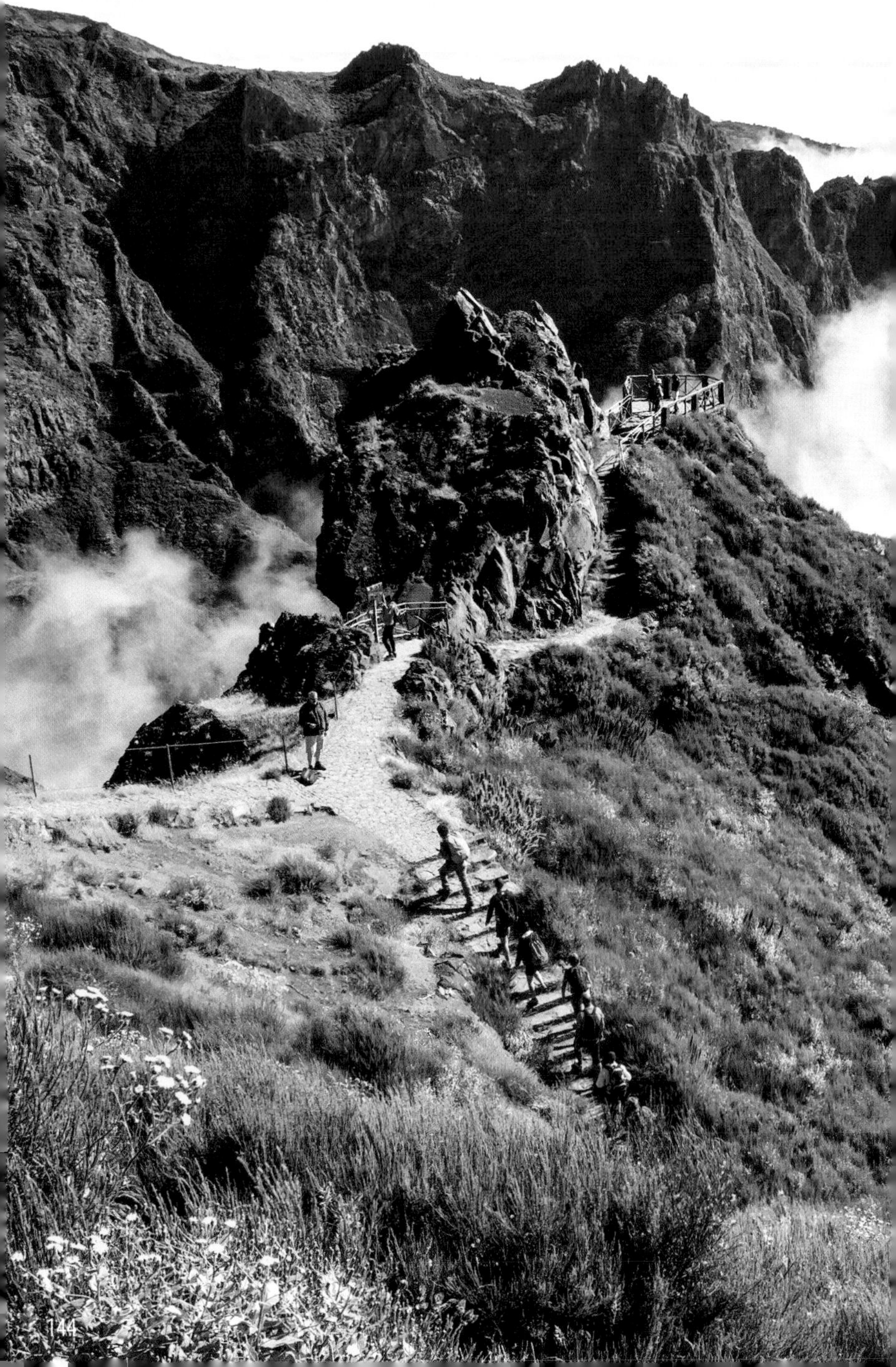

Hiking up the Pico do Areeiro is spectacular in itself, but to do it at night with rare seabirds all around is mesmerising. DZIEWUL/S

ROGER SARGENT

Assuming you get out, cetaceans should enthrall. Bryde's whale is a sizeable beast and, like sperm whale, frequently encountered. Short-finned pilot whales keep their own counsel, huddling in small pods. Atlantic spotted, common and/ or common bottlenose dolphins should make an appearance, often delighting by bow-riding. Seabirdwise, Cory's shearwater and Bulwer's petrel will be common, but the real prize is Fea's petrel, which is closely related to (and near-indistinguishable from) Zino's.

GETTING THERE Fly to Funchal on Madeira (⟨ aeroportomadeira.pt) which can be reached from many European cities (including 11 in the UK alone). The island is small but steep roads can make for slow driving.

WHERE TO GO **Pico do Areeiro** is 50 minutes (20km) by road from Funchal, following the ER103 then a minor road northwest. Park at ✳ 32.734954, -16.928621) and walk north to the mirador. Access is unrestricted by day, but limited to guided excursions at night. **Ribeiro Frio** (✳ 32.735398, -16.886380) is on the ER103, 40 minutes (18km) north of Funchal. A path leads to Balcões mirador at ✳ 32.741519, -16.890148. Depending on destinations, **pelagic trips** (including to the Desertas) depart Machico on the east coast (✳ 32.718174, -16.759374) or Funchal marina on the south (✳ 32.646253, -16.909403). **Paul do Mar** is at ✳ 32.755615, -17.227065.

SUGGESTED BASES Funchal is a logical base, but consider a rural alternative. For accommodation, see ⟨ visitmadeira.pt.

⌔ The best way to see Madeiran wall lizards? Bribe them with fruit...

This afternoon is a taster of Madeiran marine wildlife. The main course comes the following day, when you join an 8-hour cruise to the Desertas Islands. Departing Funchal marina, the trip takes two hours – longer if you slow to admire seabirds or cetaceans. Keep a particular eye out for two small storm-petrels: Madeiran and white-faced.

The Desertas – indistinct lumps, as seen from Funchal – clarify into imperious rocky islands as you approach. It's an outside chance, but keep alert for a near-mythical mammal as you near Desertas Grande. Thanks to centuries of human persecution, the once-abundant Mediterranean monk seal now dices with extinction. The Desertas hold one of the Atlantic's two remaining populations – but even this numbers just 40 individuals. Nevertheless, they are doing well here – now even venturing across the water to Madeira. Keep the faith – and myth may well become miracle.

> 66 Madeiran wall lizard is an extrovert and one that is partial to pears, bananas and other fruit proffered by walkers 99

Back on Madeira, the skies are darkening. Tempting though it is to relax, head out for one final nocturnal treat. Fewer than a thousand Madeiran pipistrelles are thought to remain. Yet seeing this small, endemic and globally threatened bat is relatively straightforward. Watch it weaving around streetlights by banana plantations in Paul do Mar, or hunting along the levada between Prazeres and Arco da Calheta. Then look upwards, longingly, towards the shepherds' souls of Pico do Areeiro, climbing nearly two thousand metres into the starlit sky.

MAKE IT A WEEK Book far ahead for Madeira Wind Birds' (see below) three-day 'Zino's petrel pelagics'. Take a two-day trip to **Desertas Grande**, staying overnight near the seabird colony which holds Cory's shearwater, Bulwer's petrel and Madeiran storm-petrel. Hike other laurel forests for pigeons and firecrests: good options include **Ribeira da Janaela** and **Fajã da Nogueira**. Take the ferry to **Porto Santo Island**, looking for seabirds and cetaceans. Seawatch from **Ponta da Cruz** (where Atlantic canary is common) or Porto Moniz. Enjoy endemic butterflies at allotments near the Parque Ecológico do Funchal office. Go diving for parrotfish, wrasse and groupers.

FLEXIBILITY Petrel: April to August (June to August best overall for seabirds); whale April to October; others: resident.

TITBITS A good source of wildlife information is ✆ madeira.seawatching.net. Operators offering Zino's petrel walks include **Madeira Wind Birds** (✆ madeirawindbirds.com). Companies running pelagic trips (including to the Desertas) include **Ventura** (✆ venturadomar. com), **Birds & Company** (✆ birdsandcompany.com), and Madeira Wind Birds.

Übercute

WHERE Lower Austria, Vienna and Burgenland, eastern Austria
TARGETS Black-bellied hamster, European souslik, particoloured bat, moustached darter, banded darter
ACCESSIBILITY ⑤
CHILD-FRIENDLINESS ⑤

For generations of kids, hamsters have made the perfect first pet. Warm and furry yet demanding minimal attention. A sufficiently short life-cycle that enables the child-owner to develop a sense of quasi-parental responsibility without being beholden for a dozen years. Yet cute though domestic hamsters may be, they are not a patch on the real thing. Black-bellied (or, more pejoratively, common) hamsters – watched in the wild as they scamper around, cheeks bulging with leaves – are übercute. They are also impressively sized, stylishly attired and – best of all – easy to see on a city break to the Austrian capital of Vienna.

△ Look at those cheeks! A black-bellied hamster on the lookout.

The range of black-bellied hamster dribbles westwards from Asia into eastern and central Europe. Within our area this rodent is an increasingly rare creature. As a result of persecution (its crime: nibbling cereal crops), hunting (its fur makes good clothing, apparently) and degradation of its original steppe habitat, the world's largest hamster has suffered very severe declines and local extinctions. Where its existence is respected rather than vigorously curtailed, black-bellied hamster is now making a decent fist of things in manmade habitats. So it is in Vienna.

A large hamster population occurs through a fair swathe of northern and, particularly, southern Vienna. Two fine places to watch them are the grave-free meadows at the central cemetery (Zentraler Friedhof, where Ludwig van Beethoven is buried) and the courtyards of Franz-Josef Hospital (particularly around the childrens' playground), where signs rightly celebrate the hamsters' presence. 'If this were Britain', says Dave Walker, a keen mammal-watcher and bird-observatory boss, 'the authorities would probably have called in pest control'. In order to avoid hungry red foxes, these normally nocturnal mammals have turned active by day in Vienna. This makes seeing them all the more straightforward – though late afternoon onwards remains the best time for a furry encounter.

And what creatures they are! Large rodents, their body size is that of a grey squirrel, but they are much more rotund. Their pelage is Titian, with contrasting white craters on the head, neck and flanks. And, as the name suggests, the belly is deep velvet. Watch the hamsters scampering around, collecting leaves in ever-fuller cheek pouches before retreating to their burrow-for-one. What could be more delightful?

Before the light fades, make for Donaupark on the banks of the River Danube. Red squirrel and (perhaps more incongruously for a city centre) brown hare abound here. Your quarry, however, is aerial. In late summer, particoloured bats migrate westwards to Vienna – and it would be rude not to try and see them. The male's call, unusually among bats, is audible to the human ear. Even more oddly, the boys tend to call to the girls while in display flight near buildings, rather than amid parkland. So stick closer to one of two iconic anthropogenic landmarks, Vienna International Centre or Danube Tower than you might have anticipated.

> 66 In the courtyards of Vienna's Franz-Josef Hospital, signs celebrate the hamsters' presence 99

Another day, another übercute ground-dwelling rodent. Bright-eyed but not particularly bushy-tailed, European sousliks are mid-sized squirrels that shun trees for a life that is part-terrestrial, part-subterranean. Active by day, they typically pose vertically (like meerkats) to keep their neighbourhood under surveillance.

European sousliks inhabit short grassland on plains and steppes. But they also more than make do with artificial equivalents such as, in this case, the grounds of an outdoor swimming lake north of Vienna (Badeteich Gerasdorf).

The best way to watch these particular sousliks is frankly bizarre. Opposite the Badeteich entrance is a grassy field. In its centre, incongruously, sits a chair.

GETTING THERE Vienna International Airport (⟨⟩ viennaairport.com) lies in Schwechat, 18km southeast of central Vienna. There are flights from many European cities, including via low-cost airlines such as easyJet from Luton, UK. You can traverse Vienna on public transport, but are better off with a hire car outside the city.

WHERE TO GO In **central Vienna**, one hamster site is **Kaiser Franz Josef Hospital** off Triester Straße (✳ 48.174025, 16.350657). From the main entrance, walk left and look for the green areas marked with signs about the hamsters. The best area is the children's playground (after hours). Another good hamster location is **Zentralerfriedhof** (a cemetery) off Simmeringer Hauptstraße. Enter through gate 2 (✳ 48.154534, 16.441899) and walk east to the meadows. Donaupark is a large urban green space between downtown Vienna and Donaustadt (✳ 48.239480, 16.411192). **Badeteich Gerasdorf** (✳ 48.302398, 16.458798) is an open-air swimming pool 1km northwest of Gerasdorf, which itself is 16km north of Vienna. **Amphitheatre Zivilstadt** lies 23km east of Vienna international airport (✳ 48.109843, 16.851157 ⟨⟩ carnuntum.at). **Neusiedler See–Seewinkel National Park** (⟨⟩ nationalpark-

⌂ On the outskirts of Vienna, European sousliks can be phenomenally tame.

GILL HOLLAMBY

Accept the implied invitation and, peanuts stashed in pocket, sit down. Within a few minutes, the (entirely wild) sousliks – habituated to the prospect of a free meal – will come to you… and scoff your nutty offering straight from the palm.

For the remainder of the weekend, three options are calling your number. You could make for Neusiedler See, Europe's largest and westernmost steppe lake, which straddles the Austro-Hungarian border. With the breeding season over, many birds are now flocking ahead of autumn migration. Black-tailed godwits have already departed, but replacement waders stocking up on invertebrate calories include ruff, broad-billed sandpiper and marsh sandpiper. August is the peak month for darter dragonflies; Neusiedler hosts eight of Austria's nine species. Good sites are along the road north of Illmitz biological station and at Sandeck. Moustached darter is abundant; southern is common; and red-veined, yellow-veined and black all fairly frequent. Rarest and most attractive is banded darter. It's a cracker!

Souslikholics may want another crack at the ground squirrel within Zivilstadt's Roman ampitheatre, east of Vienna airport. Creatures here are wilder, refusing to disgrace themselves by accepting handouts. Alternatively, return to Vienna. A former imperial hunting park comprises extensive forests and meadows, now known as Lainzer Tiergarten. Black and middle spotted woodpeckers occur. So too naturalised (and enclosed) populations of wild boar (which are both common and tame), fallow deer and red deer. There are even mouflon, the males curly horned and even more auburn than the hamsters – if not even a quarter as cute as Vienna's stellar rodents.

neusiedlersee-seewinkel.at) is a 1-hour drive (80km) along the A4 southeast of central Vienna. Start at the information centre at Illmitz (❄ 47.770525, 16.801649 ⬡ tinyurl.com/illmitz-visitor). Good darter sites are along the road north of Illmitz biological station (❄ 47.768824, 16.766568) and the 'Seedamm' at Sandeck (❄ 47.733974, 16.766890). In Illmitz and other urban areas, look for Syrian woodpecker. **Lainzer Tiergarten** (⬡ lainzer-tiergarten.at) lies just west of Vienna. Six entrances include Lainzer Tor (❄ 48.166893, 16.257109).
SUGGESTED BASES Vienna, Gerasdorf or (if you visit Neusiedler See) Illmitz.
MAKE IT A WEEK Explore Vienna! As well as the city's cultural and historical wonders, good wildlife sites include **Schönbrunn Schloßpark** and **Weinerberg Teich**, whilst **Donau-auen National Park** lies just east of the city. Check ⬡ leanderkhil.com/birding-austria/birding-in-vienna for ideas. **Leander Khil** also offers guiding services. For an entirely wildlife-focused week, you won't go far wrong by getting to know Neusiedler See, with its mosaic of habitats.
FLEXIBILITY Hamster: April to September; souslik: April to August; bat: August to October; darters: June to November, but best July to October.

GORKA OCIO Verballenas.com

Bounteous Biscay

WHERE Bay of Biscay, France and Spain
TARGETS Cuvier's beaked whale, fin whale, basking shark, ocean sunfish, Macaronesian shearwater
ACCESSIBILITY ⑤ (although ships are wheelchair accessible, check whether a lift operates to the open deck)
CHILD-FRIENDLINESS ⑤

When the trickiest decision demanded of you this weekend is whether to watch wildlife with a beer in hand or a gin and tonic (you're on holiday, remember), you must be on to a good thing. Cruising across the Bay of Biscay is a trip premised on relaxation. Marine mammals and birds greet you on a regular basis. Your side of the bargain is simply to keep your eyes open (most of the time) and focused on the ocean.

During the late nineties and noughties, mini-cruises between southern England and northern Spain were quite the rage among nature-minded folk. P&O's *Pride of Bilbao* plied between Portsmouth and the Basque city, spending ample daylight hours traversing the continental shelf where shallow waters plunge 4km. Pioneering researchers discovered that this abyssal plain was beloved of numerous whales and dolphins. What swiftly proved to be one of the world's greatest cetacean-watching spectacles became available to the masses. Enthusiasts would cruise from the UK to

⚬ You should see striped dolphins from the ferry, but join a dedicated pelagic trip to watch them this well.

Spain, potter around for a few hours, then catch the return ferry. Sadly, P&O ceased operating both route and ship in 2010… pressing European whale-watchers into a profound sulk.

Fortunately, recent years have witnessed the rebirth of Biscay's whale-watching experiences. In addition to continuing its Plymouth–Santander service, Brittany Ferries launched a route to the same Spanish city from Portsmouth (plus one to Bilbao). The timings are regrettably sub-optimal, the late-evening return journey granting fewer hours over deep water, which lies midway between the ports.

This grumble notwithstanding, there remains no finer opportunity to see a diversity of whales and dolphins in Europe, complemented by throngs of exciting seabirds. The experience is particularly poignant because the Bay of Biscay hosted the first-ever commercial whaling operation – run by Basque mariners for six centuries from 1050. So board, get your tipple from the bar and get scanning.

At dawn, bagsy your spot on an upper deck (number 10 if you are travelling on the *Pont-Aven*). Choose your location carefully. In breezy conditions, it pays to be sheltered but this involves choosing port or starboard; you can't be in two places at once. Should someone spot something exciting off one side, you may come to regret being hunkered down on the other. Ideally, site yourself on the aft deck with access to both flanks.

Enough already of the tactics. What about the action? The first life you notice will be seabirds. Gannets and fulmars predominate, the former sometimes flocking above shoals of fish. Great and Arctic skuas roam, looking for a seabird to harry into discarding its salty catch. Manx shearwaters flicker past on arthritic black-and-white wings.

If the preceding days have witnessed strong Atlantic winds, scarcer seabirds should also be present. Sooty shearwaters are bulky and swarthy, Balearic shearwaters slighter and mid-tone. A notch or two larger are great and Cory's shearwaters, the former dark capped, the latter oddly featureless. The star turn would be Macaronesian shearwater, which flutters along on auk-like wingbeats.

> **One of the world's greatest cetacean-watching spectacles became available to the masses**

As for cetaceans… on a good cruise, your species total could approach double figures. You should have no problem seeing short-beaked common dolphin – usually in small pods but sometimes in large squadrons – often close to the ship. Striped dolphin – garbed in several tones of grey – is also frequent, as is common bottlenose dolphin. The undemonstrative harbour porpoise is a tad scarcer, as is the typically battle-scarred Risso's dolphin.

A close-knit huddle of stocky, oily-black cetaceans is likely to be pilot-whales, probably long-finned. A Biscay speciality is Cuvier's beaked whale. Distinctively pale and impressively snouted ('beaked'), this is a hard cetacean to see elsewhere, yet it is a poor cruise that does not furnish good views of at least one.

And then there's the big stuff. Rorquals (or baleen whales) are typically first spotted by dint of their lungs. The size and shape of the 'blow' (an exhalation of water vapour) offer the first clue as to the whale's identity. A strong, tall column that lasts several seconds before evaporating is likely to be a fin whale, a true giant and – delightfully – Biscay's most abundant large whale. An inconspicuous plume vanishing by the time the dorsal fin appears indicates a minke whale. Less frequently observed leviathans include sperm, blue and northern bottlenose whales – but every cruise is different, so keep looking!

> **66** Distinctively pale and impressively snouted ('beaked'), this is a hard cetacean to see elsewhere **99**

While your focus is rightly on cetaceans, stay alert for other marine creatures too. A bloated, eerily pale and beady-eyed face staring out of the sea belongs to an ocean sunfish. This bizarre creature floats sideways, elongated fins splashing either side of the elemental boundary. Another 'floater', but this one hard-shelled, may prove to be a leatherback turtle. Among the world's largest reptiles, individuals can easily exceed two metres in length. Finally, look for the isoceles triangles formed by the fins of a basking shark, the second-biggest fish in the sea… right here in front of you, with beer (or G&T) in your hand!

⬜ To see a Cuvier's beaked whale this well, extend your visit with a small-boat trip from Bermeo or Santurce.

GETTING THERE 'The journey, not the arrival, matters.' For the Bay of Biscay, getting there is being there. The best option is the Portsmouth–Santander ferry service operated by Brittany Ferries (⚲ tinyurl.com/brittany-biscay; three return crossings weekly, taking 24–32 hours). Second-best is the same company's Portsmouth–Bilbao route (ditto), with a needs-must option being its Plymouth–Santander service. All services spend a few hours in port before returning, making for a three-night trip.

WHERE TO GO Stay on the ferry – on an upper deck with good visibility. You may encounter marine wildlife at any point in the journey, as long as it is light enough to see. But the best area is the Biscay abyssal plain, which is roughly midway through the cruise journey, between 48°N and 44°N.

SUGGESTED BASES The ferry! Should you wish to benefit from expert guides, Brittany Ferries partners with marine-wildlife charity ORCA (⚲ orcaweb.org.uk) to offer dedicated whale- and dolphin-watching mini-cruises (⚲ brittany-ferries.co.uk/offers/mini-cruises; Jun–Sep). These are there-and-back trips, with a short shore excursion in Spain where you may see common Iberian birds.

MAKE IT A WEEK Assuming you stay in Spain rather than returning on the first available ferry, a cracking extension would be a few days in the **Picos de Europa** (page 130), **Somiedo** (page 156) or **Pyrenees** (page 122). If you fancy more whale-watching, join a small-boat trip from northern Spain (⚲ verballenas.com; up to nine trips monthly, Jul–Oct, departing **Bermeo** or **Santurce**; €69pp, advance booking essential). These particularly excel for seeing Cuvier's beaked whale and fin whale at gobsmackingly close range.

FLEXIBILITY July to August are the best months for all targets, but cetaceans and seabirds can be seen throughout June to October.

ORCA

Experienced observers are often on hand to help everyone see Biscay's whales. ▲

The bear necessities

WHERE Somiedo, Asturias, northern Spain
TARGETS Cantabrian brown bear, wildcat, Iberian grey wolf, Pyrenean chamois, Spanish ibex
ACCESSIBILITY ②
CHILD-FRIENDLINESS ④

The greens of hillside broom bushes are coppering, but the scree slope and interspersed boulders remain intransigently greyscale. Rustling in the shrubbery intensifies into energetic rummaging. The assembled crowd – and you have quite some company this late-summer evening – holds its collective breath. All peer through whatever optics they have available, or otherwise squint a couple of hundred metres across the valley. Sixty extraordinarily long seconds later, the vegetation cedes to brute force, and a Cantabrian brown bear emerges. Game on.

Nowadays, you stand a very good chance of seeing brown bears in any of several European countries. This book alone features them in Finland, Estonia, Slovenia and Italy, and mentions them in passing for Romania. Arguably the most 'natural' way to see them – no baited hides here, unlike most other places – is in northern Spain's Somiedo Natural Park.

Here Europe's smallest brown bears are out and about, doing their stuff, at their own pace, in their own way. Durwyn Liley, a childhood friend and environmental

KENNETH BACK, SWEDEN

❝ For a month from mid-August, however, bears shed their inhibitions ❞

▲ The moment when a Cantabrian brown bear heaves into view.

ALICK SIMMONS

consultant, loved showing his kids the bears on a family holiday: 'One evening, we had an adult in view for over an hour. We all watched it climbing trees, tearing down branches and clambering over rocks. Then a second animal arrived, and they charged around together.'

Such encounters are typical in Somiedo, which is why the viewpoints at Peral, Gúa and the bottom of the track up to El Llamardal sometimes attract a dozen or more bear-watchers. All keep a respectful distance: Cantabria's bears are markedly shy creatures – the legacy of decades of illegal persecution that reduced their numbers to 70 animals in the mid-1990s. Things have improved thanks to conservation action by local organisations such as Fundación Oso Pardo (the Brown Bear Foundation), coupled with an evolution in community attitudes. Villagers have come to welcome the economic benefits of bear-inspired rural tourism. Perhaps 250 brown bears now roam northern Spain.

For most of the year, Somiedo's bears keep their own counsel, sticking to the most remote mountainsides and forests. For a month from mid-August, however, they shed their inhibitions. Unlike their northern cousins, Cantabria's bears are not particularly carnivorous. Other than scavenging carrion in spring, their diet majors on grasses, invertebrates, fruits, nuts… and berries. It is the latter foodstuff that entices the ursines out of hiding. These few weeks see a berry bonanza, as Alpine buckthorn and bilberry cascade with nutritious fruit. Focus your bear-watching time on the first and last three hours of daylight – and you should enjoy prolonged, if relatively distant, views.

Brown bear is not the only mammal for which to watch out from these viewpoints. There is a fair chance of wildcat (regular at Peral), Pyrenean chamois and wild boar too. Another Somiedo site to try for the sought-after feline is in hay meadows

Look up at rocky slopes to spot Spanish ibex such as this male.

JUAN-CARLOS MUÑOZ/BIOSPHOTO/FLPA

around Valle de Lago. August is prime time, as the felines hunt small mammals in the recently cut hayfields – and, with hungry kittens to feed, are routinely active in daytime. As you walk trails around the village, you should encounter reptiles including Iberian rock lizard, small birds such as rock bunting, large birds such as Egyptian and griffon vultures, and butterflies such as scarce copper, Chapman's blue, Queen of Spain fritillary and southern grizzled skipper.

For a much more robust chance of wildcat, you need to leave Somiedo, heading east to Riaño, south of the Picos de Europa (page 130). As you pass Riaño's large

GETTING THERE Nearest airport is Asturias (⊘ tinyurl.com/asturias-airport), to where there are regular flights from London and Paris. From Asturias airport, it is 1 hour 15 minutes (72km) to Pola de Somiedo. Santander airport is more distant (3 hours' drive; 270km).

WHERE TO GO Somiedo Natural Park (⊘ parquenaturalsomiedo.com) is centered around Pola de Somiedo, approximately 80km by road southwest of Oviedo. Pola tourist information centre and the Fundación Oso Pardo visitor centre have up-to-date information on recent bear sightings, but there are three main viewpoints (best visited at dawn and before dusk, and when cool). From **La Peral** village (✳ 43.043790, -6.249485), walk 500m east, uphill to El Principe/Mirador del Rey (✳ 43.045673, -6.245384). In the hamlet of **Gúa**, park near the church (✳ 43.079827, -6.259678) and view slopes east across the AS227. Between the two is **El Llamardal**; scan from the AS227 car park at the base of the track to the hamlet (✳ 43.047578, -6.236685). East of Gúa, **Valle de Lago** is a village centered around ✳ 43.072784, -6.200667. **Riaño** (✳ 42.973946, -5.013497) is 2½ hours (167km) east of Pola de Somiedo, at the southern edge of **Picos de Europa National Park**. Scan rocky hillsides

⚹ Seeing Iberian grey wolf involves either luck or the expertise of a local guide.

reservoir, scan slopes for Spanish ibex and the isolated Cantabrian sub-population of Pyrenean chamois, which some believe to be a distinct species. A brilliant area for wildcat – reputedly Europe's densest population – is the meadows along the LE215 between Boca de Huérgano and the butterfly hotspot of Besande. Trawl the road the first and last two hours of daylight. If you fail here, try valleys between Riaño and Vegacerneja.

Should time permit, this latter area is also where you swallow any reservations you might have about using local guides (I know, I know – but not everybody seems to want up-to-date expert advice…), and splash some cash to see Iberian grey wolf. Simply put, you'll be extremely lucky if you see them without local insights. Relatively small and with short, dark fur, these pack-dwelling canids barely resemble the grey wolves featured on wildlife documentaries set in North America. Iberia's isolated populations even differ from the subspecies found elsewhere in Europe. Some argue they are a separate subspecies, but whatever their taxonomic status, having the chance to see them is a real treat.

Wolf packs typically have extensive ranges, so there is little chance of simply bumping into them off your own back. A local guide, in contrast, spends weeks learning a pack's movements and identifying the optimum viewpoint. A typical excursion involves bundling into a 4x4 before walking a short distance. Then it's a case of sitting and scanning, ideally with a telescope because wolves are even shyer than bears and even more loath to be within sniffing distance of humans. But that's what makes the Asturias experience so natural…

around the village for ibex and chamois. A good site for the latter is the steep cliff north of Horcadas, reached via the path north from the church (✳ 42.942212, -5.043301). A good ibex site nearby is the rocky cliffs 400m west of Llánaves de la Reina (✳ 43.043654, -4.842627). Drive the N625 10km north towards **Vegacerneja** (✳ 43.035545, -5.012857), checking roadside meadows for wildcat. Do the same along the LE215, south from **Boca de Huérgano** (✳ 42.970824, -4.923402) to Besande (✳ 42.898567, -4.885564).

SUGGESTED BASES In Somiedo (⊘ parquenaturalsomiedo.com/alojamientos.html) Pola de Somiedo or Valle de Lago. Furth east, Riaño or Boca de Huérgano are convenient.

MAKE IT A WEEK The area around Resoba in the **Fuentes Carrionas y Fuente Cobre National Park** excels for Iberian wolf and wildcat, with a decent chance of brown bear. You will need a guide such as Tino García Cayón of Convientonorte (⊘ convientonorte.com).

FLEXIBILITY Bear, wildcat: August to September; others: year-round.

TITBITS For wolf-watching, you could do worse than be guided by **WildWatching Spain** (⊘ wildwatchingspain.com).

Rock and a hard place

WHERE Cádiz, Spain, and Gibraltar
TARGETS Barbary macaque, striped dolphin, honey buzzard, northern bald ibis, two-tailed pasha
ACCESSIBILITY ④
CHILD-FRIENDLINESS ④

The cork has finally popped from the bottle. After four foggy days, the skies have cleared – as the backlog of migrating storks and raptors is intently aware. The blueness above is filling with their long-winged forms, no longer frustrated by unhelpful flying conditions. From your vantage point, high on the Rock of Gibraltar, gaze upwards at a cornucopia of soaring birds.

In this flyway phenomenon, there are white storks, their lengthy bill and legs protruding perpendicular to the flying apparatus. There are honey buzzards, languid and long-tailed. There are booted eagles, stocky and compact. There are black kites, uncompromisingly swarthy. And there are griffon vultures, immense and cavalier. All are 'kettling', harnessing rising thermals of sun-warmed air to gain height before drifting towards a different continent, visible some 20 kilometres south.

ANDY BUTLER

▲ Barbary macaques are Europe's only ape and a quintessential feature of the Rock.

> **From high on the Rock of Gibraltar, gaze upwards at a cornucopia of soaring birds**

Thermals and kettling are prerequisites for the collective of soarers to make it across the Mediterranean. As thermals cannot form over sea, migrating soaring birds use the shortest crossing point to travel between Western Europe and Africa. This funnels them to the Straits of Gibraltar, between the eponymous, contested limestone buttress and the Spanish town of Tarifa. The result is one of Europe's most jaw-dropping wildlife spectacles. Up to 10,000 birds pass on the best days – with perhaps 300,000 across the entire autumn.

Wind direction and strength decree your watchpoint and how close the birds pass. In westerlies (*poniente*), observe from Gibraltar, as the birds are pressed that way. In easterlies (*levante*), Bolonia is good. In calmer conditions, use one of several sites around Tarifa. Wherever you choose, you will have company. Quite some battalion of volunteers spans the coast during migration periods, counting the flyovers. Their expertise may help you spot less abundant raptors such as short-toed eagle and Egyptian vulture, or even to discern true scarcities such as lanner falcon or Rüppell's vulture.

At some point, all the day's raptors – released from the bottle of inclement weather – will have prevailed southwards, leaving the heavens free of feather. What then? Three thrilling options stand out: exploring a political hot potato, taking to the seas or honouring conservation effort.

Let's start with the Upper Rock, a nature reserve. At sea level, 30,000 Gibraltarians cram into 6km², travelling on double-decker buses, drinking in English pubs and being surveyed by British bobbies. Higher up, a green swathe of maquis and garrigue provides rich habitat for intriguing wildlife – an invitation to explore.

Your priority should be to enjoy the Barbary macaques – Europe's only primate (*Homo sapiens* aside). Mistakenly called an ape on account of being tailless, macaques often form welcoming committees for visitors arriving by cable car atop the Rock. Other good places to see these very confiding creatures are Apes' Den (Queen's Gate) and around the Great Siege Tunnels. In total, 160 macaques, spread between six groups, inhabit Gibraltar – no mean population for this globally threatened mammal. The current population derives from introductions in the early 20th century.

Try now to complete the 'Barbary' brace. Barbary partridge is an attractive gamebird that, in Europe, otherwise only inhabits the Canaries (page 29) and

Honey buzzards are among the many species of raptors that migrate over Tarifa and Gibraltar.

Sardinia (page 62). On Gibraltar, at least, it is safe from shotguns – but bumping into one (perhaps at O'Hara's Battery) is largely a matter of fortune. An early-morning visit raises chances.

After this, mooch around Alameda Botanic Gardens – less to admire its flowering plants than to enjoy the colourful insects savouring their nectar. Among butterflies, you should see swallowtail, cleopatra and geranium bronze. The prize, however, is the year's second brood of two-tailed pasha – Europe's most glamorous butterfly. Only marginally less sumptuous is Gibraltar's sexiest day-flying moth, auspicious burnet. Aptly named, it burns with wings of crimson, velvet and cream.

Option two – weather permitting – involves taking a boat trip out from Gibraltar or Tarifa, looking for marine mammals. You rarely travel far before being surrounded by striped or short-beaked common dolphins. Numbers seem to be declining overall, but September remains a fine month for them. Many excursions also locate long-finned pilot whales, and orcas may linger from their late-summer peak. Some strike it lucky with a marine reptile, namely a loggerhead turtle paddling its way through the swell. Should you not be among them, seek solace instead in seabirds, of which Cory's shearwater is the most frequent.

The final option celebrates sterling conservation work that is seemingly set to re-establish northern bald ibis in Europe. A graph of this striking bird's population over time mirrors that of its sharply downcurved beak. Its declining numbers have long resulted in the 'waldrapp' being classified as Critically Endangered.

GETTING THERE Nearest airport is Gibraltar (⊘ gibraltarairport.gi), which takes flights from six UK airports. There is no need for a hire car if you stay solely within Gibraltar.
WHERE TO GO Migration counts in the **Straits of Gibraltar** are co-ordinated by Fundación Migres (⊘ fundacionmigres.org). In **Gibraltar**, raptor-watching vantage points include the cable-car top station (⊘ gibraltarinfo.gi/en/cable-car-3; ☀ 36.133992, -5.345713) in the **Upper Rock Nature Reserve** (entrance fee payable) and **Europa Point** (☀ 36.110515, -5.345777). Also in the reserve are Apes' Den (☀ 36.132941, -5.348880), Great Siege Tunnels (☀ 36.145194, -5.345281) and O'Hara's Battery (☀ 36.123787, -5.342925). The Gibraltar Ornithological and Natural History Society bird observatory is at Jews' Gate (⊘ gonhs.org; ☀ 36.120995, -5.345848). **Alameda Botanic Gardens** is slightly lower down, on Red Sands Road (☀ 36.131671, -5.351248 ⊘ gibraltargardens.gi). Raptor-watching locations between Algeciras and Tarifa include **Punta Carnero** (☀ 36.076474, -5.426822), **El Algarrobo** (☀ 36.090080, -5.483795), **Cazalla** (☀ 36.032963, -5.576581), and **Trafico** (Observatorio del Estrecho, ☀ 36.014573, -5.586695). A good summary of their pros and cons is at ⊘ tinyurl.com/cantelo-tarifa. Further west is **Puerto de Bolonia** (☀ 36.101629, -5.733241

ALEX BERRYMAN

In the noughties, nearly 200 captive birds were released around La Janda – and some are now breeding successfully. In September, the most reliable place to find them is Barbate marshes. Admire both the oddity of the ibis – its face only one a mother could love – and the perseverance of the conservationists seeking to prise them from between a Rock and a hard place.

tinyurl.com/cantelo-bolonia). **Cetacean-focused boat trips** run from both Tarifa (where operators include whalewatchtarifa.net, turmares.com and firmm.org) and Gibraltar (dolphin.gi). For the ibis, try marshes/grasslands along the A2231 between **Barbate** (❋ 36.193481, -5.913163) and Zahara de los Atunes (❋ 36.138363, -5.846447) or Montenmedio Golf Club driving range (❋ 36.237441, -5.910418).

SUGGESTED BASES Gibraltar (visitgibraltar.gi) or Zahara de los Atunes.

MAKE IT A WEEK **Alcornocales Natural Park** has ample raptors, butterflies and dragonflies. **Los Lances** for waterbirds, waders and possible lesser crested tern. **La Janda** for red-necked nightjar. Further afield, try **Coto Doñana** for birds, reptiles and amphibians, or even Iberian Lynx in **Sierra de Andújar** (page 22).

FLEXIBILITY Macaque and ibis: resident; buzzard and other migratory soaring birds: August to October (and February–May); dolphin: resident, but best September; pasha: May to June and August to October.

TITBITS **Inglorious Bustards** (ingloriousbustards.wordpress.com; see ad, page 234) provide expert guiding for migration-watching and more.

Conservationists have reintroduced northern bald ibis to southern Spain, and birds are now breeding successfully. ⬙

FABIEN BRUGGMANN/BIOSPHOTO/FLPA

> **❝ Abruzzo's golden-crowned brown bears may represent an undescribed and endangered subspecies ❞**

Et tu, Abruzzo?

WHERE Abruzzo National Park, Abruzzo, Italy
TARGETS Abruzzo chamois, Apennine grey wolf, Marsican brown bear, white-backed woodpecker, rock partridge
ACCESSIBILITY ①
CHILD-FRIENDLINESS ②

It may not be a *particularly* tough climb, but you may nevertheless be somewhat devoid of puff when you emerge above the beech forests of Val di Rose. The landscape now free of trees, there is nothing but Apennine meadow, rock and craggy slopes for miles around. Plus a group of Abruzzo chamois posing atop scree, appearing bemused at your gasping arrival. No mammal is more in its element in Abruzzo National Park than this mountain goat. It's also a rarity, a conservation success story and a taxonomic conundrum.

Protecting 50,000 hectares of mountain and beech woodland, birch and pine forest, heavenly meadow and sparkling river valley, Abruzzo National Park will celebrate its one hundredth birthday in 2023. If cloven hooves permitted, the chamois would raise a glass then, as the park has been the locus of an amazing turnaround in this mammal's fortunes.

Thanks to strenuous conservation attention, chamois numbers have risen from just a few score to a thousand individuals during the past 80 years. This is significant

⬧ The experience of watching Marsican brown bear is quite unlike that of seeing one from a hide.

because Abruzzo chamois is an endemic subspecies of Pyrenean chamois, which otherwise occurs only in the Pyrenees (page 122) and Cantabria (page 130). All three populations are a different species to that which ranges from the Alps eastwards (Alpine chamois).

Take time to watch these special rock-climbers. Groups typically allow close approach, enabling you to admire their proud demeanour, recurved horns, stripey faces and cinnamon coat. As you watch them, a rock bunting hops through pink-flowered rock crane's-bill and a snow finch rattles as it flakes past indigo splatters of fringed gentian. Alpine chough and Alpine accentor emphasise that your walk has brought you to a decent altitude (1,942m if you reach Passo Cavuto).

As you return to the timberline, a Cantabria pine vole – the only short-tailed vole here – scurries across the path. On your descent back to Civitella Alfedena, autumn crocus and mountain tragacanth (a vetch) splash the pathside with colour. You should bump into red deer or wild boar, both being common throughout Abruzzo. Porcines snort around open meadows, while stags are presently rutting intensely.

Once back at the village, have a quick visit to the wolf sanctuary, which rehabilitates injured lupines. Before calling firecrests distract you overly, drive northwest for 40 minutes to Gióia Vécchio. As you journey, keep an eye on roadside meadows and inclines. As well as boar and both red and roe deer, you have a chance of both remaining mammalian targets: Apennine wolf and Marsican brown bear.

From the viewpoint near Gióia Vécchio church, light scrub descends to the valley where meadows open out, ceding abruptly to forest as the slope opposite ascends. A party of boar trots through a clearing as two red deer chew the cud. In recent autumns, an Apennine wolf pack has made this area its base, granting prolonged if distant views of adults and pups. Over one hundred wolves inhabit the park; keep alert and you could encounter one anywhere.

BRUNO D'AMICIS/NPL

Abruzzo chamois are veritable mountaineers.

NEIL BOWMAN

The watchpoint has gained repute as a reliable site to observe Marsican brown bear. In spring, bears lumber through these meadows ahead of mating. They return to gorge on autumn's bounty, particularly beech nuts, apples and (up high) Alpine buckthorn berries. Some argue that the golden-crowned bears here represent an undescribed and endangered subspecies: just 40–60 adults inhabit the park. If your schedule allows, come here for the first and final two hours of each day. Overcast conditions (including rain) are better than sun. Watch for bears pondering between shadows and patches of fruit. They appear and disappear at will, so scan constantly. Like Spain's Somiedo (page 156), the joy of Abruzzo is that you watch the ursines wandering around naturally, with neither bait nor hide in contemplation.

On day two, bears aside, concentrate on trying to see two rare birds. White-backed woodpeckers here are of the race *lilfordi*, which some clever folk suspect is a species in its own right. You might bump into this rare creature anywhere there is dead wood – and some have even seen it from Gióia Vècchio viewpoint. Optimise chances by exploring beech-dominated forest either in the Pesco di Lordo Valley southwest of Pescasséroli or along the SR509 south of Opi.

Seeing rock partridge involves an hour-long journey into neighbouring Sirente-Velino Natural Park. This declining species has a world range limited to southeast Europe and usually breeds above the treeline. Little surprise that birders are keen to see it! Beyond the village of Aielli, a track winds gently towards rolling hills, the dusty ground starred by autumn crocus. A great banded grayling – a large butterfly with striped wings – greets your eventual arrival at the scree. An oddly familiar scratchy clicking alerts you to the gamebird's presence, and you eventually track it down to a rock nudging the conifer belt. Like Abruzzo chamois, this finicky bird is well worth the climb.

▲ Rock partridge is a rare mountaineer, usually breeding above the treeline.

GETTING THERE Nearest airports are both at Rome: Fiumicino and Ciampino (⏣ tinyurl. com/rome-airports). Most airlines use the former; a low-cost airline, the latter. From here it is 2 hours' (163km) drive from Ciampino to Pescassèroli in Abruzzo National Park (an additional 30 minutes/30km from Fiumicino).

WHERE TO GO Almost anywhere in **Abruzzo National Park** (⏣ www.parcoabruzzo. it/Eindex.php) is worth exploring. Much is accessible from the SS83. Visitors arriving from the north/west (eg: Rome) enter the park at **Gióia Vècchio**. Park at San Vicenzo church then watch from 100m southeast at ✳ 41.899616, 13.733992. Another **good bear area** is 5km north of Pescassèroli, at the SS83/SP17 junction (✳ 41.851848, 13.777322). For **Val di Rose**, park in Civitella Alfedena then follow the footpath south that leaves Via Nazionale at ✳ 41.764249, 13.941933. Walk uphill for 2–3 hours towards Cavuto Pass. From July to early September there is a daily limit on walkers, so book ahead (⏣ tinyurl.com/valdirose2). In **Civitella Alfedena**, the wolf centre is on Via Santa Lucia at the northern edge of the village (✳ 41.767159, 13.944999). Access **Difesa Forest** southwest from Pescassèroli along the track through Pesco di Lordo Valley. Park at ✳ 41.795292, 13.782930, then continue on foot. For beech woodland near **Opi**, head south from the village on the SR509 and explore upslope (west) from km post 8 (✳ 41.759510, 13.827998). In Sirente-Velino Natural Park, **Aielli** is north of the A25. Approaching Aielli from the south, turn off Via San Massimmo at ✳ 42.078889, 13.589444, heading northwest along a dirt track until you reach scree slopes. Good spots are ✳ 42.087117, 13.579837 and ✳ 42.107778, 13.592778.

SUGGESTED BASES Accommodation in the national park is collated at ⏣ www. parcoabruzzo.it/esog.php. Many stay in Pescassèroli, the largest town. If you plump for **Castel di Sangro**, check the church walls at night for beech marten.

MAKE IT A WEEK Stay overnight at two mountain refuges to optimise prospects of encountering bears. Local company **Ecotur** (⏣ ecotur.org) offers escorted trips. It's a 2–3 hour hike into both **Iorio** (in the Vallone di Peschio di Iorio: ⏣ ecotur.org/en/refuge_ jorio.xhtml) and **La Cicerana** refuges (⏣ ecotur.org/en/refuge_cicerana.xhtml). **Monti della Meta** is another good site for chamois, bear and wolf. Drive roads at night looking for Indian grey mongoose and Apennine grey wolf, including between Pescassèroli and Opi. Wolf has also been seen regularly by day from the viewpoint at **Gióia Vècchio**. For a botanical kick, cyclamen proliferate in the **Sagittario Gorge**.

FLEXIBILITY Bear: May and mid-August to late September; wolf: year-round but autumn/winter best; others: year-round.

TITBITS If you visit for bears in May, search for birds such as collared flycatcher and numerous orchids. UK wildlife-travel companies operating bear-and-wolf tours to the Abruzzo, include **Wise Birding** (⏣ wisebirding.co.uk; see ad, page 230).

> **" No group of animals does migration more magnificently, more abundantly and more widely than birds "**

The Great South Road

WHERE Falsterbo, Skåne, Sweden
TARGETS Visible migration of numerous raptors and landbirds
ACCESSIBILITY ⑤
CHILD-FRIENDLINESS ④ (beaches!)

The opacity of night is losing its battle against the translucence of dawn – and already the click-counters are in hand. A squadron of Scandinavian birders stands – literally as well as metaphorically – ready to help unravel the mysteries of bird migration. No such diligence is demanded of you. Your 'role' is simply to marvel at the overhead passage of tens of thousands of birds, all beating south to execute their winter-survival strategy.

Some butterflies migrate: monarch being the most famous with painted lady its European equivalent. Some dragonflies migrate – red-veined darter and vagrant emperor among them. Some mammals migrate: think caribou in North America,

On the move. Finches such as brambling and linnet pass Falsterbo in big numbers. JAMES LOWEN

wildebeest in Africa, various rorqual whales throughout the oceans. Many moths migrate – remember the pitch invasion (by silver-Y moths) at the Stade de France that delayed the Euro 2016 final? But no group of animals does it more magnificently, more abundantly and more widely than birds. This weekend – at the fabled Swedish migration hotspot of Falsterbo – celebrates this special dimension to their existence.

Migrant birds – landbirds and raptors, at least – have a thing about peninsulas such as Falsterbo. To them the ever-skinnier strip of land, wasting away into sea or even ocean, is a funnel – concentrating passage into dwindling *terra firma* or the airspace above. It also demands a decision. Should the migrants stay or should they go? The journey has to be made, but does it have to be made *today*? Why not rest while conditions are inclement, refuelling before the dangerous crossing over open water? Or if the sun is shining and the skies are clear, why not make headway while the going is good?

Weather will decree your strategy this weekend. In rain, fog or strong wind, search Falsterbo's grassland, bushes and copses for ground migrants. In clear, dry conditions, look up for what birdwatchers call 'visible migration'. Enumerating the latter is the function of those click-counters. There are simply too many birds, passing too quickly and too consistently, to assay with 'old school' pencil and paper.

Dawn sees most observers stride across the golf course to Nabben, at the very tip of Falsterbo Peninsula. Beyond here the Baltic Sea interrupts land for 20km. There is little shelter so arrive early to nab a plot on the leeward side of the sparse bushes. Almost immediately you will spot sparrowhawks zipping southwards, tummy-brushing the golf course. A single sweep with binoculars can easily reveal half-a-dozen birds, and the morning total may reach the hundreds. Marsh harrier, osprey and common buzzard are early birds too; the latter will probably prove the most numerous raptor of the day. All seek to make the most of clement conditions to continue their momentous journey south. Looking north you can see them lining up in single file, like aeroplanes arriving at London Heathrow.

Flurries of small birds similarly catch the eye as they direct themselves your way. At distance, they are a cluster of unidentifiable dots. But as they approach, their shapes become apparent: long tails or short, fat bodies or slim, narrow wings or broad. As they fleet past, you see flashes of white in the wing, along the tail or on the belly. Some of the birds call to maintain contact – perhaps a metallic pink, a nasal wheeze or an abrupt *jip*. The combination of structure, glimpsed plumage features and vocalisations leads to their identification as – whether tentative or confident – as types of finch, tit, pipit or wagtail.

Within a few hours, the 'clickers' have developed RSI. They have registered – and you have seen – tens of thousands of chaffinch, brambling and siskin, hundreds of blue tit, and scores of crossbill among others. Up to a thousand birds per minute are pouring overhead. The guesstimate of 540 million birds passing through southern Scandinavia each autumn starts to gain credibility.

As the early-morning passage abates, head slightly inland to peruse areas of cover – gardens, woodland and the like. Here you are looking for birds that are dallying before moving on. Among spotted flycatchers you may spot a red-breasted. Among the warblers, there may be an icterine. A red-throated pipit stutters along a field edge. A red-backed shrike plonks itself atop a fence post, flanked by northern wheatears and whinchats. Out of nowhere a spotted nutcracker – a striking, dark brown and white crow – flutters past on rounded wings that seem ill suited to the trials of migration. And so it proves, as the nutcracker reaches Nabben's point of no return… and loops back, deciding against migrating – today at least.

As the air warms, conditions improve for a wider variety of raptors. Assume position either at 'The Canal' or on Skänors Ljung heath. Then look up. Amongst the common buzzards, you may discern early rough-legged buzzards or tardy honey buzzards. Red kites angle past, tail-twisting. A larger form may be an eagle: probably white-tailed, but conceivably steppe or lesser spotted. All circle upwards, gaining enough height to continue journeying, travelling, migrating along the Great South Road through the Scandinavian sky.

GETTING THERE Nearest airports are Malmö (⌂ swedavia.com/malmo), 20km east of the city, and Copenhagen in neighbouring Denmark (⌂ cph.dk). From either airport it is 40 minutes (50km) drive to Falsterbo. Driving from Copenhagen involves an expensive crossing of Øresund Bridge (⌂ oresundsbron.com), made famous by 'Scandi noir' drama *The Bridge*. You can also reach Falsterbo easily by public transport from either airport, the final leg being bus 100 from Malmö central station to Falsterbo Strandbad. You could then hire a bike to get around Falsterbo.

WHERE TO GO Useful details of sites around **Falsterbo** are on the Falsterbo Bird Observatory website (⌂ falsterbofagelstation.se/index_e.html then select 'Bird sites'). Approach Falsterbo on road 100, turning left at the roundabout onto Strandbadsvägen. After 2.7km turn left onto Östergatan, then follow Sjögatan to the **bird observatory** (✳ 55.388934, 12.836902) in **Falsterbo Park**. For the peninsula, park by Flommens golf club (✳ 55.393225, 12.827862) or by **Kolabacken** (✳ 55.383629, 12.821989). Then walk, respectively, 2km south or 1km southwest to reach **Nabben Point** (✳ 55.377950, 12.810712). **Fyren lighthouse garden** (✳ 5.383700, 12.816652) is excellent for migrants. **South Flommen** (✳ 55.389882, 12.820475) can also be good. **Skänors Ljung** heath (✳ 55.400056, 12.869013) lies south of road 100, immediately west of Ljunghusen. There is parking along the road and at Falsterbo Resort campsite (✳ 55.397335, 12.865552). Further east, the southwest corner of **Falsterbo Canal** (✳ 55.396049, 12.943470) is another good base for raptor watching.

SUGGESTED BASES Falsterbo has a few hotels, the **Falsterbo Resort campsite** (⌂ falsterboresort.se) where you can rent cabins, and hostel-type accommodation at the bird observatory. Some stay in the towns of Skanör or Trelleborg.

MAKE IT A WEEK During the migration season, every day is different – so you can easily spend a week reiterating a circuit of the numerous 'birdy' locations around Falsterbo. For something different you might target waders such as broad-billed sandpiper. Other good spots for migrant birds in the vicinity include **Lilla Hammars**, **Klagshamn** and **Trelleborg**. Slightly further afield are **Börringe** and lakes around **Vombsjön**. For a different Swedish migration experience, spend a few days on the brilliant island of **Öland** in southeast Sweden. AviFauna Nature Tours (⌂ avifauna.co.uk; see ad, page 231) and Wild Sweden (⌂ wildsweden.com; see ad, page 230) offer tours seeing the best of Swedish wildlife.

FLEXIBILITY Anytime August to October is good for migration; the species composition evolves throughout the period. Earlier is better for honey buzzard, pipits and wagtails; later for thrushes and wildfowl.

JAMES LOWEN

Search for exciting migrants such as red-backed shrike. ▲

66 Olm can survive a decade without eating – truly life in the slow lane **99**

WILD WONDERS OF EUROPE/HODALIC/NPL

The cave with the dragon babies

WHERE Inner Carniola and southeast Slovenia, Slovenia, and Friuli-Venezia Giulia, Italy
TARGETS Olm, nose-horned viper, brown bear, European cave spider, autumn lady's-tresses
ACCESSIBILITY ③
CHILD-FRIENDLINESS ③

There is nothing like the olm. It is as strange an animal as you will ever see – without doubt the most remarkable creature featured in this guide. Known locally as the 'dragon's baby' or 'human fish', pretty much every key fact about Europe's largest amphibian has the wow factor.

This salamander is an unabashed troglodyte – Europe's only such vertebrate – living up to 300 metres below ground. It is thought to live for a century, double the lifespan of any other amphibian. It can survive a decade without eating – truly life in the slow lane. Sightless, what pass for its eyes are shrouded in skin. In shape, it recalls an arrow-headed eel, four short legs doing little to detract from this impression. Unlike most amphibians it does not metamorphose, retaining youthful features such as frilly gills. It has rosy skin through which internal organs contour so clearly that you can almost determine an adult's gender. Yet it also has a melanistic variant – with black skin and functional eyes. Finally, the olm is extremely vulnerable to changes in its environment – and is thus considered threatened with global extinction. Wow, wow, wow.

⬝ Olm: a unique, remarkable amphibian.

It is unimaginable that you can actually see this most alien of animals. Yet observe it you may, and easily too, in the karst limestone caverns of underground Slovenia. Postojna Cave is the country's most famous tourist destination. A spectacular network of caves showcases fragile needle-like stalactites and immense swimming-pool-length stalagmites, hefty rock curtains and sturdy river-carved bridges. It's also where you can see this ultimate specialist.

Every few months, a few olm are 'borrowed' from the wild and given temporary home in a tank where they can be admired at close range. Those seeking a more natural experience can join a guided tour. This plumbs the watery darkness in search of both speleological spectacle and subterranean salamander. You will need to tread deftly and avoid speaking as you approach the shallow pools that the olm calls home. In its dark, silent world, light or vibration can shock this salamander into sinuous disappearance.

As you explore, your guide will point out other cave-adapted life. Cave woodlouse, cave shrimp, cave herald snail, and other crustaceans eke out existence here. So too European cave spider, cave cricket, eyeless beetles, millipedes, and even the odd lesser horseshoe bat. Wow all over again.

Olm have hit the news in recent years. In 2016, one of Postojna's 'tanked' animals laid eggs, 21 of which hatched. Excited speleobiologists (yes, there really are such specialists) are now intensively studying baby 'dragons' for the very first time. In 2017, environmental DNA sampling (testing water to detect signature eDNA) revealed the olm's existence in Montenegro – the first time this technique has revealed the presence of a subterranean animal.

Emerging from the underworld, it is time to prepare for more darkness. Kočevje in southeast Slovenia is thought to have Europe's highest density of brown bears.

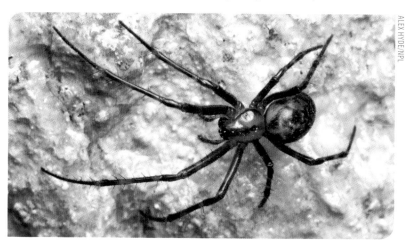

ALEX HYDE/NPL

Arachnophobes look away now: cave spiders thrive underground.

FABIO PUPIN/FLPA

Working pragmatically with local hunters (which may or may not be your thing), a couple of companies are starting to offer opportunities to watch bears from hides. Your precise destination will depend on the service-provider you select. In a typical encounter, bears (and often wild boar) emerge from the woodland early evening to nuzzle around (and usually guzzle) the proffered bait.

On your second day, head across the border into Italy. The crossing is straightforward and within no time at all you approach Carsiana botanical garden, northwest of Trieste. This *giardino* offers far more than cultivated flowers. As its name suggests, Carsiana is a celebration of the karst – above ground this time. Autumn-flowering plants include autumn crocus, purple cyclamen and winter savory. Look too for the delightful autumn lady's-tresses, its ivory flowers maypole-dancing around the delicate orchid's stem.

Stony walls and water-runnelled rocky formations dominate Carsiana. Peruse these carefully and quietly. You are looking for a coil of reptile, a nasal protrusion, a slither of serpent. Carsiana is a great place to track down what is probably Europe's most sought-after snake. Nose-horned viper does precisely what it says on the tin. This is fundamentally a large, stocky adder, with dark zigzags on a pale background. The dramatic twist comes at the snake's business end where the snout culminates in a distinct horn. Combined with an unusually large, eyebrow-like scale above an eye, this imparts a furious gaze.

Autumn is a good time to see this wonderful creature, as it readies for hibernation. Admire it – but keep your distance. This is, after all, Europe's most venomous snake. No such safety issues apply to Carsiana's other star reptile, which you are most likely to encounter in shadier terrain. Dalmatian algyroides is a stocky, brown, long-tailed lizard that occurs solely alongside the Adriatic and Ionian coast. Males have a blue face and russet belly. It is secretive, basking in secluded spots – and is swift to flee should it feel threatened. But then, with a weekend headlined by the dragon's child, 'secretive' is somewhat relative.

▲ Nose-horned viper is probably Europe's most exciting snake.

GETTING THERE Nearest airport is Ljubljana (lju-airport.si). There are flights from several European capitals, including with low-cost airlines from London. It is a 1-hour (70km) drive to Postojna. Alternatively fly to Trieste in Italy (triesteairport.it), to which a low-cost airline flies from London.

WHERE TO GO In Slovenia, **Postojna Cave** (*Postojnska jama*; 45.782641, 14.203745 postojnska-jama.eu) is 1km northwest of Postojna. The vivarium harbours olm and troglodyte invertebrates, but take a longer tour for a chance of seeing them *in situ* or visit Planina Jama caves (see below). Nearby **Predjama Castle** often has wallcreeper in autumn/winter. You can make arrangements to see **black olm** at a family farm in Jelševnik called Izletniška Kmetija Zupančič (+386 31 632636 tinyurl.com/black-olm). **Bear-watching evenings** near Kočevje in southeast Slovenia, a couple of hours' drive away, are offered by Discover Dinarics (discoverdinarics.org; see ad, page 229). In Italy, **Carsiana Botanic Garden** (45.732494, 13.739812 giardinobotanicocarsiana.it/en/) is 15 minutes (12km) from the Slovenian border, off the E70 20 minutes (14km) northwest of Trieste. It is just 40 minutes (49km) from Postojna.

SUGGESTED BASES Postojna (visitpostojna.com) is a central option.

MAKE IT A WEEK Book a tour of another world-famous karst cave, **Križna Jama**, for lesser horseshoe bat, subterranean invertebrates and bones of the long-extinct cave bear (krizna-jama.si). Even better, **Planina Jama** caves (planina.si, tinyurl.com/planina2) harbour lesser and greater horseshoe bats, steppe myotis and pond myotis, plus – most excitingly – abundant olm. Access is only by prior arrangement with local caver Zvone Samsa (mogsac5@gmail.com, zvone.samsa@studioproteus.si). Another set of caves, **Škocjan**, excels for several species of bat. You can join a guide to see these inside or wait outside to see them emerge at dusk. Hike through ancient beech and silver fir forest northeast of **Kočevje** (a good route is between 45.674978, 15.004637 and 45.674978, 15.004637); beech marten is regular here. Stroll around the seasonal lake of **Cerkniško** Jezero ('sometimes the lake is', say locals, 'and sometimes it isn't') for great bittern, reptiles including eastern grass snake, amphibians such as agile and edible frogs, and late dragonflies. In Ljubljana, at night, edible dormouse and northern white-breasted hedgehog roam the forested lower slope of Rožnik hill behind **Tivoli Park**, and red squirrels are tame here.

FLEXIBILITY Olm and spider: year-round; viper: February to October; bear: April to October; lady's-tresses: August to October.

TITBITS Slovenian company **Institute Symbiosis** (natureincolour.eu) offers hiking underground to view olm as part of a spring tour that focuses on life in cold blood (amphibians, fish, reptiles).

Autumn lady's-tresses twirl through Carsiana botanical garden.

Visit a feeding station such as Spain's Mas de Buñyol (weekend 44) for close-up views of griffon vultures.
OSCAR DOMINGUEZ deepwildphoto.com

October
November
December

Cory's shearwater – crimson speckled – autumn buttercup – Eleonora's falcon
Ibiza wall lizard – griffon vulture – Tenerife blue chaffinch
fin whale – European fiddler crab – long-eared owl – orca
humpback whale – lesser white-fronted goose
white-tailed eagle – European starling roost – wallcreeper – eagle owl

66 Scores of famished seabirds are plunging into the gloopy mess or tiptoeing delicately above it **99**

ROBIN CHITTENDEN www.robinchittenden.co.uk

Go west

WHERE Sagres Peninsula, Algarve, Portugal
TARGETS Balearic shearwater, Cory's shearwater, Wilson's storm-petrel, booted eagle, crimson speckled
ACCESSIBILITY ④
CHILD-FRIENDLINESS ④

After yesterday's storm, the calm. The transformation in weather at the westernmost extremity of continental Europe is doubly good news. Northwesterly gales have thrust pelagic birds close to land. And today's benign conditions mean that they are sitting on the sea – with you admiring them at close range from a RIB.

There's another reason that the seabirds are here, and in such numbers. They are getting a free meal. Not to be sniffed at, even if the pong from the 'chum' (diced oily fish) risks overpowering human nostrils. Five nautical miles off Cabo de São Vicente – the occidental headland beyond which the Atlantic Ocean unravels unto the New World – the skipper has paused the Zodiac. He ladles the stinky feast on to the sea surface. Scores of famished seabirds are hyperactively circumnavigating the boat, plunging into the gloopy mess or tiptoeing delicately above it.

▲ A boat trip offshore should bring you exciting seabirds such as Cory's shearwater.

The most numerous customer is Cory's shearwater, Europe's largest breeding 'tubenose'. Prominent nostrils, covered by tubes on the upper bill, give it and other family members a refined sense of smell that enables them to detect chum from miles away. Among the Cory's are striking seabirds with a white face and dark skullcap. The closest these great shearwaters breed is Tristan da Cunha. This is one of very few birds to breed in the Southern Hemisphere yet cross the Equator to winter.

As the melée intensifies, so gannets pile in, dwarfing the other seabirds. A dusky shearwater proves to be a Balearic, a seabird declining so rapidly that it is considered Critically Endangered. Even the most optimistic research puts the total world population at just 25,000. There are more than a thousand times as many Wilson's storm-petrels in the world, yet they are more unusual in a European context, as they breed on subantarctic islands. Among European storm-petrels pitter-pattering in the RIB's wake, the skipper points out a Wilson's – so close that you can see the lemon webbing separating its toes. What a pelagic!

Returning to land, the absence of cloud has enabled the sun to warm the air. 'Thermals' – columns of rising air – are developing, demanding that you make haste towards the raptor-migration viewpoint at Monte da Cabranosa. Each autumn, 20 types of birds of prey migrate southwards along the Portuguese coast. As they reach Sagres, they run out of land. This prompts them to harness solar energy, 'kettling' upwards to reach an altitude sufficient to continue safely towards Africa.

End September and early October see the peak raptor migration – which is why Iberia's biggest bird festival takes place here then. Today, you could witness a few hundred kites, eagles, buzzards, falcons, and vultures drift overhead. Booted eagle and black kite are among the most common – but griffon vultures are starting to come through. It pays to check flyovers for rarities. Eleonora's falcon visits regularly in autumn, hailing from breeding colonies in the Balearics. Scarce eagles have included lesser spotted, and even African vultures (Rüppell's and white-backed) have got caught up with fellow travellers.

Crimson speckled, a stunning day-flying moth of the Mediterranean. ▲

MATT BERRY/GREENWINGS

The next morning, return to the ocean. This time, search for marine mammals. Dedicated dolphin-watching trips take barely 90 minutes, but often produce fabulous encounters. Short-beaked common dolphin is most frequently seen, but common bottlenose dolphin and harbour porpoise are also likely. The ultimate would be for a pod to ride the RIB's bow – so close you can hear the dolphins breathe.

GETTING THERE Nearest airport is Faro (faro-airport.com), which receives flights from most European capitals and several UK cities. From here it is 1 hour 20 minutes' drive (115km) to Sagres, along the A22/N125.

WHERE TO GO Pretty much anywhere on the **Sagres Peninsula** can offer good wildlife-watching, which is one of the reasons why a major nature-oriented festival is held here each October (birdwatchingsagres.com). You can see migrating raptors anywhere, but the main viewpoint is at **Monte da Cabranosa** (37.038264, -8.954243). Good spots for migrant landbirds include the long pine hedge stretching north from Terra restaurant at **Curva do Belixe** (37.027242, -8.962768), two valleys running inland from **Telheiro beach** (37.046215, -8.978493) and scrub west of **Orbitur Campsite** (37.024269, -8.952406). Several local operators offer **RIB trips** to see dolphins and seabirds. I recommend Marilimitado (marilimitado.com), but the birdwatching festival also uses Cape Cruiser (capecruiser.org). Both depart from the harbour on the east side of Sagres (37.010403, -8.930384). You can seawatch from the northern side

▲ Jaw-droppingly beautiful and mighty large too: two-tailed pasha.

Your second boat trip over, dedicate yourself to the third element. Having done water (seabirds, dolphins) and air (raptors), it's high time to focus on land-based wildlife. Sagres's 'end-of-the-continent' location has a similar impact on migrating songbirds as on aerial birds of prey – they get 'bottlenecked'. Check areas of dense cover – the long pine hedge at Curva do Belixe or the Telheiro valleys, for example – for warblers and chats stocking up on calories before continuing their southwards journey. In the drier plains, particularly at Vale Santo, look for little bustards. These are rare residents here – an offshoot from the pseudosteppe of Alentejo further east (page 48) – but absolutely worth seeking out.

As you explore, you will doubtless come across non-avian wildlife. Moorish gecko commonly clings to buildings at night. Damp areas (including under logs and stones) are worth exploring for amphibians, notably parsley frog, stripeless tree frog and natterjack toad. Waterbodies – from puddles to lagoons such as Martinhal – attract dragonflies. Lesser emperor and broad scarlet are typically seen, but – in a good year – there could be a conflagration of thousands of red-veined darters buzzing around, each one a fiery, hyperactive spark.

Although late in the butterfly season, you have an outside chance of the sublime, multicoloured two-tailed pasha around strawberry trees. You are more likely to encounter swallowtail and Lang's short-tailed blue. Finally, look out for an exquisite day-flying moth. Crimson speckled is stunningly white, generously blotched red, yellow and black. A rarity in northern Europe, it is delightfully common at this westernmost protrusion of our continent.

of **Cabo de São Vicente** headland (☀ 37.023312, -8.996988) – a good option in rough conditions. For waders and other waterbirds, check out **Lagoa do Martinhal** (beware: sometimes dry!), southeast of Sagres (☀ 37.020014, -8.927768).

SUGGESTED BASES The town of Sagres is the logical base.

MAKE IT A WEEK Go **diving** off **Sagres** with Marilimitado. Visit the **Alentejo** steppe of Castro Verde for great and little bustards (page 48). Base yourself around Tavira to explore the wetlands of the eastern **Algarve** for Audouin's and slender-billed gulls, greater flamingo and little bittern (page 202). Keep your eye out for monarch butterflies anywhere – possibly freshly arrived in from North America!

FLEXIBILITY Seabirds: July to November; raptors: late August to early November; dolphin: year-round; crimson speckled: May to November.

TITBITS Seabirds are best after strong onshore winds. Visible migration of landbirds is best after easterlies. **Oriole Birding** (⌲ oriolebirding.com; see ad, page 235) run birding tours here.

Bloomin' marvellous

WHERE Chania and Rethymno, Crete, Greece
TARGETS Autumn buttercup, sea daffodil, Greek cyclamen, Cretan wild goat, ocellated skink
ACCESSIBILITY ④
CHILD-FRIENDLINESS ③

Northwestern Europe in October. Summer's bouquet is the faintest of scents in an olfactory memory bank. It is not merely hard-nosed botanists who crave spring's floral resurgence. We mere mortals do, too. Flowering plants mean vibrancy, mean vitality, mean life. Help, fortunately, is at hand. Or, rather, at hand four hours flight away, in western Crete, at the opposite extremity of Europe.

This is the second time that a plant-led break in western Crete features in this guide (page 64). Not only that but two of April's sites appear in the itinerary. But that's where the similarities stop. The spring visit is largely about orchids. This autumn trip concerns cyclamens, crocuses and daffodils. The colours differ; so too the textures, sizes, shapes. And that's distinct enough an experience to chivvy you through the long, flower-free winter.

Which blooms you muster – and particularly in what profusion – depends on how recently it has rained. After an arid summer, Crete's plants respond rapidly to the falling of their life source, flowering within days of the ground being dampened. Start the weekend on familiar terrain at Spili Bumps. These limestone hillocks swell

66 This weekend's most beautiful flower holds aloft subtly pink petals like an angel's wings 99

GEZA FARKAS/D

▲ Greek cyclamen are a floral highlight of autumnal Crete.

reassuringly from the green-again landscape. As you approach, an ocellated skink slouches on a rock, sunbasking lethargically. The lizard doesn't budge an inch as you admire the spotted skin that justifies the reptile's name. A clouded yellow colours the air briefly, before wending onwards.

At ground level, you spot the delicate twirls of autumn lady's-tresses – your final flourish of orchidelirium this year. The weekend's first crocus, *Crocus laevigatus*, drips delicate lilac flowers that are boldly veined purple. It grows only in Crete. Another diminutive crocus, *Colchicum pusillum*, pockmarks the ground with pale pink, its petals long and narrow, the flower overall star-shaped. More common is the pretty little blue-and-white *Solenopsis minuta* and – at last a plant granted an English name! – the gloriously yellow autumn buttercup.

Spend the rest of the day taking a comparative breather from botany before tomorrow's floral extravaganza. Head to Samariá Gorge for breathtaking scenery, the chance of lammergeier but the certainty of red-billed chough and griffon vulture, for ancient cypress trees that the wind has insisted grow squat and horizontal, and for a markedly special mammal. Samariá is the best place to see Cretan wild goat (*agrimi* in Cretan, although often erroneously called *krikri*). The subspecies you'll find here (*cretica*) occurs nowhere else in the world, yet hunting has traumatised its population to within a few hundred animals of extinction. For the best chance of seeing it, traverse the hillside along European long distance path E4 and scan the slopes. The animals may be hard to spot, but persistence should pay off.

Botanising on the beach: sea daffodils are dune specialists. ▲

Start day two on Crete's northern coast, at Kolymvari. Sand dunes here provide habitat for sea holly (a muted complex of greys, purples and blues) and sea daffodil (delightfully ivory, with a heady scent), some of which should still be in flower.

> **The subspecies of wild goat found here (*cretica*) occurs nowhere else in the world**

Check sea spurge for the strikingly ocellated caterpillars of spurge hawk-moth. Finally, wander east along the beach looking for remains of this year's (now-vacated) loggerhead turtle nests. With sensitive management of pressure from beachgoers, this globally threatened marine reptile will hopefully have enjoyed a profitable breeding season.

Then head south to the hamlet of Marathokefala, which holds an astonishing collection of special plants and quite some variety of insects. Solar-yellow goblets of *Sternbergia lutea* splash the road verges. As you walk, an Egyptian grasshopper flicks up at your tread. It's huge! Under olives and on rocky garrigue above the village Greek cyclamen flourishes. Arguably this weekend's most beautiful flower, it holds aloft subtly pink petals like an angel's wings. A swallowtail laces past. The tall spikes of sea squill – white flowers cascading around a purple stem – are prominent. Autumn squill – less closely related than its name suggests – is here in numbers too, hazing the ground with lilac. A praying mantis sways goodbye.

And so to Topolia, half-an-hour further inland. A village rather than a hamlet, but no less flower-rich than Marathokefala. Explore the rocky, scrubby hillside around Agios Thomas chapel. Sweet-smelling *Narcissus serotinus* – a tiny daffodil – rug the ground in white. Another wan-pink cyclamen (*confusum*) proliferates here,

GETTING THERE Nearest airport is Chania (⌕ chania-airport.com), which takes scheduled flights from Athens plus direct charters from north/west European cities.
WHERE TO GO From Chania, take the E75 east to Rethymno, then road 97 south to Spili. In Spili, head northeast on the road to Gerakari. **Spili Bumps** is opposite an old taverna. Just beyond the wooded stream, park at ☀ 35.214111, 24.567214, then walk south then west. At **Samariá Gorge** (⌕ samaria.gr, ⌕ samarianationalpark.wordpress.com), walk 2km east along the E4 path from Xyloskalo car park (☀ 35.308163, 23.918194) towards Neroutsiko (⌕ tinyurl.com/ep4-agrimi). Explore dunes behind **Kolymbari beach** (☀ 35.540107, 23.789838 and either side) for specialist plants. **Marathokefala** is 2km south. Park at the church (☀ 35.524979, 23.775356), then wander around the hamlet, into the hillside to the northwest then south along the road towards Spilia. About 30 minutes' drive away is **Topolia**. The best area is around Agrio Thomas chapel, 1km southwest of the village

so too further *Colchicum pusillum*. Above you, griffon vultures circle, tasting the air for death; they roost nearby in Agia Sofia cave.

It is not only flowers that you will miss this coming winter. Those solar-powered insects – dragonflies – also absent themselves. So profit from Crete's warm, sunny afternoons by culminating your trip at Agia Lake. Balkan green lizards scurry around rocks, Balkan terrapins sprawl in the shallows. A little bittern beats past, a little crake potters damply. And dragons populate the air above. Vagrant emperor is the biggest and meanest: black with a token band of blue. Scarlet darter is the most fiery and flirtatious: crimson and intense. And eastern willow spreadwing is the daintiest and rarest: a reminder that even on an unambiguously botanical trip, you should pay heed to the diversity of life.

(✳ 35.524979, 23.775356). **Agia Lake** (⌀ crete-birding.co.uk/agialake.htm) is 7km southwest of Chania, north of Agia. Park by Enasma Café (✳ 35.477131, 23.931258) or Agia Lake restaurant (✳ 35.478974, 23.932513) and watch from the lakeside path.
SUGGESTED BASES Chania has varied accommodation (⌀ tinyurl.com/chania-acc). Small hotels in Kolyambari would make a nice alternative.
MAKE IT A WEEK Imbros Gorge for Cretan dittany and other rare plants. The tiny island of **Elafonisi** for sea daffodil and spurge hawk-moth. The ruins of **Aptera** for Cretan wall lizard and ocellated skink. **Rodopou Peninsula** for extensive swathes of cyclamen. **Omalos Plateau** for more cyclamen and *Colchicum cretense* amid fruiting shrubs of Cretan maple, berberis and zelkova. **Akotiri Peninsula** for friar's cowl, autumn squill, *Narcissus* and more.
FLEXIBILITY Plants: September to October (depending on rains); goat: year-round; skink: March to November.

Cretan wild goat has suffered so badly from hunting that only a few hundred remain. ▲

The water in Mallorca

WHERE North Mallorca, Spain
TARGETS Eleonora's falcon, Balearic warbler, marbled duck, violet dropwing, Ibiza wall lizard
ACCESSIBILITY ④
CHILD-FRIENDLINESS ⑤

'The wa'a in Maj-orka don' tas'e loik wot it oughta.' OK, so you need to be of a certain vintage to remember the 1985 Heineken beer commercial. But once seen, this particular advertising classic is never forgotten. Rather like Mallorca itself.

The Balearic's largest island has a reputation for being the quintessential Club Med, bleeding badly behaved northern Europeans seeking cheap fun in never-ending sun. I well remember the look of concern rushing over my parents' face when my sister elected to celebrate finishing school with a week in Magaluf (renowned for misdemeanours and more). This weekend explores another side to Mallorca – the real island, I reckon – full of fabulous scenery and stippled with brilliant wildlife-watching locations that crave your attention.

Given that your plane will arrive in Palma, Mallorca's capital, start with a city-centre sightseeing trip. Flanking the Mediterranean, the Gothic cathedral of La Seu stands proudly, its nave higher than that of Notre Dame in Paris. At their base, the sacred walls offers safe haven for Moorish gecko and, notably, Ibiza wall lizard. As the latter's name suggests, this reptile occurs naturally elsewhere amid the Balearic archipelago, but it has been introduced here. This robust lizard is renowned for each insular population being a different colour. There are green lizards and blue ones. And turquoise, orange and yellow as well as the more expected brown. Is this Darwin's-finch-esque evolution happening, right in front of our tourist eyes?

Leave behind Palma's cold-blooded life to spend the weekend in northern Mallorca. From the northern tourist town of Port de Pollença, walk along Boquer Valley towards the sea. Ravens croak overhead as crag martins flirt with a cliff face. A blue rock thrush sallies upwards and outwards, before an Egyptian vulture slides silently between crag and plain. As you sight the sea, your chances of encountering the scrubby valley's special bird burgeon. Following up harsh tacking calls should eventually lead you to a Balearic warbler. Recently deemed a separate species from the Marmora's warbler of Corsica (page 68) and Sardinia (page 60), this spiky, blue-grey, fire-eyed insectivore should show well if you demonstrate patience.

66

99

An Eleonora's falcon eyeing up opportunities for predation. ▲

Return to Port de Pollença, then take the narrow, generously hairpinned road northeast to Cap Formentor. Below the lighthouse, sandy-grey cliffs tumble and jag into the sea. This is the domain – the *element* – of Mallorca's most famous bird of prey. Sharp, slender wings mark out the colonial, cliff-nesting Eleonora's falcon from peregrines that also thrive here.

Few Northern-Hemisphere birds breed as late as Eleonora's, a characteristic interwoven with its equally unusual shift in diet. The falcon is routinely an insectivore, but – during its autumnal breeding season – switches to 'harvesting' migrant songbirds as they fly south for the winter. Making the most of this seasonal bounty, Eleonora's falcon caches dead birds for later consumption. Remarkably, scientists recently discovered that the raptor also creates a living larder of imprisoned, immobile birds from which it has ripped both wings and tail.

To see the falcon at its best, take a boat trip around Cap Formentor to Cala Sant Vicenç. Small groups swirl and scythe around the sea cliffs. One bird breaks off to dash out over the sea. Here, incredibly, it snatches an unsuspecting migrating warbler, its epic journey into Africa abruptly curtailed.

Spend day two investigating one or both of northern Mallorca's two most renowned wetland reserves, which lie south of Port d'Alcúdia. S'Albufera marsh is the largest and best known, but aficionados profess a sneaky preference for its quieter little brother, S'Albufereta. The latter is quieter and better for a quick visit (pre-breakfast, say, if you are on a family holiday); the former, on balance, hosts better wildlife.

Whichever you start with, birds demand your attention. On the beach, an Audouin's gull chills and Kentish plovers scurry. Egrets, spoonbills and glossy ibises sift the marshland shallows. A red-knobbed coot bobs, bizarre crimson marbles adorning its forehead. A marsh harrier drifts over reedbeds, a night heron dozes in a tree. If you're lucky, a moustached warbler may scold you from a well-concealed hideout. Purple swamphens – more chicken than crake – lumber through dense vegetation. Scan carefully through hordes of wildfowl for marbled duck. Not much to look at ('subtly attractive', if you're feeling generous), this bird's interest lies in its rarity. Wetland drainage during the 20th century removed up to half the duck's habitat, rendering it Globally Threatened.

Not every denizen of the pair of wetlands is on its way out, fortunately. A relatively recent colonist is one of Europe's most sumptuous dragonflies. The male violet dropwing is a vivid pinky-plum colour. One of tropical Africa's most abundant dragonflies, it first graced Europe in the late 1970s. Violet dropwing now ranges widely across the Mediterranean – always delighting, always thrilling, always refreshing the parts that other dragonflies cannot reach. I'll raise a longneck – Heineken, clearly – to that.

GETTING THERE Nearest (only!) airport is Palma de Mallorca (palmaairport.info), which takes numerous flights from many European cities. Port de Pollença (Puerto Pollensa) is 1 hour's drive away (67km).

WHERE TO GO In **Palma**, La Seu Cathedral is set back from the seafront road of Avinguda de Gabriel Roca (✳ 39.567202, 2.648369 catedraldemallorca.org). For **Boquer Valley**, park by the roundabout with the MA2200 on the northern outskirts of Port de Pollença (✳ 39.913035, 3.084088). Walk northwest through the *finca* (private farm; respect privacy), beyond twin boulders and pinebelt, to where the path descends through scrub to the cove. Once back at the MA2200 it is a 25-minute (15km) drive northeast to **Cap Formentor lighthouse**. *En route*, stop at miradors to scan for raptors and search scrub at km16 and km17 for Balearic warbler. For **S'Albufereta Natural Reserve**, park on Carrer Bartolomé Esteban Murillo, off the MA2220 northwest of Port d'Alcúdia (✳ 39.858988, 3.098932). Walk southwest through pines to view from a mound (✳ 39.856549, 3.097749). To explore the western part of the reserve, follow the itinerary at tinyurl.com/s-albufereta. **S'Albufera Natural Park** lies immediately south of Port d'Alcúdia. There are two areas to explore (both detailed at tinyurl.com/s-albufera). Park by the MA12 roundabout (✳ 39.799249, 3.119197), then walk west along Canal de Siurana. Or park by the waterworks (*depadura*; ✳ 39.775799, 3.114923) and view from the tower.

SUGGESTED BASES Ample tourist accommodation: Port de Pollença and Port d'Alcúdia are convenient.

MAKE IT A WEEK Try for the endemic Lilford's wall lizard, which inhabits offshore islets and, on the mainland, **Colonia de Sant Jordi** harbour. Explore the **Tramuntana Mountains**, including Cúber Reservoir, for raptors. **Port de Pollença** harbour excels for Audouin's gull. The coastal heathland at **Son Real** is wonderful for Balearic warbler and Audouin's gull. **Salobrar de Campos** is good for waders.

FLEXIBILITY Warbler: year-round but spring best; falcon and dropwing: May to October; duck: year-round; lizard: February to November.

TITBITS Several websites offer excellent, detailed information and itineraries for birdwatching in Mallorca. These include birdinginspain.com, birdingmajorca.com and mallorcabirdwatching.com. Companies offering **boat trips** around Formentor include Lanchas La Gaviota (lanchaslagaviota. com/en/formentor-point). Such waterborne excursions offer a very different way to watch Eleonora's falcon, and you may even spot one hunting migrating songbirds over the sea.

JOSH JONES

As its name suggests, Balearic warbler is a local speciality on Mallorca. ▶

189

Keep calm and carrion

WHERE Aragón and Catalonia, Spain
TARGETS Griffon vulture, glossy ibis, purple swamphen, Audouin's gull, slender-billed gull
ACCESSIBILITY ⑤
CHILD-FRIENDLINESS ④

Feet stomp, wings raise, necks snake, eyes lock. Neither protagonist in this duel is backing down. There is one piece of meat, and both griffon vultures want it. A scuffle breaks out; sharp claws and mammoth beak are readied. Finally, one backs down, shuffling a return to the crowd of feather. The dust settles.

66 Rather than the villains of cliché, vultures are the ultimate goodies – nature's clean-up crew 99

ROB WILLIAMS

▲ Feeding time for Mas de Buñyol's seething morass of griffon vultures.

Each morning, *pastor de buitres* ('vulture priest') José Ramón Moragrega heaves a wheelbarrow brimming with carcasses, off-cuts and offal into a chestnut-coloured arena flanked by tiring trees and backed by looming cliffs. Up to 400 griffon vultures have been waiting – increasingly restlessly following initial patience – on Mas de Buñyol's mounds of earth.

Now they descend in a flap of urgent wings and bounce across the ground towards Moragrega. He dumps scarlet meat on the ground, where it disappears beneath the stampede – and then vanishes completely as the famished birds gobble every last morsel. You and a score of fellow visitors gawp from your ringside seats in an observatory and two hides. Camera shutters machine-gun in exultation.

Within half-an-hour, showtime is over. Vulture breakfasts are as brief and intense as they are messy and hectic. Little remains of the contents of Moragrega's wheelbarrow. The odd feather tumbleweeds – the legacy of that vulturine skirmish. Sated scavengers repair to nearby perches, digesting and dozing. This grants you time to contemplate the significance – and fragility – of what you have observed.

In the early noughties, the European Union outlawed farmers' traditional practice of leaving out livestock carcasses for vultures to 'clean', arguing that this could spread disease. Vultures starved; their populations slumped. To its credit, the Spanish government then rectified this unintended consequence. Official feeding stations such as Mas de Buñyol were established. Griffon vulture numbers are now recovering – and vulture-based tourism is burgeoning. But there's a new cloud on the Mediterranean horizon – and one that could sluice away Europe's vultures entirely.

In recent years, and despite vociferous opposition from conservation groups, the notorious veterinary drug diclofenac has been licensed for use in Spain and Italy. If vultures feed on the corpses of livestock treated with this anti-inflammatory drug, they die. Diclofenac caused the recent massive decline in African and Asian vultures. Eleven of those regions' 12 vulture species are at serious risk of extinction. (The twelfth only escapes because it is vegetarian and thus unaffected.) In several of the 11, for every 100 vultures around half-a-century ago, there is just one today.

This matters – and not just because extinction is forever. Vultures are nature's clean-up crew. By consuming carcasses, they limit the transfer of lurgies from dead animals into human communities. Accordingly, each vulture saves African governments US$11,000 per year in waste-disposal and disease-treatment costs. The unchecked spread of disease resulting from the near-extinction of vultures is costing India US$1.5 billion per year. The financial benefits may not be so evident in the more sanitary conditions of Europe, but the principle remains. Rather than the villains of cliché, vultures are actually the ultimate goodies. We misunderstand vultures – and legitimise diclofenac – at our own peril.

If this has made you despondent, frustrated or angry, cheer yourself up by heading east to the Catalan coast. Over the centuries, the Ebro Delta's sand bars, shingle and saltmarsh have created Spain's second-largest wetland (after Coto Doñana in Andalucía). Surprisingly remote in feel for an area so close to Barcelona, Ebro offers outstanding birdwatching.

The Delta is renowned for its 'long legs' – lissome waterbirds. In addition to supermodel-like black-winged stilts, there are large breeding populations of little bittern, squacco heron, night heron and purple heron. Many remain through autumn, when great white egrets join them. A dramatic recent arrival – the bird was unknown here on my first visit in 1994 – is glossy ibis. Thousands of pairs now breed; flocks of hundreds wade around the ricefields. The purple swamphen population has also exploded, with scores now turning fields a shimmering blue.

Although more than half the delta has disappeared under rice cultivation, some paddies are attractive to herons, ducks and waders. For a cracking visit, combine these with a couple of lagoons and reedbeds. Be warned though that it is easy to lose one's way here. It is best to prioritise exploration of a few key sites.

I suggest majoring on the Delta south of the Río Ebro. Start at L'Encayissada lagoon then move east to La Tancada lake and nearby salt pans. This area is particularly good for two genuinely gorgeous gulls, Audouin's and slender-billed. Riet Vell is a must-visit, as it is a demonstration farm for organic rice-growing. The paddies here really do hold more birds than elsewhere. Then explore east from Sant Jaume d'Enveja to Isla de Buda and Gola de Migjorn. If you have time, head up to the northern Delta, visiting the western shore of El Fangar. Here, with the evening sun at your back, you can end your weekend of vulture culture with close-up views of waders, gulls and terns. *Magnífico!*

▲ Purple swamphen – or purple swamp chicken, as birders affectionately call it.

JAMES LOWEN

GETTING THERE There is little choose between the airports of Zaragoza, Barcelona and Valencia ($\lozenge$ aena.es/es/pasajeros/red-aeropuertos). Each are 2–2¾ hours (140–240km) drive from the weekend›s two destinations, which lie 1¼ hours (80km) apart. There are regular flights, including on low-cost airlines, to all three airports.

WHERE TO GO Mas de Buñyol ($\lozenge$ www.masdebunyol.com; ❋ 40.842831, 0.158786) is 4km south of Valderrobres. Heading north along the A1414, 0.8km before Valderrobres, you reach Torre Sancho industrial estate on your left. Turn sharp right here. Bear left at the first fork, then right at the second. Approx 0.6km from the A1414, turn left. Continue 2km to the farmhouse, which is connected to the vulture-observation area by a tunnel. As well as griffons, vultures present sometimes include cinereous, Egyptian and even lammergeier. East of the AP7 motorway, Deltebre forms the gateway to the **Ebro Delta Natural Park** ($\lozenge$ tinyurl.com/ebro-spanish). Follow signposts to information centres at Deltebre (northern side of the delta) and Casa de Fusta (by L'Encanyissada in the south). There are several viewing platforms. In the south, **L'Encayissada** (also called El Clot on maps; ❋ 40.660022, 0.662990) is best viewed from the causeway north of Poble Nou village and from roads along the lake's northern side. Scan the east of **La Tancada** lake from Camí de Baladres (❋ 40.643892, 0.754721). Drive the sandy track south towards El Trubucador (❋ 40.620998, 0.735122) and onwards to view **La Trinitat** salt pans. **Riet Vell** organic rice farm is north of the TV3405, 0.5km west of L'Eucaliptus ($\lozenge$ tinyurl.com/riet-vell; ❋ 40.659282, 0.774691). From the TV4303/4304 junction at Sant Jaume d'Enveja (❋ 40.704019, 0.717226), head east to **Illha de Buda** (❋ 40.707557, 0.847645) and **Gola de Migjorn** (❋ 40.685956, 0.853130). In the northern Delta, view **El Fangar** bay from the southern shoreline along a road that runs from Lo Goleró (❋ 40.778359, 0.720297) to ❋ 40.762791, 0.757986.

SUGGESTED BASES Spend a night at **Mas de Buñyol** itself, where the restored farmhouse offers 6 rooms and unlimited access to the vulture hide. Then overnight in the Ebro Delta, where I prefer Poble Nou del Delta to Deltebre.

MAKE IT A WEEK The Ebro Delta is larger than you think. You could easily spend 4–5 days exploring it. A guide to birding the Ebro is at $\lozenge$ tinyurl.com/ebro-itineraries.

FLEXIBILITY Vulture: April to June and October to November are the best months; others: year-round.

TITBITS To learn more about efforts to save Europe's vultures see $\lozenge$ 4vultures.org and $\lozenge$ banvetdiclofenac.com.

Slender-billed gull is among the Ebro Delta's star birds. ▲

JAMES LOWEN

Blue-sky finching

WHERE Tenerife, Canary Islands, Spain
TARGETS Short-finned pilot whale, Tenerife blue chaffinch, white-tailed laurel pigeon, Atlantic canary, Teide viper's-bugloss
ACCESSIBILITY ③
CHILD-FRIENDLINESS ④

The mightiest of Spain's Canary Islands, Tenerife is a schizophrenic destination. As the urban sprawl along its southern coast testifies, this is package-holiday central. For wildlife-watchers, however, Tenerife is Europe's answer to the Galápagos – the famed Ecuadorian islands where isolation fostered evolution and Charles Darwin ransacked the way we comprehend the world.

Four in every ten types of plants growing on Tenerife does so nowhere else in the world. The same is true of a score of birds – eight regionally endemic species, complemented by 14 'subspecies' (a finer taxonomic grade). There is even a butterfly that occurs only within the volcanic caldera that squats beneath the towering, conical El Teide, a 3,700 metre-high peak that dominates the entire island.

It is in the hinterland of El Teide that you commence the weekend. Depending on where you overnighted, start proceedings amidt arid pine forest at Las Lajas or Pinar de Chío picnic sites, or in the exuberant botanical scrub behind El Portillo visitors' centre. These are prime sites for Tenerife blue chaffinch, which, as its name

▲ Fewer than 5,000 Tenerife blue chaffinches are thought to exist – all on the eponymous island.

suggests, is endemic to this single island. If you can't spot one instantly, peek beneath picnic tables, where Carolina-blue males and earthily toned females clean up crumbs.

> **Atlantic canaries – ancestors of birds bred to go down t'pit – are delightfully common**

Spend an hour or so at these sites and other special birds should materialise – often apparating from disconcertingly scant cover. A high-pitched call alerts you to the arrival of a 'Tenerife' goldcrest, which some ornithologists fancy as a full species. Atlantic canaries – the ancestors of the birds bred to go down t'pit, there to rejoice naively from within cages – are delightfully common. Canary Islands chiffchaffs (svelte warblers) and African blue tits (clumsily Photoshopped equivalents of our familiar garden denizens, with oversaturated colours and a surfeit of contrast) add themselves to the roll call of specialities, as do local endemic subspecies of raven and great spotted woodpecker.

As day-trippers arrive to break bread or fry meat, depart upwards to Cañadas del Teide. To do so, you may well pass through a belt of mid-altitude cloud before emerging back into the sun. Journey across the caldera floor, passing solidified lava flows and admiring endemic plants such as Teide broom and, particularly, the 3-metre-tall Teide viper's-bugloss. What a plant! Then go up in the world, taking the cable car to the summit of Spain's loftiest mountain for a high-altitude sundowner. What views!

Start day two early, for your target bird in the lush laurel forest of northeast Tenerife can turn skittish once picnickers descend on Llano los Viejos. The often mist-shrouded Anaga Mountains are home to Bolle's pigeon, which occurs solely in the Canaries. You need sharp eyes though, as these birds typically perch motionless in trees upslope from the car park. As you search, you will doubtless come across Canarian twists on three familiar birds from 'back home'. The local versions of blackbird, robin and chaffinch are all at least subtly different from those in our gardens.

Such rich habitat – and such a contrast from yesterday's desiccated landscape – merits at least an extra hour of exploration. So wander the trails in search of Tenerife lizard, plants such as golden houseleek, and butterflies including archipelago endemics such as Canary large white, Canary speckled wood and Canary red admiral. Canary this, and Canary that… this archipelago is very special indeed. If you haven't before, are you getting the Galápagos vibe now?

The bird from which the Canary Islands take their name: Atlantic canary. ▲

Assuming the day remains young, head an hour west along Tenerife's northern coast. The roads are surprisingly quick, and the distances short, so you soon arrive at Mirador de la Grimona, a viewpoint adjoining the busy carriageway. To the north, land tumbles precipitously seawards. Resist the temptation to gaze towards the watery blueness (its time will come, don't worry) and instead face southwards and scan upwards. An even steeper slope, intermittently flecked with laurel forest, rises to sheer cliffs. This is the domain of another scarce endemic, white-tailed laurel pigeon. It should not take many minutes for you to spot several loafing in naked trees or bustling between feeding grounds.

Now it is time to take to the water. First, call in at the *piscinas naturales* at Garachio. The lava-black rocks separating these tidal swimming pools burn with red rock crabs, a crustacean that swiftly brings to mind the Sally Lightfoot crabs that adorn similar habitat in (where else but) the Galápagos. Then head further west to Los Gigantes, a tourist town with a stunning beach that is also the island's whale-watching capital.

Tenerife adopts a leisurely approach to seeing marine leviathans. You venture barely a mile offshore, through invariably calm waters. Similarly guaranteed is the target cetacean. Short-finned pilot whales are rotund, gregarious and inquisitive creatures. Several groups live year-round in the narrow channel separating Tenerife from La Gomera; seeing them is a cinch. You also have a more-than-fair chance of being bow-ridden by common bottlenose and Atlantic spotted dolphins. After this culmination to such a wildlife-infused weekend, I wager that your preconceptions of Tenerife will be a thing of the past.

GETTING THERE Two international airports, with numerous scheduled and charter flights to many European cities: Tenerife Sur (⊘ tinyurl.com/ten-sur) and Tenerife Norte (⊘ tinyurl.com/ten-nor).

WHERE TO GO Several sites are in or around **Teide National Park** (useful map, including walking trails, at ⊘ tinyurl.com/teide-map), reputedly Europe's most-visited national park. If you approach Teide from the west (Chirche), go birding at **Pinar (or Merendero) de Chío** picnic site south of the TF-38 (✳ 28.267276, -16.746565). Approaching from the south (along the TF-21 from Vilaflor), stop at **Las Lajas** *area recreativa* (✳ 28.191048, -16.665205). **El Portillo** visitors' centre is just southwest of the TF-21/TF-24 junction (✆ +34 922 92 23 71); try the drinking pool in the botanical gardens behind the building (✳ 28.305463, -16.566910). **El Teide cable car** is at ✳ 28.254916, -16.625860 (⊘ tinyurl.com/teide-cable). In the Anaga Mountains, **Llano los Viejos** (✳ 28.526463, -16.285055) lies 1.5km northeast of Las Mercedes. Explore the picnic site then walk uphill to the viewpoint. **Mirador de la Grimona** (✳ 28.392750, -16.608821) lies two tunnels west of Puerto de la Cruz along the TF-5.

NICK UPTON/NPL

Garachio (✳ 28.373284, -16.766243) is 3km west of Icod de los Vinos. **(Acantilados de) Los Gigantes** (✳ 28.247532, -16.840238) lies 2.5km by road west of the TF-1/TF-82 junction. The local whale-watching provider is ⌂ whalesanddolphinsoftenerife.org.

SUGGESTED BASES Abundant tourist accommodation along the coast (⌂ webtenerife. co.uk/where-stay) plus *casas rurales* (⌂ casasrurales.net/casas-rurales/tenerife).

MAKE IT A WEEK Go star-gazing on **Mt Teide** (⌂ volcanoteide.com). Or hike to the summit (permit needed: ⌂ tinyurl.com/teide-permit). Alternatively, walk the many trails, looking for plants, butterflies and Berthelot's pipit. The **Anaga Mountains** offer a full week of walks. Watch short-finned pilot whales from the **ferry to La Gomera**, then explore that island's lush forests for both rare pigeons. Go snorkelling or diving off **Los Gigantes** (⌂ divingtenerife.co.uk).

FLEXIBILITY Year-round. Plants and butterflies are best in spring.

TITBITS A useful tourist-information brochure about Tenerife wildlife is at ⌂ tinyurl.com/ tenerife-nature. The Crossbill guide *Canary Islands – II* is a font of wildlife-focused information. **Bird Holidays** (⌂ birdholidays.co.uk; see ad, page 237) run a wide-ranging Canaries tour.

Lest you think flowers are small, enter the towering Teide viper's-bugloss. ▲

The greyhound of the sea

WHERE Counties Cork, plus Clare or Kerry, Ireland
TARGETS Fin whale, humpback whale, short-beaked common dolphin, common bottlenose dolphin, Atlantic grey seal
ACCESSIBILITY ③
CHILD-FRIENDLINESS ⑤

We've been looking, searching, questing for an hour now, and – to be frank – we're all starting to get cold, get bored and lose the faith. Colin Barnes, skipper of the *Holly Jo*, appears unperturbed. The leaden sea is barely riffled, the breeze insubstantial and the sky sombre – perfect conditions for whale-watching off County Cork. It should be just a matter of time – and sharp eyes.

'Blow! Starboard! Halfway to the horizon!'

Barnes slips the boat into gear – or whatever nautical skippers do to get things moving – and we're off, to the starboard, towards the horizon. The 'blow' is the dense exhalation of water vapour from a surfacing cetacean, in this instance specifically a 'rorqual' or baleen whale. That the shimmering cloud is markedly taller than it is wide, columnar rather than mushroom-shaped, hints strongly at the breather's identity. 'Fin whale?', someone ventures.

❝ Leaden sea, sombre sky... perfect for whale-watching ❞

BALTIMORE SEA SAFARI

▲ Participants on a Baltimore Sea Safari enjoy a close encounter with a humpback whale.

As we approach, the blow appears again, and with it, the leviathan. Its back is the colour of unoxidised iron, rather than jet black. The dorsal fin is pronounced and pointed, rather than insignificant and lumpy. The animal rolls and rolls and rolls before slipping underwater without flirting its tail flukes. My fellow passenger is correct: this is a fin whale rather than a humpback. But whether she is right or wrong, this experience is magical.

Barnes cuts the engine and we drift, giving the whale a couple of hundred metres berth. Every minute or two, it surfaces, exhales, rolls, and returns to watery concealment. Then it returns no more. It is gone – and rapidly too – plumbing the depths elsewhere. Not for nothing is the world's second-largest creature nicknamed the 'greyhound of the sea'.

Only relatively recently has Ireland squirmed its way into whale-watching consciousness. This appears to correlate with a genuine increase in the abundance of cetaceans off the southern and western coastlines, rather than merely greater awareness of their existence. In 2016, the Irish Whale and Dolphin Group collated 117 reports of humpback whales – one hundred more than five years previously.

Ireland offers two complementary approaches to watching whales; you have time this weekend to combine them. The first, as with well-established cetacean-watching destinations such as Iceland and the Azores, is to join a boat trip. Cork Whale Watch is one of a few operators in the county.

The second is to park yourself on a south- or west-facing headland – Old Head of Kinsale, Galley Head and Cape Clear Island stand out – and scan rhythmically across the sea through binoculars or a telescope. After an initial check with the

Curious and cute, an Atlantic grey seal bobs in the swell. ▲

CUBANJUNKY/D

naked eye, start scanning with optics at one end of the horizon, working your way slowly to the other side. Repeat the process, this time scanning slightly closer to shore, until you have covered the whole expanse. At first you may see nothing more than the odd Atlantic grey seal, head bobbing lethargically.

Should you spot something odd – a shadow or sudden glint, disturbance in the water, puff of sea spray or the like – keep a tight watch for several minutes. Another tip is to scan for a frenzy of feeding seabirds, most frequently gannet but occasionally Manx shearwater. This indicates a concentration of fish, usually sand eels, which are often being herded by one of more large whales.

GETTING THERE Nearest airport is Cork (⊘ corkairport.com). There are flights from several UK and European cities. From the airport it is 75 minutes' (73km) drive along the N71 to Union Hall or 1¾ hours (94km) to Baltimore, and 2½ hours (195km) to Kilrush on the Shannon Estuary. **WHERE TO GO** Land-based whale-watching locations in County Cork include the promontories of **Old Head of Kinsale** (✹ 51.604414, -8.533872), **Galley Head** (✹ 51.529359, -8.955909) and **Cape Clear Island** (✹ 51.427588, -9.526673 ⊘ capeclearisland.ie). Cape Clear is reached by a ferry from **Baltimore** (✹ 51.483005, -9.373860), where **whale-watching boat trips** are run by Whale Watch West Cork (⊘ whalewatchwestcork.com) and Baltimore Sea Safari (⊘ baltimoreseasafari.ie). Cork Whale Watch (⊘ corkwhalewatch.com) departs from further east, at **Reen Pier** (✹ 51.528781, -9.166320), 4km southwest of Union Hall. To see 'Fungie', visit **Dingle Harbour** (County Kerry). Walk southeast from Dingle Skellig Hotel (✹ 52.133627, -10.268557) to view from Dingle Lighthouse (✹ 52.121397, -10.258232) or Sláidín beach, Alternatively, venture on to the water with Dingle Dolphin Boat Tours (⊘ dingledolphin. com). Another habituated (if grumpier) common bottlenose dolphin is Dusty, which frequents

▲ Dingle Harbour's long-staying attraction, 'Fungie' the common bottlenose dolphin.

Any time of year can produce exciting cetacean-watching off Ireland. Spring and early summer sees the arrival of minke whales (which stay, in gradually diminishing numbers, until December), with harbour porpoise and small groups of short-beaked common dolphin. Humpback whales (that most aeronautical of cetaceans) are the next to turn up, followed by fin whales, with both species – plus short-beaked common dolphins – building up to a late-autumn peak. As their prey (herring and sprat) moves closer inshore towards winter, so the whales follow. The closer the better, from the watcher's perspective.

On your second day, focus on getting good views of common bottlenose dolphins. You could pay homage to 'Fungie', the habituated (but still entirely wild) dolphin that has frequented Dingle Harbour (County Kerry) for upwards of 30 years. So much a fixture is Fungie, that he even has his own booking office on the quayside. You can watch him from the Lighthouse or Sláidín beach, at the eastern mouth of Dingle Harbour. Alternatively, hour-long boat trips leave throughout the day.

Such a nailed-on experience with a dolphin that has its own Facebook page might not be to everyone's taste. If you fall into this camp, and fancy the frisson of finding your 'own' dolphins, try the Shannon Estuary (County Clare). The resident population here – just one of four Europe-wide – numbers 130-odd, so chances of seeing them are high – but they certainly crave human attention less than Fungie. Local operators offer boat trips to track them down. Alternatively you can scan from shore, particularly from Kilcredaun Point, near Carrigaholt. When it comes to cetaceans on the Emerald Isle, you always have options.

Doolin and **Fanore** (County Clare; ⊘ dustythedolphin.com). At the **Shannon Estuary**, take a boat trip with Dolphin Discovery in Kilrush (⊘ discoverdolphins.ie) or Dolphinwatch Carrigaholt (⊘ dolphinwatch.ie). Alternatively, view from land at Kilcredaun Point (✳ 52.579944, -9.709886), 3km south of Carrigaholt.

SUGGESTED BASES The city of Cork would make a logical base, although you may want to relocate, to Limerick say, if you head to the Shannon Estuary.

MAKE IT A WEEK Do another boat trip or spend another day seawatching off a County Cork headland. Take a **boat trip** to look for Risso's dolphin (and other species) around the Blasket islands and Dingle Peninsula (⊘ marinetours.ie). It's out of (botanical) season for **The Burren** (page 90) but that location provides special wanders whatever the time of year.

FLEXIBILITY Whales: August to January, but October to December best; short-beaked common dolphin: May to February; others: year-round.

TITBITS News of cetacean sightings spreads fast through the Irish Whale and Dolphin Group network (⊘ iwdg.ie).

NICK UPTON/NPL

Formosa: the Algarve in autumn

WHERE Algarve, Portugal
TARGETS European fiddler crab, Audouin's gull, Iberian water frog, Mediterranean chameleon, Moorish gecko
ACCESSIBILITY ⑤
CHILD-FRIENDLINESS ⑤

It may not quite be the Costa del Sol of neighbouring Spain (page 54), but the principle is similar. Concrete jungles ribboning the Mediterranean, existing to serve sun-craving tourists. Sounds horrible? Well… it's not. As well as resorts, Portugal's Algarve harbours internationally important tidal marshes that excel for birds and reptiles. By visiting – as the Algarve Tourism Board beseeches through nature-focused publications heavy in inspiration – you are helping the wilds resist the incursion of asphalt and breeze block. A sun-drenched, wildlife-rich, feel-good weekend? What's not to like?

Although arguably best in spring, my Algarve vote strikes an 'X' next to a late-autumn visit. Air temperatures nudge 20°C, the sea is balmier than in May, and the daily dose of seven hours sunshine bodes well for delaying the onset of mid-winter blues back home. Best of all, wherever you stay there will be a cracking wildlife-

△ A claw to stay well clear of: European fiddler crab.

watching site within an acceptably brief drive. Squeezing them all into a weekend may be a tight call, however.

Towards the western stretch of the Algarve, between the towns of Lagoa and Albufeira, Lagoa dos Salgados is an archetypal coastal lagoon. Shallow, fringed by aquatic vegetation and cordoned from the sea by soft dunes, it is also known as Sapal de Pêra. An afternoon visit is best, such that the sun shines from behind your viewpoint at the western edge of the lagoon.

> Weaving between luxury accommodation and golf courses makes for incongruous wildlife-watching

Splashes of candy-pink quickly entice your eye towards greater flamingos. Spoonbills sway their spatulate beaks rhythmically through the water. Leggy shadows transpire to be glossy ibis. Hefty, clumsy, iridescent blue footballs confess their identity as purple swamphen. Scan numerous wildfowl for the globally threatened ferruginous duck. Waders scurry, totter and stride: among others, look for Kentish plover, wood sandpiper and ruff. Thick rushes fringe the water, disguising sumptuous bluethroats. Normally skulking or otherwise sulking, eventually birds lose their inhibitions and prance, robin-like, in the open.

Heading along the coast east, almost as far as Faro airport, you arrive at Quinta do Lago, the Algarve's answer to Beverley Hills. Weaving between luxury accommodation and golf courses makes for incongruous wildlife-watching, but also means that birds and reptiles are uncommonly habituated to the passage of people. For photographers, this is a boon.

Prioritise time at Lagoa de São Lourenço. From the hide, you should see red-crested pochard, little bittern and purple swamphen. If the sun has warmed the air sufficiently, huddles of aquatic reptiles pockmark the muddy banks like hard-shelled cowpats. Spanish terrapin is the most common, with occasional European pond terrapin and even escaped red-eared sliders. Iberian water frogs abound in pretty much every freshwater pool or lake.

Black-headed weaver – a species native to Africa but introduced here – adds an unexpected glaze of yellow. Common waxbill makes the same gesture with crimson. Iberian magpies clad in baby-blue and pink flirt between parasol pines, well-named trees that characterise the coastal strip. Prolonged perusal of the tall scrub in this area may reveal the odd, neatly camouflaged Mediterranean chameleon climbing arthritically between branches.

JAMES LOWEN

Check walls after dark to see Moorish gecko. ▲

CARLOS N. G. BOCOS

The coast between Faro and Tavira is ostensibly spared development thanks to the designation of the Ria Formosa Natural Park. Tavira provides as good an access point as any to explore this beautiful (*formosa*) seaside. Scrub here and on the nearby Ilha de Tavira can provide hiding places for chameleons and stripeless tree frogs, although Moorish gecko favours stone walls. The latter are often tame particularly around human habitation: watch this spiky lizard for long enough and you may even see it lick its eyeball. Not many animals can do that.

The muddy creek fronting Santa Luzia's promenade is stippled with European fiddler crabs waving excitedly at you with their single over-sized claw. Excellent saltpans stretch east from here to Tavira, then south to Sítio das 4 Águas. These host abundant waders (including black-winged stilt but also passage migrants such as little stint) and greater flamingo, but the stars are three attractive gulls (yes, there are such things), each with a fiery red bill: Audouin's, slender-billed and Mediterranean.

Adult slender-billed gulls often show a sumptuously rosy wash to their breast. The species is also a speciality of saline lagoons at nearby Forte do Rato. This ruined monument – and indeed anywhere with scattered rocks – is a good place to search for a remarkable reptile: Maria's worm lizard. This is legless and has tiny, skin-covered eyes – adaptations to a life spent largely underground. To chance upon this pink, heavily scaled and – yes, ostensibly worm-like – animal, you will need to flip numerous stones and hope that one is secluded below, garnering heat from geology.

The marshes of Castro Marim signal both the easternmost extremity of the Algarve and your final exploration of the weekend. Saltpans rib-cage across the marshy ground and offer a similar suite of birds to that of other sites. Caspian terns hulk over the water, whilet an osprey targets larger fish. Drier areas are haunted by a small flock of little bustard. Encountering it will need fortune – but it is as *formosa* a bird as you will see anywhere in this brilliant coastal region.

▲ A Mediterranean conservation success story – Audouin's gull (with yellow-legged and lesser black-backed gulls too).

GETTING THERE Nearest airport is Faro (faro-airport.com), which takes flights including by low-cost airlines from several airports in northern Europe. All Algarve sites mentioned are within 30–45 minutes (45–65km) of the airport.

WHERE TO GO For **Lagoa dos Salgados** (aka Sapal de Pêra) leave Pêra south, following signs to Praia Grande. Park by the beach at ✳ 37.095729, -8.336487, then view from the western shore. **Quinto do Lago** is 2km northwest of Faro Airport. From Quinta de Lado, drive south along Avenida André Jordan. At the final roundabout, turn left onto Rua Douro. After 1.3km, follow the dirt track right to a parking area. Walk 500m east to the hide overlooking **Lagoa de São Lourenço** (✳ 37.024573, -8.011902). **Tavira** lies at the east end of **Ria Formosa Natural Park**. Key locations here are **Sítio das 4 Águas** (from Tavira follow Estrada das 4 south to ✳ 37.117600, -7.630861, then head southwest; boats depart hourly for Ilha de Tavira), **Santa Luzia** (east of the village, turn south off M515, signed Sopursal: ✳ 37.107335, -7.655345) and **Forte do Rato** (southeast of Tavira at ✳ 37.121444, -7.621143). At **Castro Marim**, explore south of the town, viewing from Cerro do Bufo saltpans (✳ 37.209484, -7.463586) and Sítio de Barquinha (✳ 37.197636, -7.427559).

SUGGESTED BASES Faro or Tavira (tavira.algarvetouristguide.com) are logical bases.

MAKE IT A WEEK Other areas in the Algarve to explore include coastal lagoons near **Vilamoura** and **Ria de Alvor**. The **Lower Guadiana**, north of Castro Marim, is good for black-winged kite. At the west end of the Algarve, look for reptiles and amphibians north of **Sagres** (page 178), including at Vila do Bispo and Carrapateira. Head north to **Castro Verde** for steppe species (page 48). Go east into Spain to explore the **Coto Doñana**.

FLEXIBILITY Reptiles: chameleon: February to November is best; others: year-round.

TITBITS The Algarve Tourist Board has produced an excellent and free guide to birdwatching in the region, detailing all major sites (tinyurl.com/guide-algarve). Another good online resource is wheretowatch.avesdeportugal.info.

Iberian water frogs are best admired at meniscus level, from within a pond. ▲

Parliament of owls

WHERE Kikinda, Vojvodina, Serbia
TARGETS Long-eared owl, short-eared owl, great grey shrike, hawfinch
ACCESSIBILITY ⑤
CHILD-FRIENDLINESS ③

We know *of* owls more keenly than we know them. We are acquainted with them through myth and story, yet our physical paths rarely cross in normal life. This Serbian weekend puts that right. It particularly celebrates one species of owl – long-eared – in homage to all owl-kind.

The allure of the owl is incontrovertible. As author Mike Unwin emphasises in his and photographer David Tipling's book *A Parliament of Owls*, 'encounters [with owls] are always special'. Owls have something – several things, actually – that sets them apart. First, they are enigmas, moving unseen, revealing their presence by disembodied voice. Further, they regale in a realm – night-time – that unsettles us, at best. Second, they are supreme hunters, with peerless stealth and precision. An owl's victim, unlike a lion's, knows nothing of its killer.

▲ Serbia's worthy parliament of long-eared owls. CHEDO VUCHKOVIC, courtesy of DAVID LINDO

" Serbian birders have named
the town of Kikinda the
'owl capital of the world' "

Third, on the scant occasions that owls condescend to reveal themselves, their appearance takes us aback. Uniquely among birds, an owl's massive eyes look forward. This creates a distinct face, which makes it obvious when the bird is looking at us, examining us, evaluating us, dismissing us… Our insecurities and uncertainties press us to mythologise what this means. Owls are wise, are protectors of people, are ghosts from the underworld, are agents of evil, are harbingers of death. We know of owls, but now it is time to get to know them.

So to Serbia's long-eared owls. Upon my first (special, of course) encounter with this exciting bird – in 1989, in Yorkshire – the country of Serbia did not exist. It is one of seven nations then brigaded as Yugoslavia. After a difficult birth and troublesome infancy, the country has settled down and is starting to receive attention from wildlife-watchers. Serbia's long-eared owls are integral to that.

Very few owls roost communally and none is more gregarious than the long-eared. This is nowhere more true than northern Serbia, which is dotted with 400 separate roosts. On average, each slumber party contains 50 birds. Many are 250 strong, some exceed 400. Individual trees routinely hold 25 owls.

And what owls they are. Although typically hunched at rest, when alarmed they become slender and erect. Ludicrously long ear-tufts (not ears, note) elongate the bird further. Combined with mottled, streaked and barred plumage in a palette of browns and buffs, this blends the bird with its chosen hideaway. And then there are embers for eyes, which make the owl look perpetually indignant. What an owl.

And so to seeing them. Even more remarkable than Serbia's numerous congregations of long-eared owls, indeed even more amazing than the size of those gatherings, is their location. These are urban roosters, slumbering the day away in the middle of villages and larger settlements. Serbian birders – keen to celebrate their attraction and to entice tourists – have named the town of Kikinda the 'owl capital of the world'.

And with good reason. From November to March, up to 700 owls – a full parliament – fluff themselves out in roadside pines, in frosty trees above the main shopping street, behind the church, in front of the café, along the school fence. To contextualise this, the biggest UK collective I have seen – those inaugural Yorkshire birds – numbered seven. Kikinda's offering is two orders of magnitude greater.

Owls have been roosting in Kikinda since at least the early 20th century (the date of owls embossed on masonry of a local building). Yet owl tourism has only grown wings over the past decade. 'Local people have really taken them into their hearts', says David Lindo (aka The Urban Birder), who leads tours here. Each November, Kikinda residents celebrate the owls' return with a five-day arts festival. Nowhere else in the world does *any* type of owl gather in such numbers.

The owls are attracted to Kikinda and other urban areas by the local abundance of trees in the grassland-dominated landscape of the Pannonian Plains, and by the warmth and shelter offered by buildings. There are so many owls because their prey is abundant. Serbia's long-eareds consume 150 million voles each year. And there are so many voles because Serbian agriculture is as-yet untraumatised by the European Union's environmentally deleterious Common Agricultural Policy.

GETTING THERE Nearest airport is Timișoara, Romania (⊘ aerotim.ro/en), which takes flights from several major European cities including two low-cost airlines from London. From here it is 1¼ hours (72km) to Kikinda. Belgrade airport is 2 hours (135km) south of Kikinda.

WHERE TO GO Kikinda lies 7km from the Romanian border in Vojvodina, northeast Serbia (✳ 45.827788, 20.461662). Seeing owls is a matter of walking around and checking roadside trees – particularly in the main square. **Bačko Gradište** is 1 hour (60km) southwest along road 15 (✳ 45.530260, 20.023843); look around the church. **Melenci** is 30 minutes (35km) south of Kikinda along road 13. Owls occur in the town centre, at Rusanda spa and in nearby Rusanda Park (✳ 45.537190, 20.269176). **Fantast Castle** is a rural hotel, 15km northwest of Bečej, off road 109 (✳ 45.652639, 19.901933 ⊘ tinyurl.com/fantast-castle).

SUGGESTED BASES There are a few hotels and hostels in Kikinda, of which the best is hereprobably **Bed & Breakfast Twenty** (⊘ twenty.rs). An alternative is **Kaštel Ečkea** (⊘ kastelecka.com) in Ečke, 1 hour from Kikinda. Long-eared owls roost in the courtyard,

This weekend, tour several communities graced by the owls and deepen your experience at each. At Bačko Gradište, challenge your companion to an owl-counting competition. Near Melenci, photograph the collective then wait for dusk when they stretch wings and depart to hunt. At Fantast Castle, get the ultimate close-up image. Or collect and dissect pellets to determine what the owls have eaten.

As you travel, you should spot Syrian woodpeckers banging the heck out of urban trees. Hen harrier and great grey shrike are common in the plains. So too hawfinches – with their staring eyes and massive bills – in woods. Short-eared and little owls also frequent Kikinda and Fantast Castle. But it's the long-eareds for which Serbia is special – and for which you come.

REBECCA NASON

with little and barn owls around the adjacent church. Another option is Fantast Castle (see above), which has the benefit of four species of owl residing in its grounds.

MAKE IT A WEEK Slano Kopovo (⌀ slanokopovo.com/en/ornitofauna) is a large nature reserve comprising grasslands, shallow lakes and reedbeds. It can hold thousands of common crane in autumn. Wildfowl includes thousands of white-fronted goose, among which there is a decent chance of red-breasted goose. Saker falcons hunt wildfowl here. **Bečej Fishponds** is good for pygmy cormorant and wildfowl. A summary of good places to go birdwatching is at ⌀ birdwatchserbia.rs/birdingserbia.html. In Hungary, **Hortobágy** is only 4½ hours (300km) away (page 107; ⌀ hnp.hu). In November, it excels for geese, cranes and raptors.

FLEXIBILITY Long-eared and short-eared owls: early November to mid-March; little owl: year round; shrike: October to April.

TITBITS David Lindo leads regular owl-watching tours here (⌀ theurbanbirderworld.com/tours) and local guides include **Birdwatch Serbia** (⌀ birdwatchserbia.rs).

There's no messin' with an amber-eyed long-eared owl. ▲

Swimming free, in black and white

WHERE Tromsø, Troms, Norway
TARGETS Orca, humpback whale, aurora borealis
ACCESSIBILITY ② (snorkelling/diving)
CHILD-FRIENDLINESS ③

What shocks you is not the cold, but the silence. Those early seconds underwater are mortally quiet. Your eyes feint to deceive, taking moments to comprehend the unexpectedly jade crispness that fades to navy before plunging blackly. Argent fish scales – the detritus of herring past – gently confetti downwards. A shoal of live fish, choreographed as a single entity, glistens before vanishing. Then a ghost looms from the gloaming. At first, white flashes. Then a grey curve. Then an entire, huge, piebald whale. An orca: right here, right now.

For three decades, Norway has offered the world's only opportunities to snorkel legally with orcas. The largest dolphins in the seas, killer whales (as they are also known) are attracted to Norwegian fjords and inshore seas in late autumn, following the 'herring run' along the coast until it dissipates in February. For years, Tysfjord was the fulcrum of orca-watching activity, but the herring have recently moved north, so now Tromsø or Kvaløya Island typically serve as departure points.

Norwegian operators offer a spread of services to cater for different needs. You can take a short trip in a fast RIB or a slow burn in an adapted fishing boat. You can do a live-aboard for three or six days, or have a week of daily departures from an onshore base. You can observe from above the sea surface, or kit up in drysuit and snorkel to slip underwater and join the orcas in their element.

Given this book's timescale, I suggest a three-day live-aboard. This maximises flexibility and optimises time on the water; the boat literally follows the herring. As orca-operator Solveig Molvik of Strømsholmen says, 'With the live-aboard concept, we go where the orcas are and can stay with them.'

It is still dark when you join ten or so other hardy souls aboard the boat. But that's hardly surprising. Daylight at this latitude, this near to the winter solstice, is five hours at best. As the black fades to grey, so your eager mind perceives the hillsides as upside-down orcas: largely black, with an eye-catching snowy oval up top. Togged up in defiance of the aching chill, you spot a white-tailed eagle brooding atop a rocky outcrop. A pair of long-tailed ducks arrows past, their name explained by the male, which trails preposterously long, slender central tail feathers.

Scanning the navy undulations of the sea, you start at silvery foam or imaginary slick black spikes. You muse on your target's name. Conservationists balk at 'killer whale', arguing that the cetacean is a dolphin, rather than whale, and that 'killer' makes for bad PR. But 'orca' is arguably little better. The scientific name *Orcinus orca* roughly means 'whale from the realm of the dead'. That said, when you finally spot the phantom weave towards you from the murk, the etymology has a certain sense to it.

But we're getting ahead of ourselves. First, your ship's captain needs to find the herring. She or he may do so by staying in radio contact with the Norwegian herring fleet. Orca like to stay at the head of the run. Then it's a matter of sharp eyes scanning for dark waves that actually are a whale's curved spine (rather than merely resembling one), or for the protruding scythe of a 2-metre-tall dorsal fin.

TONY WU/NPL

❝ You are mesmerised by the black and white interplay of a twisting orca ❞

Don't worry, the orca's after the fish, not you. ▲

At this point, the captain judges whether the pod – which could easily number 40 animals, an impressively extended family – are on the chase or hanging around. If it's the latter… then game on! You heave on drysuits and split into two groups of Michelin Men – one taking the port side, the other starboard. Adhering to guidelines developed by the Undersea Soft Encounter Alliance, only six snorkellers enter the water at any one time. Swimmers stay motionless, at best moving parallel to the pod, displaying bellies to demonstrate submissiveness. No constraints are placed on orca behaviour or movements. Swimmers may temporarily share the cetaceans' habitat, but they remain observers rather than participants.

Mesmerised by the black and white interplay of a twisting orca, it takes a second or two before you comprehend the meaning of the sudden blackening of the water. Humpback! Orcas are far from the only cetacean to follow the herring run. Humpback whales are commonplace too – and they are truly gargantuan. As one rolls through the baitball, it breaks the surface with its immense head and gullet – causing those still above water to gawp as well.

A few minutes on, calm has returned and you seal-flop back aboard. Darkness descends as you slurp down chowder. Beer bottles fizz open as night inks in. And then, with a soundtrack of humpback exhalations and orca blows, the light show starts. A gauze curtain twisting in the breeze, smoke ribboning through the heavens, a sky fit for a David Lynch film. Green and magenta and violet and indescribable colours. The aurora borealis, what else?

GETTING THERE The nearest airport will depend on where your chosen operator departs from, but is likely to be Tromsø (⌖ avinor.no/en/airport/tromso-airport), which has connections to Oslo and other Norwegian cities.

WHERE TO GO You will need to travel with one of several local operators. **Strømsholmen** (⌖ orcanorway.info) offers 3- and 6-day live-aboards; departure ports vary but the meeting point is normally Tromsø. Also in Tromsø are **Arctic Whale Tours** (⌖ arcticwhaletours. com/winter-safari), which offers a 6-hour excursion, and the Dutch company Waterproof Expeditions, which runs 6-day live-aboards (⌖ tinyurl.com/waterproof-orca). Three operators are based in Andenes, Vesterålen. **Northern Explorers** (⌖ tinyurl.com/northern-explorers-orca) offers a 6-night trip with hotel-based accommodation and daily departures. **Hvalsafari AS** (⌖ tinyurl.com/tromsowhale), offers a 6-hour excursion which often encounters sperm whale in winter as well as orcas and humpback; it has discontinued its Tromsø-based operation. **Lofoten Opplevelser** (⌖ lofoten-opplevelser.no) provides a 2–4 hour, RIB-based safari; it has a 90% success rate, with clients snorkelling with orcas on 80% of trips. Further south, **Orca Tysfjord** (⌖ tinyurl.com/orca-tysfjord) operates short trips from Bognes in conjunction

with the Tysfjord Turistsenter. However, the northwards displacement of the herring, away from the former Mecca of Tysfjord, suggests that these trips may currently be less successful.

SUGGESTED BASES If you need land-based accommodation, then Tromsø (visittromso. no) is a logical base.

MAKE IT A WEEK The obvious option is to do a full week cruising for orcas, whether on a live-aboard or via a land-based operation. Alternatively, there is plenty of hiking around **Tromsø**; look for Eurasian elk in forests. For something different, go sledding with huskies.

FLEXIBILITY Cetaceans: herring run is usually late October to mid-February, but Novmber to early February is best; eagle: year-round; aurora: September to March.

TITBITS Most (but not all) operators offering snorkelling trips provide drysuits – so check ahead. Book well ahead for live-aboards. In inclement weather, live-aboards may suggest diving for marine fish and invertebrates. **Wildlife Worldwide** (wildlifeworldwide.com; see ad, page 229) are among companies offering short breaks to see orcas and the aurora. For advice on aurora-watching, see Polly Evans' *Northern Lights: A Practical Travel Guide* (Bradt Travel Guides).

Humpback whales: lunge-feeding leviathans. ▲

Rewilding from A(nser) to B(ranta)

WHERE South Holland, Flevoland and Friesland, Netherlands
TARGETS Lesser white-fronted goose, tundra bean goose, barnacle goose, smew, white-tailed eagle
ACCESSIBILITY ⑤
CHILD-FRIENDLINESS ②

A shroud of colourless mizzle drapes over a sodden flatness of green. The weather, to be frank, could be more amenable. But that doesn't seem to matter one jot. For the vast field before you writhes with an Escher lithograph of life. There are barnacle geese everywhere. Thousands upon thousands upon thousands of them. Griddled forms in ivory, silver and black. Unexpectedly, spontaneously, the entire flock spooks. And lifts off. Yapping and yelping and chittering and panicking. Upwards, outwards, onwards. Winter on the Dutch polders is never static, never dull.

Whether marshes, flood plains or reclaimed land, the Netherlands does polders better than anywhere else. As a result, it also does wintering geese better than anywhere else – at least in Europe. In mid-winter, an estimated 2.5 million geese graze in Dutch fields, often with a backdrop of windmills. The farmers owning land favoured by geese are not always best pleased to have cattle silage nibbled.

▲ A blur of monochrome as thousands of barnacle geese wing upwards. OLIVER SMART www.smartimages.co.uk

REWILDING FROM A(NSER) TO B(RANTA)

> **This trip is less a wild goose *chase* and more a wild goose *extravaganza***

In response, the Dutch government has compensated producers for their losses (€16 million was paid out in early 2016). It has also sought to scare geese away from 'no-go' areas – a policy that was found to have precisely zero lasting effect, not changing goose behaviour by even a single percentage point.

But such public policy conundrums need not trouble you this weekend. Instead, enjoy both the quantity and quality of Dutch wildfowl. This trip is less a wild goose *chase* and more a wild goose *extravaganza*. Your exact destinations will depend on where the geese are – and they do move around. Typically they spend the pre-Christmas period in northeast Netherlands (Friesland and Flevoland provinces) and late winter in the southwest (South and North Holland). But there are always exceptions to the rule.

In west Friesland, a good area to go goosing is roughly bordered by Lemmer, Mirns, Workum and Sneek. Drive the roads and scan the fields, staying inside your vehicle to avoid the geese fretting. You should see tens (perhaps even hundreds) of thousands. The majority will be grey geese in the genus *Anser*: tundra bean, greylag, pink-footed and white-fronted. The remainder will be black geese of the genus *Branta*: barnacles and (in muddy, salty areas) dark-bellied brent. Sift through as many flocks as you can bear and you could conceivably turn up the rarities for which the Netherlands is renowned: notably red-breasted, lesser Canada and pale-bellied brent (all part of the *Branta* tribe).

The next day, make for Flevoland. *En route* you should come across dense flocks of diving ducks (tufted duck and pochard – particularly around Lepelaarplassen Reserve), great egrets standing sentry-like along ditches, and raptors such as peregrine, hen harrier and rough-legged buzzard. Your destination is

REBECCA NASON

Oostvaardersplassen, the country's largest wetland reserve. A famed example of rewilding – conservation seeking to restore ecological processes in a landscape – the fields are now grazed by introduced Konik ponies, heck cattle and red deer, ecological equivalents of the herbivores that once roamed here (tarpan, auroch and, erm, red deer, respectively).

Scanning Keersluisplas Lake from the visitor centre (De Kluut), you should see white-tailed eagles causing havoc amongst the wildfowl. A stroll into the reserve should produce willow tit and great grey shrike. Strike it lucky, and your sojourn

GETTING THERE From the UK, a cross-Channel ferry will put you within striking distance; one from Newcastle, Hull or Harwich across the North Sea into Dutch ports would be even better (⊘ directferries.co.uk). Alternatively you could fly into Amsterdam (⊘ schiphol.nl) or Eindhoven (⊘ eindhovenairport.nl). The Netherlands is so small that most sites are within a 2-hour drive.

WHERE TO GO A reliable area for geese in **west Friesland** lies within the area bordered by Lemmer (✳ 52.845558, 5.717044), Mirns (✳ 52.855940, 5.466132), Workum (✳ 52.976234, 5.452199) and Sneek (✳ 53.032368, 5.656106). Explore the area along roads. **Lepelaarplassen** is off the N701 in southwest Flevoland, just north of Almere (⊘ vogelkijkhut.nl/view/4); visitor centre at ✳ 52.417014, 5.221316. **Oostvaardersplassen** is a large area starting 5km to the northeast and continuing in that direction almost as far as the town of Lelystad. There are a dozen hides (⊘ tinyurl.com/oostvaard), mainly off two quiet roads (Knardijk and Praamweg), which lead south from the roundabout on the N701 (⊘ 52.493019, 5.400719). De Kluut visitor centre is at ✳ 52.457939, 5.417876. For

▲ The male smew, colloquially known as 'white nun', is a designer duck.

from any of several hides may result in an encounter with rough-legged buzzard among the common buzzards, or a hen harrier or goshawk. And everywhere, of course, there will be geese.

By now, yesterday's poor visibility is an indistinct memory. There is a welcome crispness to the air, and the light sparkles. As you leave Flevoland – and leave you must, a wrench though it is – travel via Vossemeer. Scan its length from the western bank until you locate Europe's hottest ducks. Goosander is a lengthy, svelte duck; the males a clotted cream colour with a tree-green head and spicy red bill. The closely related smew is smaller and more dapper: the drake crystalline-white with delicate black tramlines. Both epitomise icy winters.

Tracking down the ducks probably means you have had to forsake geese for an hour or two. Which, in turn, means you'll probably be craving a final fix before the weekend retires. So why not try for the Netherlands' most special gaggle of geese?

They move around a fair bit, but often a group of 30-plus lesser white-fronted geese hang out in the damp, windmill-strewn fields of Oudeland van Strijen, south of Rotterdam. These particular birds are remarkable because they form the core protagonists in a reintroduction programme in Scandinavia that is striving to haul the species back from the verge of extinction in Europe.

Squat and small-headed, with an eye-ring and forehead blaze that suggests innocence, these are demure birds in dire need of conservationists' help and farmers' tolerance. Rewilding, their presence here seems to suggest, involves returning geese to the wild just as much as resuscitating ancient landscapes.

Vossemeer, drive east along Vossemeerdijk from Ketelhaven (✳ 52.579391, 5.767223) and scan the water. In South Holland, **Oudeland van Strijen** is 3km northwest of Strijen, about 12km south of Rotterdam (✳ 51.767264, 4.512507). View from surrounding roads: Hoekseweg, Oudendijk, Molenweg and Voorweg. Another good site for lesser white-fronted goose, particularly later in winter, is **Vereenigde Harger and Pettemerpolder** (✳ 52.738683, 4.647257; also on maps as De Putten), 3km south of Petten in North Holland.
SUGGESTED BASES Lelystad on Flevoland (⌀ vvvlelystad.nl/en) is convenient.
MAKE IT A WEEK Go 'goosing' in the Delta or North Holland. Look for black woodpecker and crested tit in beech woodland near **Harderwijk**. Long-eared owls regularly roost in towns, eg: **Hoofddorp** (in Haarlemmermeerse Bos Park), in central **Swifterbant** and in **Dronten**.
FLEXIBILITY Geese: October to February, but most reliable in featured sites November to December; eagle: year-round but particularly October to March; smew: November to March.
TITBITS Try ⌀ waarneming.nl for a font of wildlife information. Much of it relates to the Netherlands, but it also consolidates interesting sightings from across the world.

51

Murmurazione?

WHERE Rome, Lazio, Italy
TARGETS Starling roost, blue rock thrush, red squirrel, European free-tailed bat
ACCESSIBILITY ⑤
CHILD-FRIENDLINESS ⑤

In the city without historical peer, natural beauty tussles with human heritage. Rome's authorities have taken umbrage at the side-effect of a wildlife phenomenon that – worldwide – has become trendy to admire. Europe's mightiest gathering of European starlings – one million is at the low end of estimates – murmurates above Rome on autumn and winter evenings. But it also poops – excessively, say the Colosseum's present-day guardians – on architecture, Vespas and expensive tailoring below. Romans want starlings out.

This would be a shame. The ballet of starlings prior to roost has the power to enchant anyone who sees it, wildlife connoisseur or not. Even TripAdvisor resounds with exultations from tourists captivated by the performance in Rome. As sunset burns the sky above Fountain and Forum, clouds smoulder and starlings smoke. The *storni* move as a collective above Piazza and Pantheon, tens of thousands of individuals coalescing into a single, humungous and quite wondrous organism. They wisp and whirl, billow and balloon. They spiral and seethe and slump. They create parabolas, columns and corkscrews – or farfalle, penne and fusilli.

For most of us, it is enough to gawp and gasp at the starling spectacle. For scientists, however, the manoeuvres beg questions as to how and why the birds move in unison. How do they not collide? And what's the point? The latest attempt to understand and explain the acrobatics – by Italian scientists, pleasingly – deploys high-speed cameras to capture movements and computers to model behaviour. Unsurprisingly, results scupper the 1930s postulation that starlings communicate by telepathy. Instead each starling tracks the tiniest movement of its six or seven closest brethren, adjusting its flight to remain synchronous. A signal to shift direction from one individual crosses a 100-metre-wide flock in a fraction of a second.

As to *why*, the smart money is on deterring predators, the wheeling and dipping and shape-shifting bewildering a hungry falcon. Starlings at particular risk from peregrines form larger, dense flocks. This 'confusion effect' makes it harder for a peregrine to single out and grab individual prey. For starlings, getting lost in a crowd seems to be a good idea.

Our appreciation bolstered by the theory, let's return to the practice. Starlings move their roost site between months and across years, but the train station (Termini) and Lungotevere (along the River Tiber) seem reliable locations. You can admire the aerial *balletto* from any viewpoint over the city. Perhaps the best is the cylindrical Castel Sant'Angelo (Mausoleum of Hadrian) in Parco Adriano. Climb the tower an hour before sunset and prepare to be enthralled.

Just one potential problem. You may need to enjoy the starlings soon, before they are ousted by 21st-century centurions. Every so often municipal busybodies resolve to rid Rome of its guano problem by introducing sonic bird-scaring devices or flying in trained raptors. To be fair, they have a point. Acrid droppings cover bus stops and pavements. Rather than cleansing the pavements, rain worsens the problem, making the ground slippery with poo. At night, people even walk with open umbrellas in the 'worst-hit' areas.

For me, this reaction to starlings is a microcosm of a wider crisis. How we refuse to co-exist with wildlife. How we insist on the pre-eminence of our needs – rather than accepting that we are just one species among many. Why can't the Italian government celebrate its starlings, laying on viewing facilities rather than fomenting vilification?

Take the cue to turn revolutionary. As you tour the sights, regale in a clandestine celebration of the Italian capital's hidden wildlife – animals that live under Romans' noses, thriving despite human indifference.

Blue rock thrushes songflight from the Forum and above the Via Sacra. Red squirrels scuttle through Villa Ada Park. A black redstart ignites the Colosseum.

JAMES LOWEN

Blue rock thrushes don't demand natural stone on which to perch. ▲

" *Nothing is quite like the ballet
of starlings prior to their roost* "

A shape-shifting murmuration of European starlings clouds the sky above Rome

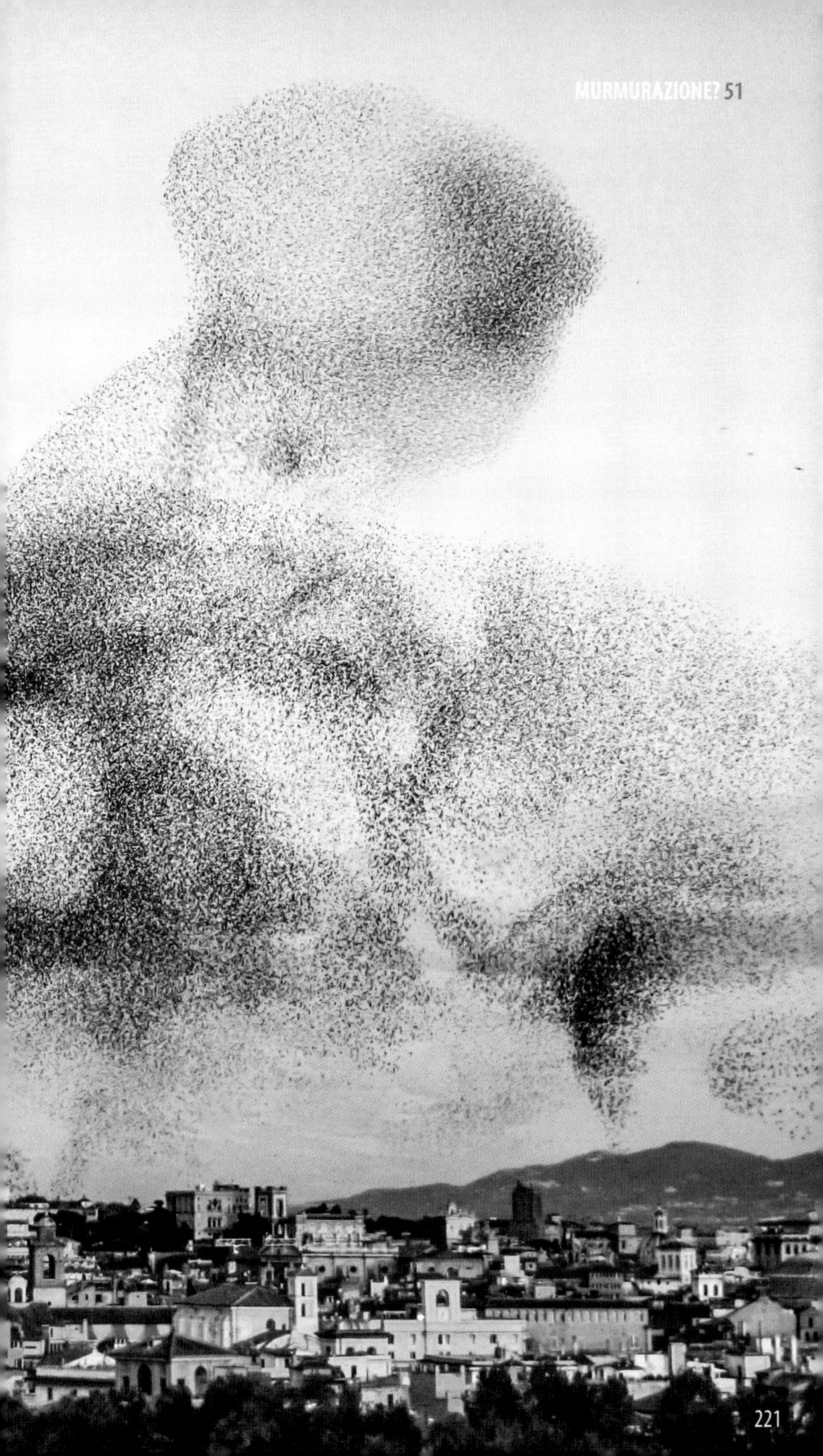

PAOLO TARANTO – ALESSANDRA TOMASSINI | www.fotografianaturalistica.org

If there is enough sun, Italian wall lizards scuttle around ruins. Ring-necked and monk parakeets exaggerate urban greenery. European free-tailed bats have colonised a building in the Quartiere Africano and emerge noisily before dusk. A yellow-legged gull surveys crowds from atop Trevi Fountain.

Hooded crows mob a peregrine over Trajan's Market. Noctule bat and three species of pipistrelle roost underneath Vittorio Emanuele bridge near Castello Sant'Angelo. Short-toed treecreepers mouse up trunks in Appia Antica Park, which also harbours Cetti's warbler, zitting cisticola, firecrest and even little bittern. Adjacent to the park, Moorish geckos emerge at night in stone walls along Appia Way. Just south of Fiumicino airport, a mixed bat-roost in ruins at Ostia Antica holds Schreiber's, Capaccini's, greater horseshoe, and both species of mouse-eared bats. Even in this most resolutely urban tourist destination, wildlife thrives, ready for your delectation. Look and you shall see.

Before departing Rome, make time for another murmuration. This is one show where every performance is individual, different, unique. Tonight the sky may brood rather than blaze. This evening the avian collective may venture high rather than stay low. There will be new shapes to decipher, new dances to appreciate, new flocks that merge to enlarge the feathered cloud. With roosting starlings, boredom is an impossibility.

▲ Cometh nightfall, cometh Rome's European free-tailed bats.

GETTING THERE Nearest airports are Rome's Fiumicino and Ciampino (tinyurl.com/ rome-airports). Most airlines use the former; a low-cost airline, the latter. Fiumicino is more convenient. You can reach Rome easily by bus or train. There is no need for a hire car. **WHERE TO GO Rome** (turismoroma.it/?lang=en) is the world's largest open-air museum. **Termini** is at 41.900507, 12.501617. **Castel Sant'Angelo** is in Parco Adriano on the west bank of the River Tiber, along which runs the Lungotevere (41.902888, 12.466287 castelsantangelo.beniculturali.it). Nearby **Vittorio Emanuele bridge** spans the Tiber (41.901054, 12.464399). **The Forum** is at 41.892542, 12.485143, **The Colosseum** slightly further east (41.890386, 12.491543), and **Via Sacra** runs between the two (41.890500, 12.489228). **Trevi Fountain** is at 41.900882, 12.483322. **Trajan's Market** is on Via Quattro Novembre (41.895665, 12.485991). **Villa Ada Park** is north of the sights (41.933843, 12.504581). **Appian Way** borders **Appia Antica Regional Park** (41.868222, 12.503203 parcoappiaantica.it): the best area is Parco Acquatico Point (41.867218, 12.510383). The bat colony in the **Quartiere Africano** is on Via Migiurtinia, which runs through 41.930661, 12.521477. South of Fiumcino airport, bats roost in the Cisterna di Nettuno inside the ruins of **Ostia Antica** (41.756446, 12.292471).

SUGGESTED BASES When in Rome…

MAKE IT A WEEK Not hard in Rome – provided you have at least one cultural bone in your body. For a wilder time, **Vasche di Maccarese** and **Macchiagrande** are both WWF reserves near the airport that hold a good variety of wildlife (wwf.it/oasi/lazio/). This includes crested porcupine, although a nocturnal visit would be necessary to encounter it. Alternatively, visit **Abruzzo National Park** (page 164). Although too late for Marsican brown bear, it's a cracking month to see Apennine wolf.

FLEXIBILITY Starling: October to January (but variable); lizard: February to December; others: year-round.

The avian performer in the aerial ballet – the starling – is arguably equally beautiful at close range.

La vie en rose

WHERE Camargue, Bouches-du-Rhône, southern France
TARGETS Greater flamingo, greater spotted eagle, eagle owl, wallcreeper, coypu
ACCESSIBILITY ④
CHILD-FRIENDLINESS ③

Alice may not have been far wrong after all. Flip the pink vision upside down, and it could well be used as a croquet stick. But I prefer my greater flamingo – my *flamant rose* – legging around a shallow French lagoon, its impossibly long neck plunging towards the briny water as this mad-billed bird feeds upside-down. If you have never seen a flamingo – an avian incarnation of Edith Piaf's *La vie en rose* – you absolutely must. When you first see one, you will gawp in amazement. And even if you have seen thousands previously, you will not tire of them. So ask Santa nicely to bring you Christmas in the Camargue.

An immense marshy plain in the Rhône Delta, the Camargue Regional Natural Park encompasses 930km² of étangs (lagoons), reedbeds and saturated grassland, all defended from the Mediterranean Sea by filaments of sand dunes. This great wetland is not what it was, the advance of agricultural intensification having exacted its toll. Yet the Camargue remains a fascinating place to visit, and one that whispers greater secrets to the patient observer.

With a single day at your disposal, focus on the eastern side of the focal (and flamingo-filled) Étang de Vaccarès, accessed via the D36B. Passing groups of semi-wild, shockingly white horses, an ancient breed that characterises the Camargue, you arrive at La Capelière visitor centre, which offers information and sells (cheap) access permits. Walk the reedbed trail here to see penduline and bearded tits, and be alert to the chance of moustached warbler. From the lakeside hide, sift through thousands of duck for compact black-necked grebes and extravagantly coiffeured red-crested pochards.

As you stroll, keep an eye on trees by the path. If the weather is clement, you may spot a stripeless tree frog. This bright green amphibian tends towards inactivity in winter, basking motionless with limbs tucked beneath its body. Return at night and you may hear its chorus: a low-pitched rasp, quite unlike other European tree frogs.

Head 6.5km south towards Salin de Badon, and up to 2km beyond, past La Bomborinette. Birds of prey ply the marshes. Marsh harrier, hen harrier and common buzzard predominate, but wintering greater spotted and white-tailed eagles and even long-legged buzzard are local specialities. Scan both sides of the road for flying, resting or roosting birds. (If you don't see these rarer raptors here, try the viewing platform at Mas Neuf, on Vaccarès's northern flank, and the road north to Mas d'Agon.)

Around Salin de Badon in particular, coypu – known locally as *ragondin* – are often seen grazing in or swimming along roadside ditches. South America's answer to beavers, coypu are not native to the Camargue but nevertheless enchant visitors with their furry buoyancy and goofy gnashers. To complete the loop, cut east to the D36 then head north to Le Sambuc (black stork winter northwest of the village).

&& Gawp in amazement at your first flamingo – an avian incarnation of Edith Piaf's *La vie en rose* &&

Simultaneously ugly and elegant: a flock of greater flamingo. ▲

JAMES LOWEN

By now the notorious *mistral* wind of southern France – pouring icy montane air into the lowlands – may force your retreat. Bid the Camargue *adieu* and recharge your batteries.

Spend day two exploring the Alpilles ('little Alps'), centered around the charmingly rocky hilltop village of Les Baux-de-Provence. Diminutive though this mountain chain is – never extending above 500m altitude – it stands majestically, rising precipitously from the stony alluvial plain of the Crau. The village is famous among birdwatchers for being Europe's most accessible place to find wallcreeper. A grey, mouse-like bird that hops up sheer cliffs with disconcerting ease, the wallcreeper morphs into a multi-coloured butterfly when it takes flight. Rounded wings flit gracefully, gloriously flashing magenta, black and white.

To see it, scan cliffs below the ruined castle from the Chemin de Trémaïé, a footpath, or the area around the Vierge Noire statue, along path reached from a paved track signposted 'Le Village', off the D78. As you search, you should encounter other avian specialists of rocky areas. Crag martins glide in lazy circles, lethargic in the winter chill. Blue rock thrushes glister in the sun. Alpine accentors hop around the castle precincts – and even on the cobbled streets.

Nearby, north of Maussane, ascend La Caume to the car park. From here, it is a gentle 45-minute walk to the summit (where there is a radar station). Scan along the mountain sides and down into valleys and you may pick up a Bonelli's eagle – one of Europe's more elusive raptors.

Finish the day, the weekend, the Christmas break and this wildlife-rich year by looking for a giant. Eagle owls are serious nocturnal predators, capable of grabbing slumbering buzzards at their roost. At two well-known sites near Les Baux, birds shuffle out from their cliffside lair shortly before dusk. They call – a throaty, bisyllabic groan – then wing into the gloaming. A Christmas treat indeed.

▲ A male wallcreeper, one of the world's most beautiful and bizarre birds.

GETTING THERE From the UK, travel by Eurostar (⬦ eurostar.com) to Lille and TGV (⬦ sncf.com/en/trains/tgv) to Avignon or Aix-en-Provence. Alternatively, the nearest airports are Nîmes, Montpellier and Marseille – all served by various European airports and within 1½ hours' drive of the Camargue.

WHERE TO GO For **Camargue Regional Natural Park** (⬦ www.reserve-camargue. org, parc-camargue.fr), take the D570/D36/D36B south from Arles. **La Capelière** visitor centre is off the D36B at ✳ 43.535243, 4.644126. **Salin de Badon** is 6.5km south (✳ 43.481441, 4.646774). **Le Sambuc** is at ✳ 43.524178, 4.705745. North of Étang de Vaccarès, **Mas Neuf** lies on the D37 (✳ 43.571736, 4.541779); **Mas d'Agon** is 2km north (✳ 43.581039, 4.542668). **Les Baux-de-Provence** (✳ 43.744091, 4.794461 ⬦ lesbauxdeprovence.com) is 35 minutes northeast of Arles along the D17/D78F. For wallcreeper, park near 'le village' signposts on the left just before Les Baux. Follow the footpath right to Vierge Noire statue and scan cliffs. Alternatively, continue along the D27A beyond the main village car park. Scan from a sharp left-hand bend. For **La Caume**, take the D27A/D5 towards Saint-Rémy-de-Provence. Park at ✳ 43.756383, 4.833828; walk east to the summit. Eagle owl frequents cliffs at the end of the track running north behind **Mas de l'Oulivié** hotel, 3km southwest of Les Baux along the D78F (✳ 43.736585, 4.776552). View from the red fire hydrant. Or try **Le Destet**, 12km east of Les Baux. Park at the first junction south of the D78/D24 junction. Walk west for 1km to view cliffs northwards.

SUGGESTED BASES Arles is perfect for both areas (⬦ arlestourisme.com).

MAKE IT A WEEK Climb **Mont Ventoux** for black woodpecker, citril finch and snow finch. Explore the **Crau** for little bustard and pin-tailed sandgrouse. Visit the **Pont du Gard** at dawn or dusk for roosting rock sparrow and wallcreeper.

FLEXIBILITY Flamingo, owl and coypu: year-round although owl often best December to April; eagle and wallcreeper: November to April.

TITBITS An excellent leaflet on Camargue sites is at ⬦ tinyurl.com/camargue-leaflet.

Although not native to France, coypu enchant visitors to the Camargue. ▲

Further information

Here is a personal selection of books to accompany *52 European Wildlife Weekends*. These focus on identification and locations for wildlife-watching.

Identification guides

A Photographic Guide to the Insects of Southern Europe and the Mediterranean Paul Brock, Pisces Publications 2017

Collins Bird Guide Lars Svensson, Killian Mullarney and Dan Zetterström, Collins 2009

Collins Butterfly Guide Tom Tolman and Richard Lewington, Collins 2009

Field Guide to the Amphibians and Reptiles of Britain and Europe Jeroen Speybroeck, Wouter Beukema, Bobby Bok and Jan Van Der Voort, Bloomsbury 2016

Field Guide to the Dragonflies of Britain and Europe Klaas-Douwe Dijkstra and Richard Lewington, British Wildlife Publishing 2006

Mammals of Europe, North Africa and the Middle East S Aulagnier, P Haffner, A J Mitchell-Jones, F Moutou and J Zima, A&C Black 2009

Wild Flowers of the Mediterranean Marjorie Blamey and Christopher Grey-Wilson, Bloomsbury 2008

Wildlife overviews

Central and Eastern European Wildlife Gerard Gorman, Bradt Travel Guides 2008

France. Traveller's Nature Guides Bob Gibbons, Oxford University Press 2003

Greece. Traveller's Nature Guides Bob Gibbons, Oxford University Press 2003

Spain. Traveller's Nature Guides Teresa Farino and Mike Lockwood, Oxford University Press 2003

Wildlife site guides

I am a big fan of the Crossbill Guides (see ad, inside-back cover), written by Dirk Hilbers and others, which provide in-depth treatments of wildlife-rich regions. Titles pertinent to trips covered in this guide include: *Camargue, Crau and Les Alpilles*; *North-east Poland*; *Extremadura*; *Hortobágy*; *Loire Valley*; *Canary Islands I and II*; *Iceland*; *Finnish Lapland*; *Southern Portugal*; and *Spanish Pyrenees*.

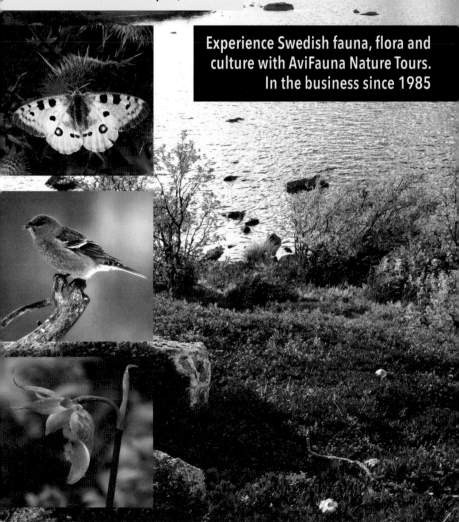

Praise for James Lowen

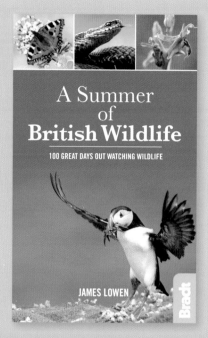

Winner, Travel Guide Book of the Year (2016 Travel Media Awards)

"A brilliant idea!" (Chris Packham, BBC Springwatch Unsprung)

"An ideal addition to any family bookshelf... a friendly, encouraging and knowledgeable companion" (*BBC Wildlife*)

"Inspiring and evocative" (*Birdwatch*)

"A delightful and invaluable aid to enjoying the outdoors with children" (Birdguides)

"Lowen is so good at evoking the sights, sounds and smells of the natural phenomena he describes" (*Bird Watching*)

"Beautifully written... both inspiring and practical" (*Nature's Home*)

"Brilliant, refreshing. An invaluable, inspirational guide." (Brett Westwood, *BBC Wildlife*)

"An indispensable resource" (*Outdoor Photography*)

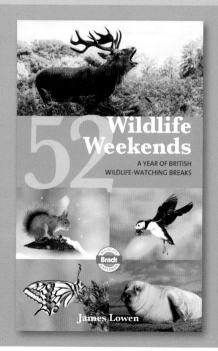

Both books published by Bradt Travel Guides.

bradtguides.com

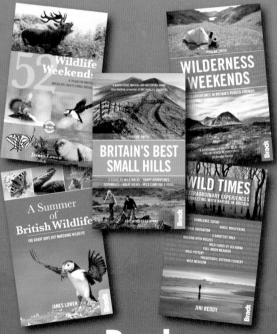

Index

Index of sites

Main entries for geopolitical areas (eg: countries, provinces) are *italicised*; sites are in plain type; photographs of locations are marked in **bold** type. Only the first mention of each entry in the main text for each weekend is specified. Country is given for each site mentioned. Sites mentioned solely in the *Practicalities* box (eg: in *Make it a week*) are omitted. For brevity, protected area status (eg: 'national park') is omitted from site names; this is mentioned in the *Practicalities* box that accompanies each weekend.

Index of advertisers

Index of wildlife targets

This index relates solely to 'target wildlife', ie: the highlights given at the start of each weekend. Scientific names follow each species in parentheses. After each scientific name is a simple descriptor of the 'type' of flora or fauna involved (eg: bird, moth, plant) where this is not evident from its name.

Page numbers in plain type indicate the first mention (only) of the species during a particular weekend; those in **bold** type indicate that the species is one of the 'targets' for that weekend; and those in *italics* relate to photographs.

First edition published April 2018

Bradt Travel Guides Ltd

IDC House, The Vale, Chalfont St Peter, Bucks SL9 9RZ, England

www.bradtguides.com

Print edition published in the USA by The Globe Pequot Press Inc,

PO Box 480, Guilford, Connecticut 06437-0480

ISBN: 978 1 78477 083 9 (print)

e-ISBN: 978 1 78477 540 7 (e-pub)

e-ISBN: 978 1 78477 441 7 (mobi)

British Library Cataloguing in Publication Data

A catalogue record for this book is available from the British Library

Photographs

Photos © individual photographers and organisations credited beside images & also from picture libraries credited as follows: Alamy.com (A), Dreamstime.com (D), Flpa-images.co.uk (FLPA), Nature Photographer Lassi Rautiainen www.wildfinland.org (LR), Naturepl.com (NPL), Rspb-images.com (RSPB), Shutterstock.com (S), Superstock.com (SS)

Author photo Sharon Lowen

Cover design Pepi Bluck, Perfect Picture

Front cover images *Top image*: brown bear (Winfried Wisniewski/Minden Pictures/FLPA); *Clockwise from top left*: Arctic fox (J-L Klein and M-L Hubert/FLPA); two-tailed pasha (Arik Siegel/Nature in Stock/FLPA); sperm whale (Hans Overduin/Nature in Stock/FLPA); little bustard (Wim de Groot, Buiten-beeld/Minden Pictures/FLPA)

Back cover images *Top* Eurasian lynx (J-L Klein and M-L Hubert/FLPA); *Bottom* Atlantic canary (James Lowen)

Title page image Mountain hare, supremely equipped for wild winters. (Oliver Smart www.smartimages.co.uk)

Map David McCutcheon FBCart.S

Typeset by Pepi Bluck, Perfect Picture

Digital conversion by www.dataworks.co.in

Production managed by Jellyfish Print Solutions; printed in the UK